AF556162

BUSINESS ENVIRONMENT

BUSINESS ENVIRONMENT

Jyotsana Singh

CENTRUM PRESS
NEW DELHI-110002 (INDIA)

CENTRUM PRESS
H.O.: 4360/4, Ansari Road, Daryaganj,
New Delhi-110002 (India)
Tel: 23278000, 23261597, 23255577, 23286875
B.O.: No. 1015, Ist Main Road, BSK IIIrd Stage,
IIIrd Phase, IIIrd Block, Bangalore-560085 (INDIA)
Tel: 080-41723429
Email: centrumpress@gmail.com
Visit us at: www.centrumpress.com

Business Environment

First Edition, 2011

ISBN 978-93-80921-07-5

PRINTED IN INDIA

Printed at Balaji Offset, Delhi.

Contents

Contents

Preface

Business environment is a set of political, economic, social and technological forces that are largely outside the control and influence of a business and that can potentially have both a positive and a negative impact on the business.

This book makes clear what the differences will be and why these differences are inevitable. Because the environment will be different, and because the firms that survive will be those best suited to this changed environment, it follows that future firms must be, and will be, different from today. My intent in this book is to describe the necessary nature of these survivors, these future firms.

The contents of this book include organizational decision-making, with particular emphasis on the effects of the organization's environment and on the use of information technology by the organization's decision-makers. I am sure that this book will prove extensively useful for all management students.

Author

1

Introduction

As the market place is becoming more dynamic and businessmen are becoming more aware of the importance of forecasting in decision-making, the organizational structure, business philosophy, corporate culture, and level of senior management's support for this function are changing. With that, the landscape of forecasting is changing. Changes are being experienced in corporate culture and business environment, public perception about forecasting, forecasters, approach to forecasting, uses of forecasts and technology.

CORPORATE CULTURE AND BUSINESS ENVIRONMENT

We are currently experiencing enormous changes in corporate culture and business environment. Command and control strategy for managing business is giving way to autonomous business units with power to develop and implement their own policies. The silo-based strategy is being replaced by collaboration and knowledge sharing not only within an enterprise but also with customers and suppliers. New products are no longer developed in isolation by one department but by a team of experts from different departments. Furthermore, there is now increasing pressure from top management to convert data into knowledge so that better decisions can be made. The current technology has provided massive amount of data, but not enough efforts are being made to translate the data into intelligence. The changes in corporate culture and environment are causing changes in the way forecasts are prepared and communicated. The breaking down of functional silos has given rise to collaboration both within and outside the enterprise. There is now more openness among different functions than ever before. More and more decisions are now made collectively rather than individually.

The S&OP (Sales and Operations Process), which many companies now have in place, is an example of collaboration within an enterprise. In a regularly scheduled S&OP meeting, people from different functions often get together to build a consensus on forecasts; if there is a gap between supply and demand, decide on the action plan to match them; and determine capacity needs. The programmes such as VMI (Vendor Managed Inventory Programme) and CPFR (Collaborative Planning, Forecasting and Replenishment) grew from the spirit of collaboration. Under both these programmes, retailers not only provide access to point-of-sale data but also agree to share information about changes in their store layout, opening and closing of stores, promotional plans, and forecasts. At present, Retail Link, Wal-Mart's electronic data interchange system, provides weekly forecasting data to more than 3500 of its 5000 vendors. If vendors know what is happening on the consumer end, as well as what retailers are planning to do, they can do a better job in preparing forecasts. A business firm is an open system.

It gets resources from the environment and supplies its goods and services to the environment. There are different levels of environmental forces. Some are close and internal forces whereas others are external forces. External forces may be related to national level, regional level or international level. These environmental forces provide opportunities or threats to the business community. Every business organization tries to grasp the available opportunities and face the threats that emerge from the

BUSINESS ENVIRONMENT

Business organizations cannot change the external environment but they just react. They change their internal business components (internal environment) to grasp the external opportunities and face the external environmental threats. It is, therefore, very important to analyse business environment to survive and to get success for a business in its industry. It is, therefore, a vital role of managers to analyse business environment so that they could pursue effective business strategy.

A business firm gets human resources, capital, technology, information, energy, and raw materials from society. It follows government rules andregulations, social norms and cultural values, regional treaty and global alignment, economic rules and tax policies of the government. Thus, a business organization is a dynamic entity because it operates in a dynamic business environment.

SYSTEM APPROACH OF BUSINESS ENVIRONMENT

All the systems are subsystems of other system in the nature except the supra-system or cosmos. We individually are also the part of our family.Formal organization or business is made of group of people for specific purpose. Very similar to the organization we personally are the members of our family and that is a component of a broader society. The same society is a component of a nation. Group of nation with similar interest are grouped in regional alliances such as SAARC and EU. World economy is made of with all these regional alliances and network. In this approach, nothing is in isolation. All are integrated and interlinked.

Organizations are open systems because they get resources from others and give output to others. A business deals with number of business kenvironmental forces. These forces from where a business gets resources and supplies resources, forces that influence the business operation, and factor that present opportunities and threats are taken as the business environment. In this sense, a business can be viewed as an internal system or controllable system of a manager or strategist. Managers can control their own businesses. Managers can collect resources such as capital, human, information, idea, land, and equipments. These components are controllable. Managers can operate their organization and use their decision to run it. Similarly, the output of the organization is also under their control. But, other broader systems that cover the business may not controllable.

Group of similar organization becomes an industrial system that comprises business organizations as its subsystems. Industry level environment is common to all the businesses running within the industry. A country and its environment is broader system that covers even the different sectors or industries such as banking, education, health, trade, manufacturing, and service industries. Therefore, it affects all the business operations inside the nation. Regional alliances influence the national policy because a country is a subsystem of the regional alliances such as SAARC and BIMSTEC. Even such regional alliances are also affected by the broader international systems such as WTO and United Nations. Relatively broader systems are uncontrollable for any subsystems. In case of a business, it is a very small subsystem that should follow the industry norms, national policies, regional agreements, and global systems.

In summary, it can be concluded that a business and its internal areas are controllable for a manager but other broader systems control the businesses. Therefore, the strategy for a manager is to control internal areas and react with the external forces to grasp the opportunity and face the threats by the external environment. This system approach can be classified into three environmental groups: uncontrollable, semi-controllable.

COMPONENTS OF BUSINESS ENVIRONMENT

A manager must follow a change in his or her structure, strategy and policies in response to the changing environmental forces. Thus, a business firm exists in two level of business environment a) Internal and b) External. Internal business environment comprises internal structure, system, culture, staff, and resources of the organization. This is sometimes identified into the internal functional areas such as marketing-distribution, finance accounting, human resources, production-operation, and research-development. All these business environment components are controllable.

External business environment comprises two layers that are task business environment and general business environment. Task environment is also known as close or industry level business environment. Such environment more directly interacts with the business operation and semi-controllable in nature. Next layer is relatively broader and more indirect in nature that covers the effect of environment emerged at national, regional, and international level.

Business environment comprises internal components of a business, which is manageable at managerial level. Internal business environmental forces are the components of the business. As discussed before semi-controllable and uncontrollable environmental forces are external business environmental forces. These forces can be classified into two levels: industry level and general level. These general environmental forces may exist at national, regional and international level. The internal environment or business components are surrounded by industry level environment and the industry level business environment is surrounded by general level business environment.

APPROACHES OF IDENTIFYING AND REPORTING ENVIRONMENT COMPONENTS

There are many distinct but similar approaches available in categorizing business environment components. Jauch & Glueck (1988) identified business environment components into three sets namely general, industry level, and internal. This concept became very popular and holistic among the many academicians.

They identified five major components including political-legal, socio-cultural, economic, technological, and climatic factors of general business environment. Industrial and general level business environment are grouped into external business environment. Many writers coined Political, Socio-cultural, Economic, and Technological factors as PEST.

- Political and legal components are sometimes separated and PESTEL is also used as an acronym. Some others address these external environment components as Social, Technological, Political, and Economic (STEP) factors. Including natural environmental factors into this set social, technological, economic, environmental and political (STEEP) model is presented. The same natural environment is also taken as a distinct component; therefore, it is sometimes addressed as Socio-cultural, politicallegal,Economic, Natural, and Technological (SPENT).
- Cartwright identified an acronym SPECTACLES to address the set of ten external environment components such as Social, Political, Economic, Cultural, Technological, Aesthetic, Customer, Legal, Environmental, and Sectoral.
- External business environment are grouped into remote environment for general and operating environment for task or industry level business environment.
- General business environment is also used as macroenvironment. Similarly the industry level environment is used as the microenvironment in many writings.
- Furthermore, industry level business environment is also taken as competitive environment.
- Some writers even merged competitive environment into a set of external or general environment.

General Business Environment Components

A variety of factors can affect company's business. Such factors can be national level, regional level, and international level environmental forces. These factors are also known as societal factors or macro level business environment factors. In general, five forces are taken as the general environmental factors namely economic, socio-cultural, political-legal, technological, and international. Some writers included natural environment as a distinct component but the growing social awareness on natural environment shows that this component can be included into the socio-cultural environment. Set of these environmental factors is mostly referred by first four factors PEST (Political-legal, Economic, Socio-cultural, and Technological).

The logic behind this is pervasiveness of the international environment because it affects all these four sectors. Fast growing technological development, outsourcing business, emergences of multinational companies, and global and regional alliances have made the world a global village. In this context, effect of international environment in four major components of general environmental factors is natural. In today's dynamic business environment Information Communication Technology (ICT) revolution and globalization are to be considered very important effect in today's international business environment.

Growing multinational companies and their influence in one national economy is clearly evident. Use of automated technology and e-commerce has replaced many of the manual works and workplace. World Trade Organization and its growing members including Nepalese 147th membership in Cancun summit has placed new opportunities and threats to the developing countries like Nepal. South Asian Association for Regional Cooperation (SAARC) is active since twenty years and it recently declared South Asian Free Trade Area

(SAFTA) charter. Furthermore, Bay of Bengal Initiative for Multi-Sectoral Technical and Economic Cooperation (BIMSTEC) and its future potentialities presented new prospectus to the local and international business entities in this sector. The term Business Environment is composed of two words 'Business' and 'Environment'. In simple terms, the state in which a person remains busy is known as Business. The word Business in its economic sense means human activities like production, extraction or purchase or sales of goods that are performed for earning profits. On the other hand, the word 'Environment' refers to the aspects of surroundings. Therefore, Business Environment may be defined as a set of conditions – Social, Legal, Economical, Political or Institutional that are uncontrollable in nature and affects the functioning of organization.

Business Environment has two components:

1. *Internal Environment*: It includes 5 Ms i.e. man, material, money, machinery and management, usually within the control of business. Business can make changes in these factors according to the change in the functioning of enterprise.
2. *External Environment*: Those factors which are the control of business enterprise are included in external environment. These factors are: Government and Legal factors, Geo-Physical Factors, Political Factors, Socio-Cultural Factors, Demo-Graphical factors etc.

It is of two Types:

1. Micro/Operating Environment
2. Macro/General Environment

   Micro/Operating Environment: The environment which is close to business and affects its capacity to work is known as Micro or Operating Environment. It consists of Suppliers, Customers, Market Intermediaries, Competitors and Public.

1. *Suppliers*: They are the persons who supply raw material and required components to the company. They must be reliable and business must have multiple suppliers i.e. they should not depend upon only one supplier.
2. *Customers*: Customers are regarded as the king of the market. Success of every business depends upon the level of their customer's satisfaction.

Types of Customers:

- Wholesalers
- Retailers
- Industries
- Government and Other Institutions
- Foreigners

3. *Market Intermediaries*: They work as a link between business and final consumers.

Types:

- Middleman
- Marketing Agencies
- Financial Intermediaries
- Physical Intermediaries

4. *Competitors*: Every move of the competitors affects the business. Business has to adjust itself according to the strategies of the Competitors.
5. *Public*: Any group who has actual interest in business enterprise is termed as public e.g. media and local public. They may be the users or non-users of the product.

Macro/General Environment: It includes factors that create opportunities and threats to business units. Following are the elements of Macro Environment:

1. *Economic Environment*: It is very complex and dynamic in nature that keeps on changing with the change in policies or political situations.

It has three elements:

- Economic Conditions of Public
- Economic Policies of the country
- Economic System
- *Other Economic Factors*: Infrastructural Facilities, Banking, Insurance companies, money markets, capital markets etc.

2. *Non-Economic Environment*: Following are included in non-economic environment.
   - Political Environment: It affects different business units extensively.

Components:

- Political Belief of Government
- Political Strength of the Country
- Relation with other countries
- Defence and Military Policies
- Centre State Relationship in the Country
- Thinking Opposition Parties towards Business Unit

- *Socio-Cultural Environment*: Influence exercised by

social and cultural factors, not within the control of business, is known as Socio-Cultural Environment. These factors include: attitude of people to work, family system, caste system, religion, education, marriage etc.

- *Technological Environment*: A systematic application of scientific knowledge to practical task is known as technology. Everyday there has been vast changes in products, services, lifestyles and living conditions, these changes must be analysed by every business unit and should adapt these changes.
- *Natural Environment*: t includes natural resources, weather, climatic conditions, port facilities, topographical factors such as soil, sea, rivers, rainfall etc. Every business unit must look for these factors before choosing the location for their business.
- *Demographic Environment*: It is a study of perspective of population i.e. its size, standard of living, growth rate, age-sex composition, family size, income level (upper level, middle level and lower level), education level etc. Every business unit must see these features of population and recongnise their various need and produce accordingly.
- *International Environment*: It is particularly important for industries directly depending on import or exports. The factors that affect the business are: Globalisation, Liberalisation, foreign business policies, cultural exchange.

Characteristics:

1. Business environment is compound in nature.
2. Business environment is constantly changing process.
3. Business environment is different for different business units.
4. It has both long term and short term impact.
5. Unlimited influence of external environment factors.
6. It is very uncertain.
7. Inter-related components.
8. It includes both internal and external environment.

2

Concept of Environment

Leaders of important enterprises are often heard to have remarked, *"If I had only known—, I would have chosen a different strategy."* The blank may have been end of the Cold War, downsizing of the defence establishment, the run-up of interest rates, the bursting of the real estate price bubble, or similar events. Some of these events are purely economic; some have significant political components; others may have large sociological or legal components.

They all affect the functioning of enterprise, and it is up to the business strategist to try to look ahead to make sure that an appropriate work force is at hand, that inventory stocks (raw materials or finished goods) are adequate, that key items of fixed capital are on order or already installed.

The economic forecaster's job is to try to look ahead, unconditionally; to assess the implications of "what-if" conditional options; to present appropriate error bands of judgment; and to recommend some appropriate lines of action. we plan to tell you something about our latest investigations to make very short-run economic forecasts—up to six months, with frequent replication, weekly or even daily—but also to comment on both medium term forecasts—up to 3 to 5 years—and longer term forecasts—up to 10 years.

Some economists have an eye on longer horizons for several decades into the future—but those are highly conditional scenarios and not, strictly speaking, forecasts in the usual sense of the term. Forecasting for business may overlap considerably with forecasting for public bodies but the targets in the bottom-line may be quite different and the scope may be quite broad. The national public sector is particularly interested in macroeconomic forecasts of total production (GDP), inflation (change in the CPI), the unemployment rate, the number of jobs created, the internal balance (surplus or deficit) and the external balance (current account), representative interest rates and currency exchange rates. International public organizations have the same bottom-line interests but they also follow distributions among countries or regions. Local government units have a much more restricted scope, but usually are interested in local area analogues of the same magnitudes that national governments follow.

The primary targets for private business are company sales, profits, debt ratios, debt service burdens, market valuations of equities, company inventory positions, and the impact of state, local, or national legislation. The biggest private companies, whose sales may be as large as one-half per cent or more of GDP, may have direct interest in the national macroeconomic magnitudes, but for the most part their interest is indirect; they are mainly interested in macroeconomic magnitudes because they shape the environment for company performance.

At the present time, however, the most frequent inquiry that is posed to economic forecasters is "Where are interest rates headed?" In our service as a board member and chairman of the economic policy committee of an investment banking company, we find ourself being quizzed mainly about the course of interest rates.

But this firm's revenues are partially indexed to inflation; so there is corresponding curiosity about the course of inflation. Overall macroeconomic performance is less interesting for this company, except as it has indirect effects on the company's bottom line.

BUSINESS ENVIRONMENT COMPONENTS

There are many factors in the macro-environment that will effect the decisions of the managers of any organisation. Tax changes, new laws, trade barriers, demographic change and government policy changes are all examples of macro change. To help analyse these factors managers can categorise them using the PESTEL model.

This classification distinguishes between:

- *Political factors.* These refer to government policy such as the degree of intervention in the economy. What goods and services does a government want to provide? To what extent does it believe in subsidising firms? What are its priorities in terms of business support? Political decisions can impact on many vital areas for business such as the education of the workforce, the health of the nation and the quality of the infrastructure of the economy such as the road and rail system.
- *Economic factors.* These include interest rates, taxation changes, economic growth, inflation and exchange rates. As you will see throughout the "Foundations of Economics" book economic change can have a major impact on a firm's behaviour. For example:
  - Higher interest rates may deter investment because it costs more to borrow
  - A strong currency may make exporting more difficult because it may raise the price in terms of foreign currency
  - Inflation may provoke higher wage demands from employees and raise costs
  - Higher national income growth may boost demand for a firm's products
- *Social factors.* Changes in social trends can impact on the demand for a firm's products and the availability and willingness of individuals to work. In the UK, for example, the population has been ageing. This has increased the costs for firms who are committed to pension payments for their employees because their staff are living longer. It also means some firms such as Asda have started to recruit older employees to tap into this growing labour pool. The ageing population also has impact on demand: for example,

demand for sheltered accommodation and medicines has increased whereas demand for toys is falling.

- *Technological factors:* new technologies create new products and new processes. MP3 players, computer games, online gambling and high definition TVs are all new markets created by technological advances. Online shopping, bar coding and computer aided design are all improvements to the way we do business as a result of better technology. Technology can reduce costs, improve quality and lead to innovation. These developments can benefit consumers as well as the organisations providing the products.
- *Environmental factors:* environmental factors include the weather and climate change. Changes in temperature can impact on many industries including farming, tourism and insurance. With major climate changes occurring due to global warming and with greater environmental awareness this external factor is becoming a significant issue for firms to consider. The growing desire to protect the environment is having an impact on many industries such as the travel and transportation industries (for example, more taxes being placed on air travel and the success of hybrid cars) and the general move towards more environmentally friendly products and processes is affecting demand patterns and creating business opportunities.
- *Legal factors:* these are related to the legal environment in which firms operate. In recent years in the UK there have been many significant legal changes that have affected firms' behaviour. The introduction of age discrimination and disability discrimination legislation, an increase in the minimum wage and greater requirements for firms to recycle are examples of relatively recent laws that affect an organisation's actions. Legal changes can affect a firm's costs (e.g. if new systems and

procedures have to be developed) and demand (e.g. if the law affects the likelihood of customers buying the good or using the service).

Different Categories of Law Include

- *Consumer laws*: these are designed to protect customers against unfair practices such as misleading descriptions of the product
- *Competition laws*: these are aimed at protecting small firms against bullying by larger firms and ensuring customers are not exploited by firms with monopoly power
- *Employment laws*: these cover areas such as redundancy, dismissal, working hours and minimum wages. They aim to protect employees against the abuse of power by managers
- *Health and safety legislation*: these laws are aimed at ensuring the workplace is as safe as is reasonably practical. They cover issues such as training, reporting accidents and the appropriate provision of safety equipment

Typical PESTEL factors to consider include:

Factor	Could Include
Political	e.g. EU enlargement, the euro, international trade, taxation policy
Economic	e.g. interest rates, exchange rates, national income, inflation, unemployment, Stock Market
Social	e.g. ageing population, attitudes to work, income distribution
Technological	e.g. innovation, new product development, rate of technological obsolescence
Environmental	e.g. global warming, environmental issues
Legal	e.g. competition law, health and safety, employment law

By using the PESTEL framework we can analyse the many different factors in a firm's macro environment. In some cases particular issues may fit in several categories. For example, the creation of the Monetary Policy Committee by the Labour government in 1997 as a body that was independent of government but had the ability to set interest rates was a political decision but has economic consequences; meanwhile government economic policy can influence investment in technology via taxes and tax credits. If a factor can appear in several categories managers simply make a decision of where they think it best belongs. However, it is important not to just list PESTEL factors because this does not in itself tell managers very much. What managers need to do is to think about which factors are most likely to change and which ones will have the greatest impact on them i.e. each firm must identify the key factors in their own environment. For some such as pharmaceutical companies government regulation may be critical; for others, perhaps firms that have borrowed heavily, interest rate changes may be a huge issue. Managers must decide on the relative importance of various factors and one way of doing this is to rank or score the likelihood of a change occurring and also rate the impact if it did. The higher the likelihood of a change occurring and the greater the impact of any change the more significant this factor will be to the firm's planning.It is also important when using PESTEL analysis to consider the level at which it is applied. When analysing companies such as Sony, Chrysler, Coca Cola, BP and Disney it is important to remember that they have many different parts to their overall business - they include many different divisions and in some cases many different brands. Whilst it may be useful to consider the whole business when using PESTEL in that it may highlight some important factors, managers may want to narrow it down to a particular part of the business (e.g. a specific division of Sony); this may be more useful because it will focus on the factors relevant to that part of the business. They may also want to differentiate between factors which are very local, other which are national and those which are global.

For example, a retailer undertaking PESTEL analysis may consider:

- *Local factors* such as planning permission and local economic growth rates

- *National factors* such as UK laws on retailer opening hours and trade descriptions legislation and UK interest rates
- *Global factors* such as the opening up of new markets making trade easier. The entry of Bulgaria and Rumania into the European Union might make it easier to enter that market in terms of meeting the various regulations and provide new expansion opportunities. It might also change the labour force within the UK and recruitment opportunities.

This version of PESTEL analysis is called LoNGPESTEL.

	Local	National	Global
Political	Provision of services by local council	UK government policy on subsidies	World trade agreements e.g. further expansion of the EU
Economic	Local income	UK interest rates	Overseas economic growth
Social	Local population growth	Demographic change (e.g. ageing population)	Migration flows
Technological	Improvements in local technologies e.g. availability of Digital TV	UK wide technology e.g. UK online services	International technological breakthroughs e.g. internet
Environmental	Local waste issues	UK weather	Global climate change
Legal	Local licences/planning permission	UK law	International agreements on human rights or environmental policy

In "Foundations of Economics" we focus on the economic environment. We examine issues such as the effect of interest rate changes, changes in exchange rates, changes in trade policy, government intervention in an economy via spending and taxation and economic growth rates. These can be incredibly important factors in a firm's macro-environment.

The growth of China and India, for example, have had massive effects on many organisations. Firms can relocate production there to benefit from lower costs; these emerging markets are also providing enormous markets for firms to aim their products at. With a population of over 1 billion, for example, the Chinese market is not one you would want to ignore; at the same time Chinese producers should not be ignored either. However, the relative importance of economic factors compared to other factors will depend on the particular position of a business.

Exchange rate fluctuations may be critically important to a multinational but less significant to a local window cleaner. Rapid economic growth or economic decline may be very significant to a construction business that depends heavily on the level of income in the economy but may be slightly less significant to a milk producer whose product is less sensitive to income. So whilst the economy is important to all firms on both the supply side (e.g. unemployment levels affect the ease of recruitment) and demand side (e.g. income tax affects spending power) the relative importance of specific economic factors and the relative importance of the economy compared to regulation or social trends will vary. Whilst we hope this book provides a good insight into the economy and the possible effects of economic change on a business these must be considered in the light of other macro and micro factors that influence a firms' decisions and success.

During the years when we was responsible for much of the work at Wharton Econometrics, we had to serve hundreds of users, some in specific microeconomic investigations but mostly in overall macroeconomic studies, we found that it was necessary to be prepared to relate overall economic performance to the fortunes of many diverse users of forecasts.

FORECAST ACCURACY

Economic forecasters, whether by judgment or by formal system, are well aware of the inevitable presence of error. Also, those who engage in this activity with a strong scholarly background are well aware of the orders of magnitude of error and their root causes; nevertheless we serve as the butt of jokes by many outsiders who do not realise just how difficult it is to forecast the economy accurately.

Most economists aside from those actively engaged do not replicate their forecasts or keep score for their "track records," but I do believe:

- It is possible to forecast the economy correctly, on average, and to provide useful information to business and to the public sector.
- Forecasting systematically by econometric model techniques have gradually improved over the last 50 years, but user demands have become increasingly severe.
- There remain promising avenues for improvement in accuracy and usefulness, but these gains are likely to be modest and steady; no breakthrough is on the horizon, especially knowing what we do about the sources of error.

Roughly speaking, we can project overall growth in an industrial economy, where there is a good data base, within about 1 percentage point, or slightly more, with a time horizon of one year. Accuracy slips to 1.5 to 2.0 percentage points for 2 to 3 year horizons.Inflation, interest rates, and unemployment rates are predicted more accurately than the GDP growth rate, and the errors might be as low as one-half the size of the error for the latter.

Within the GDP, the dominant components like total consumer spending (expenditure side) and total wage payments (income side) are projected about as accurately as the grand total, but such volatile components as consumer durable spending, business fixed investment, inventory change, net exports, the federal budget deficit, corporate profits and currency exchange rates are much less accurate. It is particularly the case that net balance or "residual" estimates are difficult to forecast. If these estimates fluctuate near zero, their percentage valuations of error deviations are highly erratic.

Forecast accuracy is affected by:

- Accuracy of observation of the target magnitudes,
- Behavioural changes by producers and consumers,
- Unpredictable shifts in noncontrollable factors (weather, natural disasters, military actions),

- Sampling error,
- Poor economic analysis (wrong model).

The GDP of the US is prepared by economists in the Department of Commerce, and they have carefully tabulated the ranges within which they revise GDP estimates every month. If the ranges are wide enough to encompass two-thirds of the revisions that have been made over the past several years, then we can say that carefully structured econometric forecast errors are well within such ranges.

The other sources of error (b,c,d,e) cannot be evaluated from "live" data, but in stochastic simulation experiments, replicated on computers, we have found that econometric forecasts do not lie outside expected error bands. Granted that these errors are larger than forecasters or users would like to see, there is nevertheless an inherent need to try to look ahead. Forecast, we must, and it makes sense to do it carefully and systematically.

High Frequency Forecasting

The computer and the provision of comprehensive national income and product accounts (NIPA) were two technical breakthroughs for me in our own way of building statistical models and forecasting from them. At the present time, we are investigating the possibilities of using advances in telecommunications to make a step forward in enhancing the precision of economic forecasts. The technique is based on the use of "high-frequency" information.

Fifty years ago, especially in preparing for post-war economic policy judgments our information base and statistical modeling interval was one year. For the present discussion, this would be called "low-frequency." When quarterly information on the NIPA became available in the 1950s, we shifted to a "higher-frequency," namely quarterly, and this became common during the 1960s. But, within a quarter, we gradually gain information on a daily, weekly, and monthly basis that tells us a great deal about the course of quarterly economic developments, not only in the current quarter but also in the subsequent quarter, by virtue of high serial dependence within the economy. This is purely a judgment, but the dependable influence of serial dependence on future extrapolations lasts no more than about six months in the US economy.

There are two objectives in the use of high frequency information. One is to make use of the up-to-minute flow of latest economic information in judging the current situation. This is for the purpose of pure, unconditional forecasting. A second objective is to tune medium range models so they start off a forecast exercise with plausible values for major economic magnitudes. In the present high-frequency model for the US economy, the steady flow of reports on monthly or weekly performance is put into a time-series model for rapid prediction of the quarterly NIPA. This can be done as frequently a$ desired, but presently is done at the end of every week, when the working days' reports for the completed week are assembled.

This is a purely objective system without subjective adjustment. It relies on more than 75 monthly indicators and generates values for more than 150 NIPA entries (real, nominal, and associated deflators). To get an idea how our view of the economy is sensitive to the information flow, we present two sets of graphs, dealing only with the real growth rate (GDP rate) and inflation rate (consumption deflator), showing the relationship between official reports and high-frequency forecasts—(1) made 3 months prior to a quarter's end, (2) 2 months prior to a quarter's end, (3) 1 month prior to a quarter's end and (4) a week prior to the first official report (approximately 2 or 3 weeks after the quarter's end but prior to the official report release).

It is evident that the accuracy of forecast improves as we get closer and closer to release date. More information becomes available about part of the quarter's performance, week-by-week. It is this flow of partial information (at high frequency) that we are trying to exploit in order to improve forecast accuracy, and it appears to be able to do that. In addition, it is a replicable process; we can provide exact arithmetic steps for others to follow in order to arrive at this same result.

Averaging Properties

One aspect of our particular approach to forecasting that has not been dealt with explicitly is its "averaging" property. An average of forecasts can reduce forecast risk. It is simply a variant of the practice of diversification, well known to investment practice and theory. If there is independence, to some degree at least, among forecasts or forecasters, then forming an average of forecasts spreads risks. We form averages in two dimensions. First we use our technique for three bodies of data, each one arriving at the same national total of interest, namely GDP. We forecast the expenditure side of the GDP from high frequency indicators of consumer and producer final expenditures. We also forecast the income side of the same GDP total from high frequency indicators of factor income payments (wages, interest, profit, rents, etc). The third estimator is obtained from principal components of important cyclical aggregate indicators such as monthly industrial production, personal income, and total consumer expenditures, together with several other general indicators. The principal components are not related directly to components of GDP, simply to the total and the associated deflator. GDP and its deflator are thus averaged across the three separate estimates.

It is worthwhile pointing out that official US practice allocates all the statistical discrepancy between the expenditure side and income side estimates of GDP to the latter. This is obviously an arbitrary decision and highly debatable, but it does tend to favour, in a relative sense, attribution of greater accuracy to expenditure side estimates. Nevertheless, it still pays to average our three forecasts of GDP.

There is another form of averaging implied by our procedures, namely that the large aggregates, especially GDP, are determined from a "bottom-up" calculation. The forecast of the grand total, GDP, is computed by adding or subtracting forecasts of several elements of accounting identities—types of expenditures or types of income. We do not want to compare this averaging process with "so-called" consensus forecasts, averaged across scores of different forecasters—some using objective methods and some using subjective methods. These "consensus forecasts" are unwieldy for responding instantaneously to situation changes or to "what-if" questions. Our approach, especially if tied to larger mainstream econometric models, can simulate, on demand, at very high frequency.

Forecasting Meetings

Information being the key concept in improving forecast accuracy, we would like to point out another important source that can be tapped. The practice developed over the years at Wharton Econometrics was feedback between forecast provider and forecast user, through the medium of the forecast meeting.

Every quarter a model-based forecast would be prepared and distributed to Wharton participants (subscribers) who would come to a meeting where the outlook was viewed critically by scores of business and institutional economists who had a great deal of firsthand information about sectors of the economy in which they were directly involved. On the basis of their critique of a pre-meeting forecast, the Wharton group prepared a post-meeting forecast, to take account of latest information. In this way, eight basic forecasts were made each year, and the post-meeting analyses gained considerable accuracy in the light of information supplied by business participants. They, in turn, gained from having an overall, consistent view of the macroeconomy.

3

Economic Environment

Rating agency responsiveness to the changing environment facing utilities is essential. Ratings that ignore significant macroeconomic and industry changes do not provide investors with the best information. Develops a logistic regression model to compare rating agency evaluations of preferred stock between a stable operating period, 1969-1972, and an unstable one, 1978-1981.

The results indicate that Standard & Poor's changes the weight it places on key variables to reflect changes in the operating environment of a utility. Preferred stock ratings are used as the basis for the analysis because preferred stock is a significant source of financing for electric utilities (as compared with industrial firms) and there is a paucity of research on the preferred stock rating process and on preferred stock valuation.

Preferred stock ratings are tied closely to bond ratings. Consequently, utility bond rating studies provide a foundation for the analysis of preferred stock ratings. Pinches, Singleton, and Jahankhani find that fixed charge coverage ratios, measures of the regulatory climate, firm size, profitability, growth rate in profitability, and construction expenditure activity are among the most important variables determining utility bond ratings.

Bhandari, Soldofsky, and Boe find that the level and trend in fixed charge coverage, debt ratio, and return on assets can predict up to 90 per cent of the rating changes for electric utilities. Wingler and Watts find that utility bond rating changes are influenced heavily by the amount of noncash earnings (allowance for funds used during construction (AFUDC)). Research dealing directly with the rating and valuation of preferred stock provides additional insights useful in evaluating the responsiveness of rating agencies to a changing economic environment facing electric utilities. Emanuel develops an option-hedging model for the valuation of preferred stock that supports the importance of coverage ratios and debt ratios in the valuation of preferred stock. Zumwalt uses principal components analysis and multiple discriminant analysis on a large set of financial variables to examine their ability to classify a sample of preferred stocks into their respective Standard & Poor's (S & P) rating categories.

He finds that the best classification factors changed significantly over the three years of his study period. The observed lack of stability of the factor parameters in the Zumwalt study suggests that the rating process is a dynamic one. Related research dealing with the valuation of preferred stocks also suggests that investors and rating agencies may focus on different variables over time. Sorenson and Hawkins (SH) find a significant clientele effect associated with preferred stocks bearing sinking funds, resulting in valuation differences over time.

Gombola, Kahl, and Nunn question the findings of SH and argue that the shift in returns between sinking fund and nonsinking fund preferred stock can be attributed best to shifts in Federal Reserve Board monetary policy. In summary, prior work on bond and preferred stock ratings suggests that over time, rating agencies focus on and may place different weights on the set of factors considered to be important in determining the ratings of fixed income securities. The proposition that rating agencies emphasize different factors over time, depending on the economic environment. Evidence is found that supports this proposition.

Methodology

The ordered logistic regression model is utilized to classify a sample of preferred stocks into their respective S&P assigned ratings. The logistic regression model estimates weights of the logit function in order to maximize the likelihood of predicting the outcome of events, given a set of independent variables. In the current study, the logistic model indicates the probability of a given preferred stock belonging to the next higher rating, conditional on the values of the explanatory variables. The logistic model has been shown to be superior to multiple discriminant analysis (MDA) and probit models for rating municipal bonds and for bankruptcy forecasting even for small samples. Ederington, in a comprehensive comparison of various bond rating prediction models, finds that the unordered logit and the ordered probit models were statistically superior in performance to the MDA and OLS regression models.

The inferior MDA and OLS regression model performance was attributed primarily to the violation of the joint multivariate normality assumption and the assumption of an interval scale dependent variable, respectively. Logistic regression also provides a more convenient test for the significance of coefficients than is possible with MDA.

Sample

The logistic model was developed using a sample of newly issued electric utility preferred stocks rated by Standard & Poor's. New issues of preferred stock reflect the latest rating agency assessment of quality. The models were estimated for preferred stocks issued over two periods - 1978-1981 and 1969-1972. The period prior to 1973 was one of relative stability in financial markets, oil prices, regulatory climate, and construction spending. After 1973, particularly during the 1978-1981 period, electric utilities have been subject to high and volatile levels of interest rates, oil price shocks, increased regulatory risk, and problems associated with nuclear plants and construction. It is clear that 1978-1981 was unstable, characterized by high and volatile interest rates, high business risk (as evidenced in lower profit margins, higher fuel costs, and increased utility construction expenditures), and increased regulatory risk (as reflected by the AFUDC measure.) The 1969-

1972 sample includes 71 preferred stocks with a mean issue size of $28.6 million and a standard deviation of $18.7 million. The S&P ratings for the sample are: BBB (9), A (32), AA (27), AAA (3). There were no issues with a BB rating or less. All preferred stocks in the early period sample had a call feature with an average call deferment period of 5.5 years.

Of the 71 preferred issues, four were immediately callable, 46 were callable in five years, 16 in seven years, and five in ten years. Four of the 71 issues had a sinking fund. The 1978-1981 sample included 49 preferred stocks with a mean issue size of $44.5 million and a standard deviation of $24.4 million.

The S&P ratings of the sample are: AA (11), A (16), BBB (17), and BB (5). There were no issues with an AAA rating. All preferred stocks in the later period sample had a call feature, with an average call deferment of 5.0 years. Of the 49 issues, three were immediately callable, 43 were callable in five years, and the remaining three in ten years. Twenty-nine of the 49 issues had a sinking fund.

The major difference between the two samples is the greater frequency of the sinking fund feature in the later period sample. This difference should not influence the ratings received because, as stated by S&P: "The preferred stock evaluation does not accord different rating treatment to a perpetual issue versus a sinking fund obligation".

Variable Selection

The variables included in the model have been identified by rating agencies and earlier studies as being important in determining utility bond and preferred stock ratings.

IPCOV	=	Earnings before interest and taxes divided by interest plus preferred stock dividends;
D	=	Debt ratio, measured as long-term debt divided by long-term debt, preferred stock plus common stock;
ARE	=	Return on common equity, defined as earnings available to common stockholder divided by beginning of the year common equity;

PS	=	Size (dollar amount) of the preferred stock offering;
PAFUDC	=	Ratio of allowance for funds used during construction (AFUDC) divided by net income;
MB	=	Ratio of market price to book value per share of common stock;
SD	=	The standard deviation of the return on assets.

IPCOV measures a firm's ability to meet its debt interest and preferred stock dividend obligations. A positive coefficient is expected because high coverage ratios should result in lower risk of default, a lower risk of the suspension of preferred stock dividends, and thus, higher ratings. The debt leverage ratio (D) is an indicator of the risk of the firm being unable to meet preferred stock obligations. IPCOV and D indicate the dynamic (cash flow) and stock (balance sheet) dimensions of default risk and are major variables used by rating agencies. The return on common equity (ARE) is expected to have a positive relationship with ratings. A high return on equity is indicative, ceteris paribus, of a lower probability of default.

Consistent with the approach used by Cohan, the size of the preferred stock issue (PS) is included as a measure of marketability. Larger preferred stock issues (or preferred stock offerings from larger firms) generally are considered to be more marketable and, therefore, may have higher ratings, ceter, ceteris paribus.

PAFUDC is used as a measure of earnings quality and the risk of a utility's construction programme. Some regulatory commissions have allowed current revenues to reflect at least a portion of construction expenditures. Other commissions have not permitted utilities to earn a current return on construction work in progress (CWIP).

In the latter case, the utilities are permitted a noncash earnings entry reflecting the financing costs of construction. This treatment results in a cash flow burden that may be particularly severe, given the long lead time before a major nuclear or coal plant comes on stream. The expected sign for PAFUDC is negative. MB is a measure of the ability of the firm to earn its true cost of capital. It provides a measure of the return being earned relative to risk and thus may be viewed as a measure of overall regulatory risk. French and Trout demonstrate a statistically significant relationship between market-to-book ratios for electric utilities and the factors contributing to regulatory risk for the period 1978-1981. In addition, the equality of means of the MB ratios across the three Value Line regulatory climate rating groups were tested.

At the 0.01 level of significance, the null hyphothesis that the mean MB is equal across the three Value Line regulatory climate categories is rejected. Using the Bonferroni multiple comparisons test, it is found that the MB ratios are significantly different between all pairs of Value Line categories.

The mean MB ratio for the above average category was 0.90. For the average category, the mean MB ratio was 0.81. For the average category, the mean MB was 0.72. The differences between all pairs of these means are significant at the 0.05 level. The MB measure of regulatory risk was used rather than a direct measure of regulatory risk because regulatory climate measure were not available until the mid- to late 1970s. A positive relationship between the MB ratio and preferred stock ratings if expected.

The standard deviation of return on assets (SD) is expected to have an inverse relationship with preferred stock ratings. Because preferred stock dividends are paid with after tax earnings, the higher the variability in the ratio of net income to total assets, the greater is the default risk for preferred stockholders. Because SD is controlled to some extent by a company's regulators, SD also may proxy for a portion of the regulatory risk dimension.

All variables were measured for the year prior to the issuance of the preferred stock except for ARE, PAFUDC, and SD. ARE and PAFUDC are averages for the three years prior to the issuance of preferred stock. SD was estimated using annual return on asset figures for the three years prior to the issuance of new preferred stock. The SD measure was computed over a three year period, rather than a longer period to reflect the recent actions of the utility commission. Three years was chosen because this period corresponds to the term of many state regulatory commission appointments.

Analysis of Results

The estimated coefficients indicate that higher ratings are associated with firms having a high interest and preferred dividend coverage ratio, a low debt ratio, a low proportion of AFUDC to net income, a high market price to book value ratio, and a low standard deviation of return on assets, all at a 5 per cent significance level. The significance of PAFUDC and MB suggest strongly that capital costs of preferred stock (to the extent lower ratings imply higher costs of financing) are affected adversely by earnings quality concerns and regulatory risk. An examination of the correlation matrix for the independent variables revealed no significant multicollinearity problems.

Because the model was estimated using standardized variables, it is possible to determine the relative importance of the individual variables from the size of their coefficients. The order of importance of the statistically significant variables was found to be: IPCOV, MB, D, PAFUDC, and SD. The importance of the coverage ration (IPCOV) is consistent with the emphasis of rating agencies on the firm's cash flow ability to meet its fixed obligations.

The relative importance of the MB ratio is indicative of the role played by regulatory risk in establishing preferred stock ratings during this period. Of the sample of 49 stocks, 28 or 57 per cent were classified correctly. This is somewhat better than the accuracy obtained by Zumwalt (approximately 50 per cent) and similar to the accuracy achieved in electric utility bond rating models. The model's ability to classify ratings in the extreme groups (AA and BB) is significantly that for the intermediate groups. All misclassifications are within one rating of the original.

Within sample classification procedures are biased upward if used as a measure of predictive ability. To test properly for predictive ability, the estimated model should be used to classify a holdout sample of bonds. The limited sample size precluded this approach. Instead, the Lachenbruch jackknife approach is used. This procedure involves estimation of the model using n-1 observations, where n is the sample size. The estimated model then classifies the one omitted observation. This procedure is repeated n times, omitting a different observation each time. The overall accuracy across ratings is 45 per cent. The classification ability was lowest for the BB rating group.

In contrast, the 1969-1972 period was one of stability in terms of the capital costs, oil prices, construction expenditures, and the regulatory climate for utilities. Only three of the seven variables were found to contribute significantly to explaining the ratings. These are IPCOV, PS, and ARE in order of importance.

During the stable period of 1969-1972, marketability and profitability measures, in addition to coverage measures, were among the most important determinants of preferred stock ratings. In contrast, ratings in the period of 1978-1981 were impacted more by measures of default, earnings quality, and regulatory risk. Thus, it appears that rating agencies emphasize different factors depending upon the economic environment, becoming more conscious of solvency and earnings quality factors in an unstable period compared to a stable period. A particularly interesting result is that the measure of regulatory risk, MB, was significant in the 1978-1981 period but not in the 1969-1972 period.

During the earlier period, the risks of plant disallowances, prudency reviews, and significant regulatory lag, to name a few, were practically non-existent. To the extent that ratings determine capital costs, firms currently operating in adverse regulatory climate areas incur higher costs for their preferred stock financing. The logistic model accurately classified 61 per cent of the sample. All misclassified ratings were within one rating category of the original. Fiftyseven per cent of the issues were classified correctly. Additional insight into the dynamics of the rating process was obtained using the estimated model for each period to classify the sample of preferred stocks from the other period. If the rating process placed relatively greater emphasis on default risk, earnings quality, and regulatory risk in the 1978-1981 period compared to the 1969-1972 period, then the model estimated over the 1978-1981 period systematically should underpredict the ratings for the sample of bonds taken from the 1969-1972 period. Conversely, the model estimated over the period 1969-1972 should overpredict ratings for preferred stocks in the 1978-1981 period.

The analysis was confined to BBB, A, and AA ratings, as these are the only ones common to the sample for both periods. The models were estimated using the standardized variables discussed earlier in order to avoid confounding effects of changes in the relative importance of explanatory variables and secular and cyclical shifts in the levels of the variables.

For instance, of the 32 AA bonds in the 1969-1972 period, 23 were classified correctly by the 1969-1972 model. The 1978-1981 model, however, classified only 13 correctly, and 15 were classified in the lower BBB rating. The bottom half shows the classification results for the 1978-1981 preferred stock issues using the 1969-1972 model parameters. The 1969-1972 model overpredicts the ratings. For example, for preferred stock rated BBB, the same period model correctly predicted the rating of 13 of the 17 issues. The 1969-1972 model predicted the rating of only one issue correctly and classified 15 issues in the higher A rating category.

The logistic model of preferred stock classification shows that during the unstable period of 1978-1981, interest coverage, regulatory climate, default risk, and earnings quality were primary considerations in the rating process. During the stable years of 1969-1972, the coverage ratio, profitability, and marketability were more important in determining preferred stock ratings.

These results imply that the preferred stock rating process for electric utilities reflects over time changes in the business risks facing utilities. The results also indicate that the parameter estimates derived from statistical models designed to replicate bond and preferred stock ratings are not stable over time. The actual rating process is dynamic (and judgmental) with respect to the emphasis of factors used in the determination of ratings. Thus, it appears that rating agencies rationally emphasize different factors over time, depending upon the economic environment-becoming more conscious of solvency and earnings quality factors in an unstable period compared to a stable period.

From a regulatory perspective, the results indicate that ratings are affected adversely by low quality earnings. To the extent that low earnings quality leads to lower bond and preferred stock ratings (and hence higher capital costs), the impact is not favourable to ratepayers, ceteris paribus.

The results of this study also have implications for investors who may use similar models to classify nonrated preferred stocks. Utility preferred stock issues that are placed privately normally are not rated. A rating model such as the one derived in this substance should be useful to institutional buyers of private placement preferred stock. The results suggest the need for institutional investors to update the rating models they use when there are fundamental changes in the business risk facing a firm or industry.

ECONOMIC PLANNING IN INDIA

The non-economic aspects of India's economic development in the recent past and the future. Since independence was attained in 1947 India has made significant economic progress. A three-year moving average of the national income over the last decade shows that the real national income has increased at an average annual rate of about 3 per cent. Productive capacity in the Indian economy has increased through increasing investment and the rate of economic performance has been quickened. There is little doubt that the Indian economy is moving away from dead centre and cannot be characterized as "stagnant," a term which could have been applied to it with some justification during the earlier decades.

It is, however, clear that this rate of growth is small relative to the rate of population increase, which has been estimated to be 1.5 per cent per annum. The rate of increase of per capita income, therefore, comes to 1.5 per cent per annum.

If the rate of increase of population accelerates in the future, as some experts forecast on very good grounds, the present rate of increase of national income will be found to be completely inadequate and India will have to run faster and faster even to keep herself at the same level of per capita income.

Could India have done better than she has during this period? If so, why did she not? And if we know why, can she be made to perform better in the future and by what means? These are big questions, and no student of Indian problems can be expected to have all the correct answers. We are here trying to indicate in a tentative way some of the answers to these questions.

There is considerable evidence, both official and nonofficial, from Indian and foreign observers, to indicate that the development effort in India during the last decade has been characterized by much inefficiency and waste; that the available economic resources have not been as productively used under the given conditions as they could have been. And when one begins to consider and analyse this, he soon comes up with the fact that the causes lie deep in the whole Indian cultural and social setup and that it involves the whole problem of the social efficiency of the Indian society. But this is to anticipate. Let me first substantiate the opening gambit that the Indian development effort during the fifties was inefficient.

Perhaps we can begin by noting the observations of the latest Indian delegation to China, which visited that country early in 1959 to study the Chinese achievements in the conservation and maximum utilization of water, including rain water. What the delegation found most impressive, it is reported, was the type of organization employed for achieving the remarkable results in this field rather than the use of any new techniques which were being used in China and which were not known or used in India.

This is an important observation because in India' irrigation is not a new problem, and a failure in this respect cannot be explained away by pleading lack of know-how or inexperience. Yet the failure in this field is glaring and extensive. At the end of the First Five Year Plan the irrigation potential created by major irrigation works was 559,000 acres in Bihar and 465,000 acres in West Bengal, of which only 265,000 and 223,000 acres respectively were actually irrigated, thus leaving about half of the potential unutilized. In many of the irrigated areas water is available for more than one crop per year. Yet a recent survey showed that only about 12 per cent of the land under irrigation has more than one irrigated crop per year.

This failure of organizational effort is by no means unique or solitary. Many others can be easily met with in India today. Take the programme of Community Development Projects launched in 1952 with the express purpose "to set free the creative energies of the people so that they may build up through their own effort and through their own institutions a richer and improving social life." The recent appraisals, both official and non-official, of the achievements of this programme have indicated that this objective has not been reached; that there has been more concentration on welfare aspects than on productivity aspects; that the programme has settled down to a dead administrative routine so as to smother the growth of local leadership and initiative. It is again very largely an organizational failure.

This list of failures need not be added to except to note that the same kind of failure is evident, in more or less degree, in regard to land reforms, population control, education, social legislation, etc. The failures are too widespread and blatant to be explained away by such factors as inexperience or expediency. We should try to probe deeper, if we can.

An interesting aspect of the situation is that there is consciousness in the country regarding these failures. In the examples here given the appraisals and observations of responsible Indians have been principally cited. Many Indian leaders have drawn attention to them from time to time, have deplored them, and have emphasized the need for their speedy removal. If one mentions these failures in India today, there would be no reluctance to admit them. There would also be almost unanimous agreement regarding the desirability of removing their causes. But this candor will not be in evidence as soon as one goes on to discuss the reasons underlying them. A common view would be that these defects and failures are not abiding but passing and that they require only like remedies. A variation of the argument would be to take a historical view and attribute them to the long period of foreign rule in India. Self-rule, given time, will almost automatically cure them. No wonder there is complete apathy or reluctance to undertake a deeper appraisal of the situation.

The causes of the present *malaise* in Indian society lie deeper and cannot be explained by the superficial arguments. Our reflections on this theme were sparked a few years ago when we began to assess the success of economic planning in independent India. We have since been struck again and again by the repetition of similar mistakes in government policy with similar consequences. The failure to learn from experience was everywhere patent in the economic sphere. For some time we attributed this to the political element that dominates everything in India today. Politicians are notoriously shortsighted, and we thought that this was the main reason for repeated failures in the economic sphere. But later we realised that the same kind of failure was also evident in the political sphere in India, and in many other spheres also. We was forced to the cease that the causes were more pervading and deeply embedded in the whole society than we had suspected.

An analysis of these causes, however, is not easy. First,our own limitations as a social scientist are overwhelming. Secondly, it involves introspection, a difficult art to practice anywhere. Being a part of the Indian society and having been born and brought up in it, we are not sure of our ability to look at it from outside from a critical angle. we decided, however, to make the effort, perhaps in a foolhardy way, because we thought somebody must begin to do this sometime, and if we are wrong at least it would provoke abler minds to attempt the task sadly neglected so far. We have to examine for this purpose the social efficiency of the Indian society as a whole in relation to economic and social development. *But as Davis observes*: in the matter of societal efficiency we have a concept but little else. In practice it is hedged about by the preconceptions and institutions of a going society; in social science it is handicapped by the unreality of ignoring these practical limitations and by the lack of an adequate set of measuring devices. The concept says: Given a certain quantum of natural resources and human population, there exist numerous ways of bringing the two together for the production of goods and services, some of these ways being more effective than others. But it does not tell us how to measure effectiveness with respect to the non-economic parts of the social system. We can make use of such makeshift indices as exist, but in the last analysis we are thrown back on speculation and general theory.

Davis goes on to warn: "Depending on verbal description and intuitive judgment, one tends to see causal relationships *in principle* and then to assume erroneously that they exist in fact. The case of India is particularly difficult because of the country's extreme cultural diversity." The analysis that we are attempting here is of course subject to all these limitations and should be understood as such.

One must, we think, begin by analyzing the basic ways and *mores* of the traditional Indian or Hindu society, note the changes that have taken place in them in modern times under British rule, and then try to see if these in principle and in fact give some clues to the analysis of the complex problem.

Max Weber's analysis of the sociology of Hinduism is perhaps the best point of departure for this purpose from many points of view. Weber found that in religion, cultural values, personality, motivation, and social structure come together, and he discussed Hindulsm from that point of view. In summarizing his analysis, we quote the able summary given by Dr. Bellah:

Weber finds the notion of *dharma,* religiously prescribed obligation, to be the core of Hinduism, especially in its deep inner connection with the idea of *karma,* the endless chain of causation working itself out in successive rebirths. The orthodox view is that whatever position one finds oneself in, in this life and one's obligation is to fulfill the *dharma* of one's position so that one will improve one's chances in the next incarnation. The intellectuals, revolting against this notion, always sought escape from the wheel of rebirth through some sort of individualistic salvation. Weber shows how these conceptions hindered cultural rationalisation beyond a certain point.

On the one hand they contributed to the development of special technologies appropriate to the *dharma* of each profession — from construction technique to logic as the technology of proof and disproof to the technology of eroticism — but at the same time they hindered the development of levels of generalisation above the technological because of the fragmentation involved in the notion of occupational *dharma*. On the other hand, the intellectuals were so completely preoccupied with the problem of salvation that all philosophy was made subservient to this end. With respect to the social structure, it is the *dharma* concept as integrated with the idea of caste, which is the key to the situation.

In spite of the remarkable achievements of certain castes, there is always a limit imposed by the traditionalistic definition of the caste *dharma* itself. Further, the division of society into innumerable watertight compartments, while engendering a very stable integration of sorts allows a minimum of flexibility and especially limits the generalisation of political power making the society an easy prey to foreign conquest. The major religious movements which reject this mode of social organisation either fall back into it in the form of a new caste, or, as in the case of Buddhism, remain an individualistic and socially negative group existing symbolically in relation to traditional society and unable to generate any really different mode of social organization.

In terms of personality, the *dharma* idea results in the fragmentation of response directed to the external demands of ritual obligation on the one hand, or a passive withdrawal into mysticism on the other. There is no basis of inner unification of personality for action in response to the command of a transcendental God. The Indian alternatives tend to be action without unification and unification without action. Theoretically, nobody would disagree that this kind of socioreligious framework is not very suitable to modern economic development. But many have denied its relevance to the day-to-day life of the people as actually lived in India in the past and the present. Some have stressed the tradition of practical values in India which, it is said, is evident throughout her history. Others have insisted there exists an ethic in Indian life which can "sanction" the materialistic values of an industrial society.

Whether the main beliefs and ideals embodied in Hinduism shape and influence the actual *mores* of Hindu society today is a question that can be answered on the basis of such reliable and well- tested information as may be available on this point. So far as we know, the available information is not very ample; nevertheless what is available is, in our opinion, significant.

O'Malley has discussed such information in his *Popular Hinduism, the Religion of the Masses*. He cites the work of Miriam Young, in 1931 in the Punjab, who after a three-year study concluded that *karma* was a practical philosophy colouring the villager's whole outlook on life. He also refers to Crooke's study in the same region in 1897, which takes an opposite stand. O'Malley also refers to several inquiries bearing on this carried out in different regions in India at the 1891 and 1901 censuses. He refers to these discussions and to his own extensive experiences in India and arrives at the following, we think, balanced judgment:

Materialistic, however, as the villagers may be in their relations to the outside world and in the conduct of their everyday life, there can be no question that their general trend of thought is strongly devotional and that religion is deeply ingrained in thought and feeling and is a very real thing to them. One impelling force is undoubtedly the desire to accumulate merit in the expectation of a higher or better life in the next existence, and of eventually obtaining release from the burden of individual existence, though it is doubtful how far the attainment of such a distant goal as the latter is actually a motive idea among the masses.... Another factor is the absence of a nationalistic spirit and lack of scientific knowledge. Two recent studies using modern anthropological and psychoanalytical methods broadly confirm the importance and influence of the Hindu belief systems in the day-to-day life of the people.

These recent studies focus on the cumulative effect of attitudes towards each other, towards the social order, and towards the supernatural on the formation of adult personality. W. S. Taylor, who worked and lived in Madhya Pradesh, concluded that Orthodox Hinduism is able to create a basic personality pattern in which personal initiative is replaced by the sense of conformity, in which responsibility is exercised without personal authority, in which security is associated with the sense of dependence and self-respect with a sense of helplessness, and in which opportunities for frustration and acute anxiety are minimized. It is a basic personality whose integration and stability are primarily a function of the cultural system to which it belongs and are not organized around any system of personal choices.

G. Morris Carstairs, who intensively studied a village in Rajastan, confirmed generally Taylor's findings and tried to take the analysis further in psychoanalytic terms. These two recent studies in fact go deeper than the two cited before, because they delve into the personality formation process which governs the conduct of individuals throughout life, and both of them show the great influence of the basic values embodied in Hindu culture. They also show how the institutions of joint family and caste play a dominant role in this set up. We submit that an analysis accepting this, at least as a hypothesis, is likely to be more fruitful than one which loses itself either in arguing away its significance or rejecting it altogether. We proceed by accepting the hypothesis that the institutional structure and functioning of Hindu society was and continues to be inimical to the development of a community. This together with its *mores* gives rise to a widely common personality pattern devoid of personal initiative, purposefulness, involvement, etc. To attribute all the evils resulting in social inefficiency in India today to British rule is surely to ignore realities. The basic framework of Hindu society was complete and in full operation before the British and also before the Mohammedan conquest of India.

The lack of social and political cohesion in the Indian society made it, as Weber notes, an easy prey to foreign conquest. So far as the basic attitudes, personality patterns, motivations, etc. are concerned, they were independent of the British and the Mohammedan rulers. It is, of course, true that they were influenced by foreign rule. So far as the Mohammedan rule is concerned, the Mohammedans seemed to have been themselves influenced by Hindu social institutions, as witness the development of castes among Mohammedans in India. So far as British rule is concerned, it is possible to note more specifically what it did to Hindu society.

This is neither the occasion nor the place to dilate at length on the whole theme of British impact on India. We shall confine myself here to the influence of British rule on the caste structure, the pivotal structural parameter of the Hindu social system. Under the British many things happened to weaken as well as to strengthen the caste system but on balance the latter outweighed the former. The British, in contradistinction to their predecessors, progressively refused to perform certain social functions, perhaps the most important of which were those connected with the regulation of a caste society involving the functioning and relative status of castes.

The pre-British rulers, including the Muslims, by performing these functions helped maintain, even in a caste society, a degree of social integration. Thereby the process of continuous adjustment and wider integration was always at work. This process of over-all social regulation and integration could no longer be maintained when the British refused to perform these functions; as a result the social structure lost its adaptability and integration. In the preBritish days caste loyalty was tempered by the sense of loyalty to the Hindu society as a whole which was maintained by the secular authority. The loyalty to one's own caste increased under the British as occasions and opportunities for emphasizing or exhibiting the over-all sense of Hindu loyalties decreased. It is in this manner that the institution of caste became more rigid than before in the period of British rule.

Under the British also economic and social dividing lines in society became parallel, which they were not before. J. S. Furnivall has observed that the impact of the West on India has been less violent than, for instance, on Burma, because of the caste system in India which afforded considerable protection to the social system in India. It is true that it prevented social disintegration, so characteristic of other societies, but it also left the Indian society loose and weak and hampered its transformation into a modern social and industrial community.

British rule also brought to India new ideas from the West -bureaucracy, the judiciary, and an effective system of laws. It also gave rise to nationalism. As suggested, try to assess their effects, briefly in the reverse order. The development of nationalism in India was sparked by British rule and, though it began as a movement allied with social reformism, it gradually lost this aspect and became more and more a purely political movement. Only the negative aspects of nationalism developed in India, i.e., its aim were the negative one of driving away the foreign ruler, but the positive aspects of nationalism did not appear. In 1947 India acquired nationhood but has not been able to develop as yet sufficient unity and emotional integration for the effective functioning of a modern society.

The judiciary and the law system developed by the British brought about far-reaching changes in the concepts of private property. Together with the bureaucracy, they smothered village self-rule and helped to bring about a malfunctioning of the social system. The bureaucracy developed by the British effectively killed whatever little self-rule there was and furthered the demise of most vestiges of initiative. Perhaps the bureaucracy as an impersonal machine, with its impersonal character, its hierarchical order, its prescriptions of definite action in definite contexts, etc., was well suited to the general social structure of caste society. We suspect that this is one of the reasons the bureaucracy developed so well in India as compared to other underdeveloped countries and still continues to flourish. It finds a social background that is very favourable to the growth of its formal structure, though not necessarily to its working efficiency.

With British rule came English education, and this opened up the whole world of Western knowledge to educated Indians. This knowledge was and has been absorbed more at the theoretical than at the practical level. The intellectual tradition in India, which is mainly the Brahmin tradition, has that characteristic. It is singularly free from restrictions or inhibitions regarding intellectual speculation. In India there has rarely been a persecution for holding certain opinions, even heretical opinions.

This was partly because, though intellectual speculation was free, the translation of any new ideas into practice was hidebound by the prevailing ethics and modes of behaviour. The Brahmins themselves had laid down the rule that though many things might be rationally obvious and good, they should not be brought into practice if they were not in tune with the traditional behaviour pattern and against popular folkways. Such a tradition would naturally be much more ready to absorb ideas on the philosophical plane than in actual life. Today, therefore, the intellectual climate in India appears to be much more pronouncedly Western than in Japan or China.

Taking everything into account, it would be fair to say that British rule did introduce some bad kinks into the old social structure and its functioning, but it cannot be held responsible for all the evils. It would be perhaps better to say that the Indian social structure responded to the British impact in a way in which some of the bad characteristics were scored deeper while some of the good characteristics could not develop much further than they perhaps would have done in the absence of British rule. But the basic cultural and institutional patterns have very largely remained unchanged.

As a result, in India today we find in the people a widespread lack of personal initiative, involvement, and purposefulness in life, a tendency towards empty ritual, general apathy, casteism, communalism, indifference, and absence of a feeling of participation in national endeavor. This has often been noted and deplored by Indians themselves with reference to the two plans of economic development undertaken by the Government of India in recent years. It represents a position of confusion and social ambivalence not conducive to social or economic efficiency.

A critical and historical examination of the Hindu social organization brings out the fact that Hinduism is not a religion in the Western sense of the word. It is really a social system, a method of organizing society. In its earlier stages it proved a powerful instrument of absorbing diverse kinds of peoples and tribes into the Hindu fold without disturbing their individual rituals and practices. It is conceivable that if this process had gone on, perhaps caste rigidity would not have developed and the social and occupational mobility would have been maintained so as to weld all the Hindu people into an integrated community.

This grand process, however, did not go on but stagnated. The Hindu society today is an unfinished social experiment that has rigidified the social institutions into a mold. In understanding this it is necessary to realise that the doctrines of *karma, dharma,* etc. in their philosophic context would not have mattered much had they not had in Hindu society their social institutional counterparts in terms of the caste system and the joint family. Weber has referred to the developments in China and Japan, where this did not happen to the same extent as in India.

As a matter of historical fact, the growth and development of nationalism should have accomplished many of the things that are needed for the rejuvenation of Hindu society. But the growth of nationalism in India has not done this. The Hindu social institutions have subdivided the social organism in such a way as to make the units (caste and family) smaller and smaller and unrelated to the general society. *"Thus it denies the entire theory of community and bases the organization of Hindu life on the opposite principle of disintegration and division."* Nationalism in India has not been able to reverse this process. In fact, it bent the nationalist movement in its own direction rather than the other way round. Nationalism struck flame on foreign rule. The first generation of the English educated Indians was completely bowled over by Western culture as brought to India by the British.

The effective suppression of the Mutiny in 1858 impressed on them the superiority of the British. Fired by the ideas imbibed through English literature they came to the view that the old Indian ways had to be remodelled on Western lines. They came to regard British connexion with India as a providential dispensation for the good of India. They visualized political and social development to go hand in hand and believed that social reform was of basic importance even for political advancement. The Brâhma Samâj in Bengal and the Prârthana Samâj in Bombay (founded in 1865) which bore the stamp of Christian ideas were manifestations of this tendency in the social and religious field. The Indian National Congress was founded in 1885.

The next generation that came of age around the 1880's developed a more virile strain of nationalism. It was backward-looking and appealed to India's past glory. The ideology of resurgent Hinduism as put forth by Vivekananda, provided the social and religious basis for this school of nationalists. While acknowledging the benefits of British rule, this school refused to recognise it as a providential dispensation. It further maintained that these benefits will be nullified if they were not followed by home rule which was their logical culmination. The demand for self rule cannot be satisfied by good rule by a foreign bureaucracy. Political advancement was primary to all social reform. The latter will automatically follow political independence and therefore the national movement must not dissipate its strength in fighting for social reform but must concentrate on the struggle for liberation from the British yoke. For that, all means, whether constitutional or otherwise, should be used. This stand was more nationalistic than that of their predecessors. If the first generation suffered from an inferiority complex with regard to the West this generation was overcompensating for it. The neglect of social reform further underlined their backward looking orientation and made them line up with socially reactionary elements. It inevitably took a Hindu colour and ensured in time the development of a separate Muslim nationalism as a reaction. The Muslim League was founded in 1906. The more direct type of action in the struggle for independence assumed the form of the Swadeshi movement, which included the use of Indian goods and the boycott of British and foreign goods. This suited the newly rising class of industrialists and brought them into the fold of the national movement.

Gandhian orientation of the nationalist movement in the 'twenties of this century was pronouncedly Hindu, anti-intellectual and more backward-looking than that of the generation that had gone before. It condemned Western science and technique and advocated revival of cottage industries, village uplift, etc. It gave to some of the religious terms of Hinduism, like *satyâgraha, ahiEsa, cwaraj,* etc., a political meaning, and political doctrines were clothed in spiritual terms. Its intellectual content was very much inferior but its emotional appeal was great as was evidenced by the various mass movements that were conducted under the leadership of the Indian National Congress in the period after 1914. It can perhaps be said that without a watering down of the severe intellectualism of the earlier movement, it could not have appealed to the masses. It also became progressively more political, and its already declining social content gradually dwindled into insignificance. It only came to the surface when political exigencies required it, as for example, in the case of the untouchables in the 1930's.

Nationalism in India has been oriented much more towards the negative goal of ending foreign rule and much less towards evolving the positive content of what was to be done after achieving that goal. This we have called the lack of positive aspects of nationalism. The social content of positive nationalism therefore remains to be developed in India, and that is the task facing the present national leadership. The immensity of the task of bringing about the necessary extent of social change in India can be gauged from the fact that it is nothing short of the whole problem of the remaking of a nation. History affords examples of such problems being solved by violent as well as peaceful methods, and perhaps the examples of the former kind are more numerous than those of the latter kind.

India has chosen the latter and, perhaps, the harder path of change, but possibly has not yet appreciated the wide ramifications of the problems and the all-sided and clear-sighted effort that is necessary for accomplishing the difficult task. Attention and effort have been focused primarily on economic development and change. The other fields have not received as much attention.

4

Industrial Policy and Licensing

Deep into his novel Ishmael, author Daniel Quinn uses a metaphor to describe our civilization as it has arisen out of the first industrial revolution and the agricultural revolution before that. He likens our civilization to one of those early attempts to build an airplane—the one with the flapping wings and the guy pedaling madly to make the wings go. In Quinn's metaphor, the man and the plane go off a very high cliff and the guy is pedaling away and the wings are flapping, the wind is in his face, and the poor fool thinks he's flying. But the fact is, he's in free fall and just doesn't realise it because the ground is so far away. He's not flying because his plane is not built according to the laws of aerodynamics.

Quinn says that our civilization is in free fall, too, for the same reason: it wasn't built according to the "laws of aerodynamics" that allow civilizations to fly. We think we can just pedal harder and everything will be okay; pedal harder still and we can fly to the stars. But as suggested, surely crash unless we redesign our craft—our civilization—according to laws of flight that will permit us to wing into what author Paul Hawken calls the next industrial revolution.

The next industrial revolution? Is that realistic? Clearly, the first one is just not working out very well, as Quinn's metaphor so aptly demonstrates. In fact, according to economist Lester Thurow, we've already passed through the second industrial revolution and are into the third. In his 1999 book Building Wealth: The New Rules for Individuals,

Companies and Nations, Thurow holds that the first industrial revolution was steam-powered. The second, which was electricity-powered, made possible the third, which is the information revolution, ushering in the information age. Clearly, all three stages have emerged with vastly different characteristics, and all three are revolutionary in scope.

Yet they all share some fundamental characteristics that lump them together with an overarching, common theme; they were and remain an unsustainable phase in civilization's development. For example, someone still has to manufacture your 10-pound laptop computer, that icon of the information age. If you count everything processed and distilled into the manufacture of those 10 pounds, going all the way back to the mines for materials and wellheads for energy, the weight will be as much as 40,000 pounds.

Not much has changed over the years since the beginning of the industrial revolution except the sophistication of the finished product. So we refer to all three of Thurow's stages collectively as the first industrial revolution, and we believe the next truly revolutionary industrial revolution will be predicated on sustainability.

FOSSIL FUELISHNESS

I run Interface Inc., a manufacturing company that annually produces and sells over a billion dollars worth of carpets, textiles, chemicals, and architectural flooring for commercial and institutional interiors. Our factories process raw materials into finished, manufactured products. Our raw materials come from suppliers who operate their own factories. A few years ago, we decided we wanted Interface to become the first fully sustainable industrial enterprise—a company that could fly on its own into the next industrial revolution. In 1995, the year we set our sights on the stars, our sales were slightly more than $800 million.

Our first task was to examine Interface's entire supply chain, to find out where the materials came from that produce so great an amount of carpets, textiles, and other items. What we discovered horrified me. We found that to manufacture

$800 million worth of products, our factories and suppliers, together, extracted from the Earth and processed mote than 1.2 billion pounds of material—that's 1.2 billion pounds of materials from Earth's stored natural capital.

Of the roughly 1.2 billion pounds, about 400 million pounds represented relatively abundant inorganic materials, mostly mined from the Earth's crust. The remaining 800 million pounds was petrobased, coming from oil, coal, or natural gas. What troubled me the most was that roughly two-thirds of that 800 million pounds of irreplaceable, nonrenewable, exhaustible, precious natural resources was burned up to produce the energy to convert the other third—along with the 400 million pounds of inorganic material—into products used in offices, hospitals, schools, airports, and other facilities.

That fossil fuel, with its complex, precious, organic molecular structure, is gone forever—changed into carbon dioxide and other waste products, many of them toxic, that were produced in the burning of the fuel. These substances, of course, were dumped into the atmosphere to accumulate and to contribute to global warming, to melting polar ice caps, and someday, in the not too distant future, to flooding coastal plains, such as much of Florida. In the longer term, the lapping waters may even flood the streets of Boston, New York, New Orleans, and other coastal cities. Meanwhile, we breathe what we burn to make our products and our livings.

This uncontrolled consumption of natural resources cannot go on indefinitely. Our company, and essentially every other company we know of, is plundering the Earth.

Mea Culpa

Of course, no one other than me is accusing me of such wasteful practices. In fact, in terms of our civilization's prevailing attitudes, I'm a kind of modern-day hero, a captain of industry who founded a company that provides over 8,500 people with jobs that support some 27,000 family members, all of whom depend on those factories that consumed those materials. Besides, Interface pays fair market prices for every pound of material it buys and processes. Shouldn't that assuage our guilt? The answer is, only if the market's price covers the full cost, and unfortunately, it doesn't. Who paid for the military power our government sent into the Middle East to protect the oil at its source?

You did, through your taxes. Who is paying for the damage done by storms, tornadoes, and hurricanes that result from global warming? You are, through your insurance premiums. Who will pay for the losses of coastal lands in Florida and the cost of the flooded, abandoned streets of Boston, New York, and New Orleans in the distant future? Future generations, your progeny, that's who.

Bill McDonough—architecture at the University of Virginia, business entrepreneur, and a leading proponent of green design—uses the term "intergenerational tyranny" for this taxation without representation levied by us on those yet unborn. These points emphasise how the revered market system of the first industrial revolution allows companies like mine to shift those costs to others, to externalize those costs, even to future generations.

In other words, the market, in its pricing of exchange value without regard to cost or use value, is opportunistic and permissive, if not dishonest. It allows the externalization of any cost that an unwary, uncaring, or gullible public will permit to be externalized. So are we a thief, too? Yes, in terms of the definition that we believe will come into use during the next industrial revolution.

The perverse tax laws, by failing to correct the errant market and force it to internalize those externalities such as the costs of global warming and pollution, are our accomplices in crime. We are part of the endemic process that is going on at a frighteningly accelerating rate worldwide. This process, if it's not stopped, will rob our children and their children, and theirs, and theirs, of their futures.

No industrial company on Earth and—I feel pretty safe in saying—not a company or institution of any size is sustainable, in the sense of meeting its current needs without, to some extent, depriving future generations of the means of meeting their needs. When the Earth runs out of finite, exhaustible resources and ecosystems collapse, our descendants will be left holding the empty bag.

Kinder, Gentler Technology

If Interface is to become the first industrial company in the world to attain environmental sustainability, as suggested, have to focus on more than just doing no harm; as suggested, have to restore some of what's been lost since the first industrial revolution. To restore means to put back more than we take. The way to become restorative is first to become sustainable ourselves and then to help or influence others to move towards sustainability.

At Interface, we have undertaken a quest, first to become sustainable and then to become restorative. And we know broadly what that means for us. It's a daunting challenge, and it means creating and adopting the technologies of the future—kinder, gentler technologies that emulate nature. That's where we think as suggested, find the model.

Someone recently mused that a computer is mundane, but a tree is a technological marvel. A tree operates on solar energy and lifts water in ways that seem to defy the laws of physics. When we finally understand how a whole forest works and learn to apply its myriad symbiotic relationships analogously to the design of industrial systems, we'll be on the right track. That right track will lead us to technologies that will enable us, for example, to operate our factories on solar energy.

A halfway house for us may be fuel-cell or gas-turbine technologies. But ultimately, we believe we have to learn to operate off current income the way a forest does and, for that matter, the way we do in our businesses and households, not off stored natural capital. Solar energy is current energy income, arriving daily at the speed of light, in inexhaustible abundance, from that marvelous fusion reactor just eight minutes away.

Those technologies of the future will enable Interface to feed its factories with recycled raw materials—recycled raw materials that come from harvesting the billions of square yards of carpets and textiles that have already been made. Nylon face pile can be recycled into new nylon yarn to be made into new carpet; backing material can be recycled into new backing material for new carpet; and, in our textile business, polyester fabrics can be recycled into polyester fibre, to be made into new fabrics.

These recycling processes represent a closed loop—using those precious organic molecules over and over in cyclical fashion, rather than sending them to landfills, or incinerating them, or downcycling them into lower-value forms by the linear processes of the first industrial revolution. Linear must go; cyclical must replace it. Cyclical is nature's way.

In nature, there is no waste; one organism's waste is another's food. For our industrial process, so dependent on petrochemical raw materials, this means technical "food" is to be reincarnated by recycling it into the product's next life cycle, and the next. Of course, the recycling operations will have to be driven by renewable energy, too.

Otherwise, as suggested, consume more fossil fuel for the energy to recycle than as suggested, save in virgin petrochemical raw materials by recycling in the first place. We want a gain, not a net loss. If we get it right during the next industrial revolution, as suggested, never have to take another drop of oil from the Earth for our products or industrial processes.

Those technologies of the future will enable us to send zero waste and scrap to the landfill. We're already well down this track at Interface. We have become disciplined and focused in all Interface's businesses on what is sometimes called the low-hanging fruit, the easier savings to realise. We named this effort QUEST—Quality Utilizing Employees' Suggestions and Teamwork.

In the first five years of this effort, we've reduced total waste in our worldwide business by nearly 50 per cent, which has saved $133 million, and those savings are paying the bills for all the rest of this revolution in our company. We are on our way to saving $80 million or more per year when we reach our goals.

Cradle to Cradle

We're redesigning our products for greater resource efficiency, too. For example, we are producing carpets with lighter face weights—less pile—but better durability. It sounds paradoxical, but its actually working in a measurable way. We're making carpets with lower pile heights and higher densities, using carpet face constructions that wear better in high traffic but use less materials.

This is just one example of the kinds of technologies that will help drive the next industrial revolution. Those technologies of the future will enable us to operate without emitting anything into the air or water that hurts the ecosystem. We're just beginning to understand how incredibly difficult this will be, because the materials coming into our factories from our suppliers are replete with substances that never should have been taken from the Earth's crust in the first place.

Those technologies must enable us to get our people and products from Point A to Point B in resource-efficient fashion. In our company alone, at any hour of the day, we have more than 1,000 people on the move, while trucks, ships, and sometimes planes deliver our products all over the world. One potential solution for our transportation needs is the hypercar developed by Rocky Mountain Institute physicist Amory Lovins.

When operational, Amory's super-lightweight, super-aerodynamic hypercar will use solar energy for electrolysis of water to extract hydrogen to power its fuel cells. A flywheel or an ultra-capacitor with nothing moving and nothing to wear out will store energy, including the recaptured energy generated in braking the car, with this energy going to power electric motors on each wheel, dispensing with the drive train altogether.

To complement and reinforce these new technologies, as suggested, continue to sensitize and engage all 8,500 of our people in a common purpose, right down to the factory floor and right our there face to face with our customers. We must also redesign commerce in the next industrial revolution and redesign our role as manufacturers and suppliers of products and services. Already, we are acquiring or forming alliances with the dealers and contractors that install and maintain our products, requiring an investment of some $150 million in the United States alone since 1995. With these moves downstream into distribution we are preparing to provide cyclical—what Bill McDonough calls cradle-to-cradle—service to our customers, as the distribution system becomes a collection and return system as well.

In our reinvented commercial system, carpet need not be bought or sold at all. Leasing carpet, rather than selling it, and being responsible for it cradle-to-cradle is the future and the better way. Towards this end, we've created and offered to the market the Evergreen Lease, the first ever perpetual lease for carpet. We sell the services of the carpet—colour, design, texture, warmth, acoustics, comfort under foot, cleanliness, and improved indoor air quality—but not the carpet itself. The customer pays by the month for these services.

In this way we make carpet into what Michael Braungart—a chemist and partner of Bill McDonough— terms a product of service, what Paul Hawken describes as licensing in his book The Ecology of Commerce, and what the President's Council on Sustainable Development calls extended producer responsibility. Walter Stahel, Swiss engineer and economist, was perhaps the first person to conceptualize such a notion.

Environmental sustainability, redefined for our purpose as taking nothing from the Earth that is not renewable and doing no harm to the biosphere, is a mountain, but we've begun the climb. Teams all through our company in manufacturing locations on four continents are working together on hundreds of projects and technologies that are leading us towards sustainability.

STEPS TO SUCCESS

We've embraced the Natural Step—the frame of reference conceived by Kari-Henrik Robert of Sweden to define the system conditions of ecological sustainability—as a compass to guide our efforts. In the thousands and thousands of little things, the Natural Step framework is helping provide what we have termed the sensitivity hook-up, among our people, our communities, our customers, and our suppliers. We want to sensitize all our constituencies to Earth's needs and to what sustainability truly means for all of us.

We started this whole effort at Interface on two fronts. The first was focused on waste reduction. That's the revolution we call QUEST. We define waste as any cost that goes into our product that does not produce value for our customers. Value, of course, embraces product quality, including aesthetics, utility, durability, and resource efficiency. Since any waste is bad, we're measuring progress against a zero-based waste goal. A revolutionary notion itself, our definition of waste includes not just poor quality and scrap—the traditional notions of waste. It also means anything else we don't do right the first time—a misdirected shipment, a mispriced invoice, a bad debt. In QUEST, there's no such thing as "standard" waste or "allowable" less-than-perfect quality.

QUEST is measured in hard dollars and, as we said, we took nearly 50 per cent, or $133 million cumulatively, out of our costs in the first five years, on our way to our goal of more than $80 million per year of waste reduction. Scrap to the landfills from our factories is down over 60 per cent since the beginning of QUEST in 1995, in some factories, 80 per cent.

We've also begun to realise that conceptually it might be possible to take waste, by its current definition, to a level below zero as measured against our 1994 benchmark. For instance, if we substitute recycled materials for virgin materials, we are eliminating someone else's wastes and thus are creating, in effect, negative waste when measured against the old norms. If successful, as suggested, have replaced the old system, now obsolete, with the new, nonwasteful system.

Among the other initiatives we've launched is EcoSense, which is based on a concept we call EcoMetrics. As an example, consider the following hypothetical tradeoff. One widget consumes 10 pounds of petrochemically derived material, a nonrenewable resource. Another, functionally and aesthetically identical to the first, consumes only six pounds of petrochemically derived material, substituting four pounds of an abundant inorganic material, but also requires a small amount of a chlorinated paraffin. That chlorine could be the precursor of a deadly dioxin. How does one measure the true cost or value of that chlorinated paraffin?

EcoMetrics explores some perplexing tradeoffs and is predicated on a scale that weighs such diverse factors as toxic waste, dioxin potential, aquifer depletion, carbon dioxide emissions, habitat destruction, nonrenewable resource depletion, and embodied energy.

In February 1996, we brought together these two revolutionary efforts—QUEST, the hard-dollar effort, and EcoSense, the environmental effort. We merged the two task forces and formed 18 teams with representatives from our businesses worldwide. Each team had an assigned scope of investigation.

It turned out to be a wonderful marriage, integrating these closely related efforts, positively changing our corporate culture, and finding a whole new world of opportunities and challenges. Today, there are more than 400 projects—from persuading our landlord to install compact fluorescent light bulbs in our corporate headquarters office, to creating sustainable businesses within our company.

FORMULA FOR SUCCESS

In the 21st Century, as the new industrial revolution gathers speed, we believe the winners will be the resource-efficient. Meanwhile, the argument goes on between technophiles and technophobes, one insisting that technology will save us, the other contending that technology is the enemy. We believe the next industrial revolution will reconcile these opposing points of view, because there is another way to express the differences between the first industrial revolution and the next. The well-known environmental impact equation, popularized by ecologists and authors Paul and Anne Ehrlich, declares that environmental impact is a product of population size, affluence, and technology.

This can be expressed mathematically as:

$$E = P(A)(T)$$

An increase in population, affluence, or technology results in worse environmental impact. Technology—at least the technology of the first industrial revolution—is part of the problem, reinforcing the technophobes' position.

But just what are the characteristics of the technologies of the first industrial revolution? For the most part, they are extractive, linear—take, make, waste—fossil fuel-driven, focused on increasing labour productivity per worker, abusive, and wasteful. And they are unsustainable.

What if the characteristics of technology were changed? Let's say they were renewable, rather than extractive; cyclical (cradle-to-cradle), rather than linear; solar-or hydrogen-driven, rather than fossil fuel-driven; focused on resource productivity, rather than labour productivity; and benign in their effects on the biosphere, rather than abusive. And what if they emulated nature, where there is no waste?

Might not it then be possible to restate the environmental impact equation as:

$$E=P(A)/T$$

By moving technology from the numerator to the denominator, we change the world as we have known it. The technophiles, the technophobes, the industrialists, and the environmentalists could be aligned and allied in their efforts to reinvent industry and civilization. The mathematically minded see it immediately. In the new equation, the more technology the better because there would be less impact. Furthermore, it would begin to put the billion unemployed people of Earth to work, increasing resource productivity, using an abundant resource-labour—to conserve diminishing natural resources.

Technology would become the friend of labour, not its enemy. Technology would become part of the solution, not part of the problem. What will drive technology from the numerator to the denominator? we believe getting the prices right is the biggest part of the answer. That means tax shifts and, perhaps, new financial instruments, such as tradable emission credit, to make pollution cost the polluter. In any event, it means eliminating the perverse incentives and getting the incentives right for innovation, correcting the market's fundamental dishonesty in externalizing societal costs and, instead, harnessing honest, free-market forces. If we can get the incentives right, entrepreneurs everywhere will be thankful; there will be new fortunes to be made in the next industrial revolution.

But what in turn will drive the creation of tax shifts and other politically derived financial instruments? Those will ultimately be driven by a public with a high sense of ethics, morality, love of the Earth, and a longing for harmony with nature. When the people—through the marketplace-show their appreciation for these qualities and vote with their pocketbooks for the early adopters, the people will be leading; the good guys will win in the marketplace and the polling booth. And the rest of the political and business leaders will have to follow.

As a politician once said, "Show me a parade and I'll gladly march in front of it." So, too, will business and industry respond to the demands of this new marketplace, and Earth will gain a much-needed reprieve.

5

New Economic Policies

Ever since India gained its independence nearly 40 years ago, the state has intervened strongly in some sectors of the country's economy. It has taken and kept the lead in setting priorities, formulating and implementing policies, and determining the direction and pace of change in industry, foreign trade, finance, transport and energy infrastructure where it has worked hand in hand with private Indian capital, allowing it a prominent role.

But two of the largest sectors—agriculture and internal trade—together constituting the major part of the Indian economy, have been allowed to remain outside state control, with intervention limited to providing irrigation, fertilizers, and other inputs into agriculture at highly subsidized prices; buying wheat and rice at high support prices to build buffer stocks; and selling foodstuffs at relatively moderate prices in government shops in urban areas.

The partnership of the public and private sectors in controlling and running some parts of India's so-called mixed economy, has been more or less stable, continuous, and consistent over the last four decades, making due allowance for the usual quarrels that all such "marriages' have. What has made this possible is the fact that in India, so far, no one social class has emerged as dominant over all the others.

Rather, several dominant social classes are evenly matched, obliging them to share political power and work out arrangements for dividing the economic surplus. This partnership of dominant classes consists of the rich farmers, the middle peasantry, the industrial and financial capitalists, the middle and top layers of the state bureaucracy (including the officers in the armed forces), the middle and large traders, and the unionized, relatively well-paid white- and blue-collar workers of very large enterprises and the transport and energy infrastructure.

This dominating collection of social and economic forces represents the interests of the middle and upper classes, both rural and urban, as well as of the so-called labour aristocracy of high-wage organized workers—a conglomeration of about 150 million people forming the top 20 per cent of the total population. These groups have formed the support base of not only the Congress Party, which has ruled India at the centre and in most of the 22 states of the federal union for more than 35 years, but also of several other non-Communist parties which have been in government for brief periods at the centre and in some states.

In this sense of sharing power at the centre and in the states, through the Congress and other political parties, this collection acts as a loose de facto coalition. There are three major reasons why the political parties are beholden to this collection of dominating classes: first, the rich and middle farmers control the rural votes, thus deciding the outcome of general elections (75 per cent of India's population is still rural); second, the industrial and financial capitalists, along with the traders, finance the parties; third, the white-collar workers and the high-wage organized blue-collar workers, if antagonized, can halt the state machinery and modern infrastructure, as well as make the towns and cities ungovernable.

In this ruling coalition, the state has played the role of orchestrator, mediator, and arbitrator, thus ensuring for itself the dominant position. This arrangement has conferred on the state, and especially on the top echelons of the bureaucracy, a status of semi-autonomy within the state structure as a whole. Given this evolution, it is not surprising that the state and in particular the top state bureaucracy has internalized the conviction and propagated the message that it is the patriotic guardian of the national interest, standing specific sectarian and class conflicts and pursuing the goal of transforming India into a prosperous and strong nation-state and a great power. The main strategy chosen by the state in moving towards its goals took shape in the closing stages of the first Five Year Plan (FYP) in the mid-1950s and was put into operation during the second FYP period, 1955/56-1959/60.

The strategy underwent two fundamental revisions, in the mid-1960s and again in the mid-1980s, in response to severe crises. The post-independence history of India can therefore be divided into the three periods 1950-1965, 1966-1984, and 1985 onwards. The first encompasses the first three FYPs; the second begins with the suspension of planning during the three years 1966-68 (euphemistically called the "Annual Plan' periods) followed by the revival of planning on a much reduced basis in the fourth, fifth, and sixth FYPs; and the third period dates from the start of the seventh FYP.

"To plan is to choose,' said Julius Nyerere once. This self-evident truth has been sublimely ignored by the authors of the plan documents. The plans they have produced on paper envision the realization of numerous desirable objectives, all of which have been accorded priority. Constraints have been wished away. Between the all-encompassing rhetoric of the plan documents and the actual economic goals and economic strategies of the implemented parts of the plan there is a vast gap. The reason for the rhetoric is clear: since the proclaimed ideology of the state is that it is the promoter of the national interest and the welfare of all parts of the population, it is necessary to show that there is something for everybody in the Plan, that nobody has been forgotten.

In what follows, as suggested, try to identify and discuss the actual economic goals and strategies, ignoring the rhetorical trimmings. It is most important to recognize one fact of great significance right away: the related goals of substantial employment generation and substantial poverty reduction, although stressed in all Plan documents, have in reality been relegated to the bottom of the list. In relation to the needs of these two goals, the commitment of resources has been puny, the strategies weak, the impact of the programmes marginal. The state claims that there has been a noticeable reduction in proverty, but that is hotly contested by many analysts. But even if these claims are judged to be marginally true, any reduction in poverty has come about not because of, but irrespective of, the state's intervention.

THE FIRST PERIOD, 1950-1965

The overriding economic goal during the first period (1950-1965) was self-sustaining growth in industry, transport, and energy. The major constraint was diagnosed to be the lack of adequate capital stock and technological skills. It was argued that if physical and human capital were rapidly created, the result would be dynamic growth in the three sectors.

This meant giving the highest priority to:

- Importing and producing of capital goods required for the manufacture of not only intermediate and consumer goods but also other capital goods, i.e., machines for making machines, including equipment for the production and distribution of electricity and for the railways and other means of transport;
- The rapid expansion of higher education in science and technology. In addition, priority was given to the manufacture of iron and steel, cement, fertilizers, and heavy chemicals.

This strategy of going all out for the domestic manufacture of capital goods and some key intermediate goods, often termed the "heavy industry strategy,' was worked out for the Indian context by Mahalanobis and his team at the Indian Statistical Institute in Calcutta. To get it started, priority was given to the import of machinery and technological knowledge.

The investments required were huge. Foreign capital, however, was highly skeptical and reluctant to take part in this venture, which in the early 1950s was quite a novel and bold idea for a third world country. Even the biggest among the private capitalists in India were too small at that time to risk taking part in this individually, and the state discouraged the formation of cartels since it wanted to keep overall control of this strategic sector. Hence, partly by default of foreign and domestic private capital, and partly by ideology and design, the Indian state planned, financed, built, and controlled most of the capital-goods and large chunks of the intermediate-goods industries. The central and dominant position it thus acquired in Indian industry has continued into the mid-1980s. On the other hand, all consumer-goods manufacturing, including consumer durables and motor vehicles, as well as substantial parts of intermediate-goods production, was left to private Indian capital.

Access to domestic markets by both state and private industry was ensured by a ban on the import of goods that could be locally manufactured, by stringent import quotas, and in some cases by very high import duties. The import of technological knowledge and managerial expertise through royalty and lump-sum payments was permitted for limited periods, generally long enough to internalize the knowledge. The principal instrument of control for enforcing the strategy of industrialization through import substitution was not tariffs, but import bans and the granting of import licenses and industrial-production licenses on a highly selective basis.

The general criterion for granting import licenses was that the imported goods should be essential for the production of other already licensed goods for which there was as yet no domestic productive capacity. Similarly, criteria were set up for licensing increased productive capacity and starting new production. The authority to grant licenses was invested in the central bureaucracy in New Delhi.

In the ensuing scramble for scarce licenses, the really big fish in the private sector won out over their smaller rivals, because of superior ability to offer generous kickbacks and commissions to powerful politicians and bureaucrats and generous contributions to the funds of the ruling political party. As is already well known and well publicized, one of the results of this aptly named "Licence-Raj' was infiltration of corruption into the interstices of public administration and the political establishment. The other major plank of the economic strategy of the first period was public investment in huge dam-building projects for irrigation and the generation of hydroelectricity in a few selected parts of the country, which in the event accrued to the benefit of the rich and middle farmers and industrial entrepreneurs in those few chosen states. Economic and social programmes for ameliorating poverty have been in existence since the late 1950s but at a very low level relative to the allocations and efforts put into the "modern' sector.

The policy instruments included expenditures on food to be exchanged for work, other rural community development projects, and easier credits and loans to small peasants and artisans. As can be inferred from the foregoing, during the first period, agricultural development was given low priority: its contribution to the Net Domestic Product (NDP) grew at an annual rate of 2.4 per cent in contrast to manufacturing industry, transport, and electricity, which grew respectively at 7, 7, and 13 per cent, at constant 1960 prices.

At the end of the first period (1950-65), the state had succeeded in its major objective of establishing the base for a self-sustaining and fast growing integrated industrial sector, with good forward and backward interindustrial linkages among capital goods, intermediate goods, and consumer goods. Self-reliant industrialization had taken off. But in all the other objectives proclaimed of the first three FYPs, in particular agricultural development, employment generation, and poverty reduction, the state had failed dismally.

THE SECOND PERIOD, 1966-1984

The start of the second period (1966-84) was marked by several grave crises. The war with China in 1965 and the widespread famine in 1966 and 1967 (triggered off but not entirely caused by the droughts of 1965 and 1966) diverted resources to more expenditure on defence and to imports of foodstuffs. Meanwhile, the costly imports of machinery and equipment to lay the base for industrialization in the first period had eaten deeply into the foreign-exchange reserve. Western governments suspended credits in 1966, and under pressure from the IMF and the World Bank, the rupee was devalued to give a boost to exports. But neither the expected large increases in foreign aid nor the spurt in exports materialized. The food and foreign exchange crises thus forced the state to change its earlier economic goals and strategies. Planning was effectively suspended from 1966 to 1968. Investment in industry, transport, and energy was cut back sharply and concentrated instead on pursuing the goals of food self-sufficiency and export promotion.

On the food front, the strategy chosen was to invest in the new technology of high-yielding varieties (HYV) of staple foodgrains in a few states—wheat in the Punjab, Haryana, and Western Uttar Pradesh; rice in the deltas of the Godavari river in Andhra Pradesh and the Kaveri river in Tamil Nadu. With irrigation assured in these areas, farmers were offered the HYV package of seeds, fertilizers, and pesticides at highly subsidized prices. And electricity, which was already being generated in these states from earlier hydroelectric projects, was also supplied at cheap rates to pump water up from tube-wells. Credit was made available on easy terms, and the state offered to buy the farmers' produce at good support prices. Those who were able to invest in this new technology, including farm mechanization, were the large and middle farmers.

The size of their landholdings and the credit facilities available to them on the basis of their assets made the new technology a viable strategy. The results were dramatic: wheat production jumped from 11 million tons in 1960/61 to 23.8 million in 1970/71; rice from 34.6 to 42.2 million tons in the same period. As we go deeper into the second period, we notice the so-called Green Revolution spreading to only a few more districts in a small number of states, e.g., Jammu and Kashmir, Gujarat, Karnataka, Maharashtra, and West Bengal. However, seen in an all-India perspective, the production of both wheat and rice has registered remarkable increases since the introduction of HYVs in the late 1960s: by 1984/85 total wheat production was 44.2 million tons and rice 58.6 million tons, nearly a quadrupling and doubling respectively over two decades. But for other food crops the increases on a total national basis have been extremely modest, being nearly at a standstill for legumes and very low for oilseeds. One reason for this is, of course, that HYV technology has not yet been developed for the other major Indian crops. The public food grain stock held by the state for distribution through "fair price' shops, through food-for-work and other related programmes, and for emergency distribution in times of crop failure due to droughts and floods, reached 29.2 million tons in June 1985 (the highest so far), declined somewhat to 24 million by early January 1986, but is expected to climb to about 30 million by the end of 1986.

This is the best news on the food front in the sense that the state now has enough food stocks to distribute at relatively modest prices through "fair price' shops, thus keeping staple food prices down, and for distribution in case of national emergencies. The dependence on foreign imports of food grains seems to be definitely over. However, this can by no means be interpreted as having reached food "self-sufficiency,' as domestic and foreign publicists for the Indian state are claiming. The reality is different as the following facts reveal. The food distributed through "fair price' shops reaches only the urban population and is equally available to the richest and the poorest urban families at the same price, which of course means yet another increase in the purchasing power of the urban middle and upper classes at the expense of the poor. Further, some 300 million, out of a total rural population of about 560 million (in 1985), are net buyers of food grain.

These are the poorest of the poor, comprising landless laborers and marginal and small peasants, below the so-called "absolute poverty line,' which is defined by the World Bank as "that income level below which a minimal nutritionally adequate diet plus essential non-food requirements is not affordable.' The purchasing power of those below this "absolute poverty income level' (at present estimated to be about 1,400 rupees per capita per year in the rural areas, less than a tenth of a middle-class income) has seriously declined over the last few decades. The reason is that the price of coarse grains on which the poorest spend the bulk of their income has steadily increased. The theoretical net availability per capita per day of cereals remained the same, about 415 grams during the second period, while that of legumes has actually declined by a factor of one third from 60 grams in 1965 to 40 grams in 1985!

This protein availability in 1985 was about half of the 75 gram minimum world standard protein intake set up by the FAO. If to all this is added that 20 per cent of the net theoretical availability is held unsold in the state's public stock of foodgrains, it follows that the actual purchases by the poorest 300 million is bound to be well below the theoretical net availability. The stark dimensions of the malnutrition of 40 per cent of India's population thus stand clearly revealed.

What the huge unsold and unsaleable stock of foodgrains of about 24 million tons in 1986 means is that the poorest 40 per cent do not have the cash income to buy food in sufficient quantities. This "food mountain,' acquired at high subsidized support prices from middle and rich farmers in a few states, is imposing a very heavy financial burden on the state, which is of course being passed on to the poor (some 80 per cent of the total population) in the form of indirect taxes.

Irrigation, fertilizers, pesticides, farm mechanization, and good storage facilities for grain are the essential technological ingredients in the high-yielding-variety (HYV) strategy of the Green Revolution. The essential economic ingredients are credit facilities and good support prices for the farmers. The unequal availability of these technological and economic ingredients has produced a sharp worsening of existing disparities between states and between different classes of farmers within the states.

Irrigation-rich states where middle-level farmers constitute the bulk of the cultivators, like the Punjab, Haryana, and Uttar Pradesh, showed annual rates of growth in cereal production of 4.3 to 7.2 per cent, against an all-India average of 2.8 per cent during the period under consideration (1967-1985).Most of the Green Revolution has happened in these three states. Irrigation-poor states with small and marginal peasants and landless labourers making up the rural majority, like Bihar, Orissa, and Madhya Pradesh, have recorded very poor cereals growth rates of between 1 and 1.7 per cent. Broadly speaking, not more than half a dozen of India's 22 states (excluding the 9 union territories) have benefited so far from the HYV strategy, and within them the benefits have gone in the main to middle and large farmers.

A fundamental change in agrarian structures took place in this period, consolidating itself by the mid-1970s. It was brought about by abolition of the absentee landlord system and partial implementation of "land-to-the-tiller' demand. Very large landowners were obliged by the land reform law to sell land area above a certain ceiling to their tenants. Further, any amount of alnd, however small, not cultivated by the owner or his family members also had to be sold to the peasant household which cultivated it.

This gave rise to the emergence of a middle land-owning peasantry from the former tenant-cultivating part, comprising about 10 per cent of the rural population, which became very influential economically, socially, and politically. The pre-independence "patron-client' relationship between the very large landowners and the rest of the village population began to give way in some parts of the country to a class dominance by the middle peasantry which took the lead in local, regional, and even national affairs, organizing effective "farmers' agitation,' coopting a wide range of the rural population in support of improved material incentives like highly subsidized irrigation, electricity, and fertilizers, higher prices for state purchase of grains, cancellation of earlier loans, etc. The middle peasantry, together with the rich large farmers, now constitutes the dominant classes in rural India.

For the rest, however, the so-called land reform is a total sham. Of the massive amount of legislation on paper, the one thing of any significance to be implemented was the expropriation of absentee landlords, whose lands became the property of their former middle and large tenant farmers. Landless labourers and marginal and small peasants got virtually nothing out of it. Over the last four decades less than 0.6 per cent of the total cultivated area has actually been distributed among the landless. The single most important feature of Indian economic policy has been, and continues to be, not to collect direct taxes from farmers, irrespective of the size of their landholdings, other assets, and cash incomes. It is staggering that this sector of the economy which produces more than one third of the total net domestic product pays no direct tax. As though that in itself was not enough, from the mid-1960s onward the terms of internal trade began to move against industry and in favour of agriculture. This is the enormous price the state and the other members of the dominant coalition have had to pay to keep the semi-feudal landlords, the rich farmers, and the middle peasants happy, for they wield immense political power through their control of the rural population.

Turning now to the other major economic goal of the second period, i.e., export promotion, one notes that the strategy of devaluation of the rupee in 1966, coupled with a temporary suspension of export subsidies, failed to bring the expected results. Moreover, there was no net increase in the inflow of aid. Instead net aid fell by over 40 per cent in real terms. Without the hoped-for large increases in foreign aid, the state soon found it necessary to reinstate export subsidies.

The combined effect of all this was that there was no dramatic increase in export earnings, or significant change in the structure of exports in favour of modern manufactures. In the period 1968-80 exports grew at an annual rate of 5.5 per cent, but fell sharply to 1.8 per cent between 1981 and 1985 at current prices, which means that the real absolute value of exports has been falling over the last five years. As for the composition of exports, primary agricultural and mineral products, and traditional manufactures like tea, iron ore, jute, textiles, leather manufactures, gems and jewelry, etc., account for 85 per cent, the remaining 15 per cent being made up of modern manufactures like capital goods, chemicals, and clothing. The fact that in 1985 the export revenue from gems and jewelry was nearly twice that from chemicals speaks volumes for the weakness of India's exports of manufactures compared to the exports of the other industrially advanced third-world countries. On the other hand, it is no surprise that among the exports of modern manufactures, the relative newcomer, capital goods, has taken the lead, beating textiles and chemicals to the second and third places respectively. Indian manufacturers discovered that there was some demand for relatively "non-sophisticated' and "non-up-to-date' metal products, machine tools, and machinery in a few industrializing South East Asian and oil-rich West Asian and North African countries.

Examples of such goods are non-numerically-controlled, non-computerized lathes, and 1950s vintage machinery in the cement and sugar and glass industries. Indians were able to make a modest entry into these markets with the excess production that the capital goods strategy had promoted but which could not be absorbed by a stagnating domestic industry. Low wages and government export subsidies helped a good deal in the price competition against other countries' exporters. Indian government export promotion bodies also provide market-information service, warehousing facilities, and other infrastructural support to exporters of manufactured goods. Another factor that has contributed to the relatively better performance of the capital goods sector in the export field within the Indian context (absolutely insignificant though this still is in the context of the world export trade in capital goods) is that there are some very big Indian firms in this sector with the minimum of financial, organizational, and managerial resources essential for entering the export market.

The reduction in investment in public-sector industry by the state at the start of the second period had a negative effect on the whole industrial sector, which suffered from both recession and structural retrogression up to the mid-1970s. But as investment rose again, industry pulled itself out of this recession, showing substantial real growth rates of around 10 per cent per annum during the fifth FYP period (1974-79). However, it failed to maintain this momentum during the sixth FYP period (1980-85), dropping to an annual rate of 5 per cent. From the end of the fourth FYP period (1969-1974), i.e., from the mid-1970s, the emphasis on state ownership of Indian industry began a gradual decline. The claims of the private sector for a greater share became more insistent, as it sensed that the government was becoming more sympathetic to its arguments. Large-scale private industry demanded and obtained state subsidies and tax relief. Step by step, it became easier to import the latest in Western technology, signalling a retreat from the earlier ambition for indigenous development of the latest technology.

THE THIRD PERIOD: 1985 ONWARDS

By the onset of the third period, four things of fundamental significance had been achieved and consolidated in India: self-reliance in food production and food supply, self-reliance in modern industry, one of the highest savings rates (22 per cent of GDP) in the third world, and a good foreign exchange reserve of about $6 billion, 15 per cent of which came from remittances of Indians working abroad, especially in the Middle East.

Side by side with this "comfort-giving' picture of plenty, stands the reality of the poverty of 80 per cent (600 million) of the total population (750 million), of whom at least 40 per cent (300 million) are the poorest of the poor, in World Bank terminology "the absolute poor' who cannot afford a "minimal nutritionally adequate diet plus essential non-food requirement.' It is against this background that as suggested, attempt an analysis of the sectoral objectives and allocations in the seventh FYP (1985-90). The accompanying table presents a comparison of the allocations in the fifth, sixth, and seventh FYPs.

Although the transition from the second to the third period is not sudden, the departures are radical enough to signal the beginning of another era. Partly this shift is attributable to the change in the political leadership at the centre following the assassination of Mrs. Indira Gandhi. In theory, the main purpose of Indian planning is to allocate money to the development of various sectors of the economy. The Five Year Development Plans which are drawn up by the Planning Commission in New Delhi, are thus indicative financial plans. They are not the detailed material balance plans of the Soviet and East European type, governing the division and flow of raw material and other physical resources as well as labour and skills among the various economic and social sectors.

The Planning Commission estimates the financial resources, both in domestic and foreign convertible currencies, that would be required for achieving the development targets set in a five-year-plan period, for both the state-owned sector and the private sector. It proposes certain total volumes and sectoral allocations of development investment and development expenditure in the state-owned sector. In addition, it forecasts how the private sector, following the lead of the public sector, will make its own investments. The Prime Minister is the chairman of the Planning Commission.

The Indian Union consists of 22 states and 9 so-called union territories. While the latter are directly administered by the central government in New Delhi, the former have their own state governments and state legislatures. The states make their own state-level five-year development plans within the overall framework and targets set by the central five-year plan, and on the basis of the financial resources they expect to receive from the central government in New Delhi, as well as the resources they expect to raise themselves. Like the central plan, the state-level plans are in essence financial.

The states of the Indian Union are supposed to be able to influence the drafting of the central five-year plan not only through direct consultations between state and central officials and planners, but in particular also through the National Development Council, consisting of the Chief Ministers of all the states, which has the right to scrutinize the central plan and make changes in it. Here too, the Prime Minister of the central government of India acts as the chairman.

The central plan has to be approved by the national parliament in New Delhi, before it can be implemented by the central and state governments. The state-level plans have to be approved by both the state legislatures and the central parliament. Thus, the central national parliament sitting in

New Delhi is the final authority whose approval of the plan is mandatory. But that is only a formal facade. The real decisions about how to allocate resources and which parts of the plans to implement are made by a relatively small group of people in control of the coalition of the political, social, and economic interests outlined earlier.

The central planning commission was relatively autonomous and influential during the Nehru era (1950-1964). Its rapid decline began with the assumption of supreme political power by Indira Gandhi. Today it is no more than a service department of the central government, drafting plans to order by the powers that be. And the national parliament, with its huge Rajiv Gandhi Congress Party majority, has been reduced to a rubber-stamp body.

While it is the task of the five-year plan to propose the allocation of financial resources to meet development targets in the state-owned sector and recommend and forecast corresponding investments in the private sector, it is the responsibility of the annual central-government budget to find those resources. The expenditure part of the annual budget thus has two sides: the yearly development spending that the plan requires, the so-called plan outlay, and the yearly non-developmental spending for the day-to-day running of the state and the general economy and society, the so-called non-plan outlay. The budget announces how much revenue in domestic and foreign convertible currencies the central government expects to take in during a year, how this money will be divided into plan and non-plan outlays, and how the deficit between expected revenue and intended expenditure will be financed.

The budget determines what taxes will be levied on whom, how much and from whom the government will borrow, and how much more money will be printed. Like the plan, the budget too has to be approved by parliament. While the plan is a shopping-list of desirable and desired "goodies,' it is the annual budget that really determines which ones will in fact be bought. It is the budget that makes sure that the political and economic interests of the ruling coalition are taken care of. Like state-level plans, the state governments also have their own annual budgets, but there are subservient to the all-powerful central government budget. For the first time in 35 years of planning, public-sector gross investment will be lower than private sector gross investment. On comparing the fifth, sixth, and seventh Plans, one sees that this declining public investment will continue the trend of the last ten years of reducing the share of public investment in industry and increasing it in the energy, transport, and communications sectors. The private sector is thus clearly expected and invited to take the leading role in the industrial sector, which the state is now preparing to relinquish.

However, the seventh FYP is reassuring the private sector that the state will not only continue its traditional role as a supplier of cheap energy and infrastructural services, but will also improve those services in quantity and quality. The single largest allocation (30.4 per cent) of the Plan goes to energy; and almost all of this to modern forms— electric power (19 per cent), petroleum (7 per cent), coal (4 per cent)—used by modern industry, modern transport, and upper—and middle-class households; for the "other' forms of energy, which are presumably meant for the bulk of the population living in the rural areas, there is only 0.3 per cent.

The allocation for "rural development' is 5 per cent. Its purpose is, among other things, reduction of poverty and unemployment in the rural areas, through such programmes as the "Integrated Rural Development Programme (IRDP),' The "Rural Landless Employment Guarantee Programme (RLEGP),' etc. It is marginally less than the 5.5 per cent allocated in the sixth Plan. Considering that 40 per cent of the population is below the "poverty line,' the allocation of an insignificant 5 per cent of the Plan outlay towards their welfare expresses eloquently the very low priority, even in theory let alone in practice, that the state assigns to the poor.

And this impression is strengthened if one takes account of the miniscule 1.5 per cent allocated to "village and small scale industries,' a category which is supposed to absorb a substantial part of the massive numbers of the unemployed and underemployed in the rural areas. Although the transition from the second to the third period is not sudden, and the characteristics that define the third period have been maturing in the womb of the second, still the departures are radical enough to signal the start of another era.

They are:

- Aceleration of the entry of private capital into the public-sector domain, in particular the industrial sector;
- Rtreat of the state from the "commanding heights' of the economy;
- Te fiscal crisis of the state brought about by the contradictions of a "mixed' economy and the contradictions within the dominant coalition;
- Icreasing dependence of the state on internal and external borrowings and the replacement of the strategy of "self-reliant-import-substitution' by the strategy of "luxury-consumption-led-growth' in the industrial sector.1

The real absolute value of public-sector investment in industry in the seventh Plan is less than in the sixth Plan. For the first time in 25 years of planning, there will be no new public-sector projects in industry; the 197 billion rupees (about $16 billion at the 1986 exchange rate) allocated in the seventh Plan is barely enough to service the ongoing public-sector industries whose aging equipment needs modernizing.

The central government budgets of 1985/86 and 1986/87 amply confirm the above patterns and trends.2 The 1985/86 budget caused a great stir and was rapturously welcomed by the private sector and the upper and middle classes for making the following proposals:

- Substantial cuts in individual and corporate income tax.
- Abolition of capital gains tax, wealth tax, and death duties on inherited estates.
- Imports of capital goods and project packages (i.e., embodied and disembodied technologies) are to be further liberalized by adding 200 additional items

from the capital-goods sector to the Open General License list.

- The entry of private capital into some industrial sectors formerly reserved for the public sector is to be allowed, such as in the electronics and telecommunication equipment fields.
- Industrial branches formerly barred to foreign capital are to be opened up for foreign investment, even on a foreign-majority share-ownership basis.
- "Whitewashing' of "black' money (i.e., tax-evasion money) by allowing it to resurface into the visible economy without fear of penal action, as long as tax is paid on the resurfaced money at the new low rates ("black' money is variously estimated to equal between 30 and 50 per cent of the total annual GDP3).

Cuts in personal income and corporate taxes and attractive terms offered to both domestic and foreign private investors are meant to liven up the demand for and supply of luxury consumer durables (automobiles, consumer electronics, household electrical appliances, etc.), in the hope that the industrial sector will again show high growth rates.

The cuts in direct income tax are of no benefit to the poor 80 per cent of the population who pay no income tax. But the poor do pay indirect taxes on the purchases of food and a few other essential commodities which absorb 75 to 85 per cent of their income. Indirect taxes are the source of the great bulk (80 per cent) of the country's tax revenue, and they have been increasing. Between 1975-76 and 1984-85 when direct taxes as a proportion of GDP decreased, indirect taxes increased from 11.7 to 14.0 per cent. Thus, the poor will, as usual, pay for the increased luxury consumption of the middle and upper classes, and the increased profits of the private corporate sector.

The 1986/87 budget did not generate the same euphoria among the private sector and the upper and middle classes, who were highly disappointed that there were no further tax cuts, indirect allowances, or hidden subsidies. Rather, the private sector was worried by the fact that the finance minister was backtracking to a certain extent on the liberalization of imports; this partial retreat was due to the fact that within one year imports had jumped by 20 per cent without any noticeable increase in exports, punching a sizable hole in the foreign-exchange reserves. In other respects, however, the 1986/87 budget continued the main trends initiated by the 1985/86 budget.

A deepening fiscal crisis of the state and increased deficits necessitating borrowing from internal and external sources are the hallmarks of the beginning of the third period. They are intimately linked to one another, and they will profoundly affect the economy and society of India in the coming years.

Let us begin by stressing that by the mid-1980s, the Indian economy was showing the following striking features:

- Icreases in wheat and rice production and the piling up of huge public food stocks had continued steadily for a number of years.
- Bth the industrial sector and the economy in general had settled down to a respectable growth rate of about 5 per cent per annum.
- Te gross domestic savings were very high relative to GDP (22 per cent).
- Freign exchange reserves continued at the $6-billion level.
- Te untaxed money ("black' money) circulating in the non-agricultural sector alone was between a third and a half of GDP.

Therefore, there in no resource crisis now, nor is one looming on the horizon as far the general economy is concerned. However, there happens to be a crisis in the resources available to the state for investing in the public sector. As the seventh Plan Document freely admits, there is a serious resource crunch in the public sector, i.e., there is a fiscal crisis of the state. The reasons for the paradox of the above-mentioned apparent "strengths' in the economy co-existing with a fiscal crisis are not hard to locate.

The non-developmental expenditure of the state has been rapidly increasing such as on defence (17 per cent); on interest payments on borrowings (17 per cent); on subsidies (9 per cent); to farmers, private industrialists, and urban consumers; on public administration (9 per cent); and on inflated prices of goods and services bought by the state. The revenues of the state have not kept pace with these accelerating expenditures.

No direct taxes are being collected from the farmers, i.e., the biggest productive sector in the economy is not taxed. Further, the minute proportion of the population which is obliged to pay direct tax (most of them being in the middle- and high-income brackets of urban wage-workers and salaried employees) has had that tax reduced. A variety of direct taxes (on profits, capital accumulation, etc.) paid by private enterprises have also been cut. And the public-sector enterprises are suffering heavy losses.

The middle- and upper-class households, constituting less than 20 per cent of the total population, contribute an overwhelmingly large proportion to the total gross domestic savings in the visible economy; their share of savings has remained roughly constant at between 70 and 75 per cent from 1950 to 1985. The public sector's contribution to savings has also remained steady at about 17 to 18 per cent during the same period. But the share of the private corporate sector has declined from 9 to 7.7 per cent.

During the period 1980-85 the annual average revenue deficit was 9.1 per cent of expenditure. It nearly doubled to 17.7 per cent in 1985-86 and to 18.7 per cent in 1986-87. There is no new factor in the economy that can realistically be expected to increase the average annual growth rate of exports from the meager 4 per cent of 1984/85. In fact, the U.S. dollar value of exports fell in 1985/86 as compared to 1984/85. The so-called "export-oriented-growth-strategy' of the Indian official policy pronouncements is mere wishful thinking, not least because of the import-protectionist measures of the developed countries of the West.

The current levels of export subsidies have not induced the expected dynamism among India's exporters, and there is no way the Indian state can increase these subsidies to much more substantial levels, given its fiscal crisis. The public sector has been the locomotive that has pulled along the Indian economy over the last three decades. The ongoing and proposed new reductions in public-sector investment will slow down that locomotive. The private sector is incapable of providing the extra pull expected of it, at least in the short and medium term. Although the growth rate may go up a few percentage points in the next few years due to increased luxury consumption of the middle and upper classes, it will register a downward trend in the medium and long term if the present reductions in public-sector investment continue.

The proximate cause for this reduction is the fiscal crisis of the state, which in turn will become worse as the economy slows down, starting a downward vicious spiral. The fundamental underlying cause is not the fiscal crisis of the state as such but the refusal by the state to extract the required surplus from the resource-rich sectors of society, which also happen to be partners in the ruling coalition of dominant classes.This refusal is the real explanation for the apparent paradox of the coexistence of a very high rate of domestic savings with slow rates of growth in the economy. The state borrows heavily from, and pays high interest to, the household-sector savers, in order mainly to finance its non-developmental, non-productive branches, e.g., defence spending and interest payments which together make up as much as 80 per cent of the total tax revenue, or one third of total budget expenditure!4

ECONOMICPOLICIES OF THE INDIAN STATE

Under the slogans and fanfares of "rapid economic growth,' "efficiency,' "modernazation,' and "export promotion,' the Indian state in collaboration with big Indian private capital, has launched its latest policies and strategies in a stream of specialist committee reports and policy documents, followed by the seventh Plan and the two budgets of 1985/86 and 1986/87. The state promised to lead India into the computerized-paradise of the twenty-first century on the tidal wave generated by this new economic strategy. We would like to offer a different interpretation of the aims and actions of the Indian state and Indian capital. Let us that Indian industry suffered a serious recession from 1965 to 1973, from which it recovered briefly during the fifth Plan period 1974-79, only to slide back again to slow growth rates during the sixth Plan period 1980-85.

The relative stagnation of Indian industry and large parts of the Indian economy over the last two decades, in comparison with, the rapid growth and dynamism of the East Asian industrialized economies, can be aptly summed up in the phrase "low-level equilibrium trap.' The proximate cause of the inability to get out of this trap is the fiscal crisis of the state, but the underlying explanation lies in the contradictions within the dominant coalition of the ruling classes. Deficit financing and increased indirect taxation are two of the main sources of financing the seventh Plan (1985-90).

The burdens of both of these are carried almost exclusively by the poor majority (80 per cent of the population) through price-inflation of their essential consumption goods and services. The state is using the bulk of the economic surplus squeezed out of the poor through indirect taxation and inflation, as well as its huge internal borrowings from the savings of the middle and upper classes, to finance its non-developmental and non-productive expenditure. So it has to cut back on productive investment in the public sector, which of course perpetuates the industrial and infrastructural crisis, leading to a vicious cycle of stagnant incomes and markets.

Since the state cannot break out of this crisis without mortally endangering its social support base in the dominant coalition, it sees its choice as necessarily restricted to two strategies:

- Luxury consumption-led growth,
- Export-led growth.

The first requires inducements on the supply side to private industry to produce more of the latest East Asian brands of consumer durables, and on the demand side to upper-middle and upper classes by freeing more of their incomes for purchases through cuts in direct taxes. And Indian industrialists, even the biggest among them, will not take the road of export growth unless they are molly-coddled by the state through export subsidies, credits, and guarantees. Moreover it is essential for both strategies that a reliable and adequate supply of electricity, petroleum, and coal be available at subsidized prices as prime movers in industry, transport, and upper-income households (what good is an air conditioner or a refrigerator or a car, if electricity is cut most of the day and petrol consumes a quarter of the take-home pay?).

This is the context for lavishing 30 per cent of the seventh Plan's total outlay on the energy sector, the largest allocation to any one sector, almost all of it earmarked for modern forms of energy like electricity, petroleum, and coal, and almost nothing for traditional fuels used by the poor. Further, both strategies depend on the import of advanced technologies to produce and market the latest type of consumer durables, which only the transnational corporations can provide. The recently adopted industrial and technological policies make perfect sense against this background.

We know that the domestic costs of this ruling-class extravaganza will be borne by the poor in India. But, pray, who will bear the foreign exchange cost? That is nicely taken care of by foreign debt. India is highly creditworthy at present, with "only' $22 billion of foreign debt. The commercial banks, the official agencies, the World Bank, and the IMF are pressing India to go in for more. On present calculations, India's foreign debt will double by 1990 to $46 billion. Foreign creditors will be happy as long as India regularly services its debts, which after all today absorb "only' about 18 per cent of export income.

India's ruling coalition has launched the country on a journey which, unless cut short through internal political, economic, and social processes, will soon take India into the exclusive club of the largest debtors of the third would which now claims Argentina, Brazil, and Mexico as its leading members. The "laundering' of foreign loans and "aid' through India back to safe and lucrative repositories in the West and East Asia—so-called net capital flight—seems to be accelerating: it is estimated at $10 billion for the period 1976-85(5). The "Latin Americanization' of India may well be on its way in more senses than one!

6

Political Environment

The separation of powers, also known as *trias politica,* is a model for the governance of democratic states. The model was first developed in ancient Greece and came into widespread use by the Roman Republic as part of the uncodified Constitution of the Roman Republic. Under this model, the state is divided into branches or estates, each with separate and independent powers and areas of responsibility. The normal division of estates is into an executive, a legislature, and a judiciary.

The opposite of separation of powers is the fusion of powers, often a feature of parliamentary democracies. In this form, the executive, which often consists of a president and cabinet ("government"), is drawn from the legislature (parliament). This is the principle of responsible government. Although the legislative and executive branches are connected in parliamentary systems, there is often an independent judiciary. Also, the government's role in the parliament does not give them unlimited legislative influence.

The union government, as India's central government is known, is divided into three distinct but interrelated branches: legislative, executive, and judicial. As in the British parliamentary model, the leadership of the executive is drawn from and responsible to the legislative body. Although Article 50 stipulates the separation of the judiciary from the executive, the executive controls judicial appointments and many of the conditions of work. In addition, one of the more dramatic institutional battles in the Indian polity has been the struggle between elements wanting to assert legislative power to amend the constitution and those favouring the judiciary's efforts to preserve the constitution's basic structure.

THE INDIAN LEGISLATURE

Parliament consists of a bicameral legislature, the Lok Sabha (House of the People—the lower house) and the Rajya Sabha (Council of States—the upper house). Parliament's principal function is to pass laws on those matters that the constitution specifies to be within its jurisdiction. Among its constitutional powers are approval and removal of members of the Council of Ministers, amendment of the constitution, approval of central government finances, and delimitation of state and union territory boundaries .

The president of India has a specific authority with respect to the function of the legislative branch . The president is authorized to convene Parliament and must give his assent to all parliamentary bills before they become law. The president is empowered to summon Parliament to meet, to address either house or both houses together, and to require attendance of all of its members.

The president also may send messages to either house with respect to a pending bill or any other matter. The president addresses the first session of Parliament each year and must give assent to all provisions in bills passed. India is a "sovereign, socialist, secular, democratic republic." India has a federal form of government. However, the central government in India has greater power in relation to its states, and its central government is patterned after the British parliamentary system.

The government exercises its broad administrative powers in the name of the president, whose duties are largely ceremonial. The president and vice president are elected indirectly for 5-year terms by a special electoral college. Their terms are staggered, and the vice president does not automatically become president following the death or removal from office of the president. Real national executive power is centered in the Council of Ministers (cabinet), led by the prime minister. The president appoints the prime minister, who is designated by legislators of the political party or coalition commanding a parliamentary majority. The president then appoints subordinate ministers on the advice of the prime minister. India's bicameral parliament consists of the Rajya Sabha (Council of States) and the Lok Sabha (House of the People). The Council of Ministers is responsible to the Lok Sabha.

The legislatures of the states and union territories elect 233 members to the Rajya Sabha, and the president appoints another 12. The elected members of the Rajya Sabha serve 6-year terms, with one-third up for election every 2 years. The Lok Sabha consists of 545 members; 543 are directly elected to 5-year terms.

The other two are appointed. India's independent judicial system began under the British, and its concepts and procedures resemble those of Anglo-Saxon countries. The Supreme Court consists of a chief justice and 25 other justices, all appointed by the president on the advice of the prime minister.

India has 25 states* and 7 union territories. At the state level, some of the legislatures are bicameral, patterned after the two houses of the national parliament. The states' chief ministers are responsible to the legislatures in the same way the prime minister is responsible to parliament. Each state also has a presidentially appointed governor who may assume certain broad powers when directed by the central government. The central government exerts greater control over the union territories than over the states, although some territories have gained more power to administer their own affairs.

Local governments in India have less autonomy than their counterparts in the United States. Some states are trying to revitalize the traditional village councils, or panchayats, which aim to promote popular democratic participation at the village level, where much of the population still lives.

7

Fundamental Rights and Directive Principles of State Policy

The Fundamental Rights, Directive Principles of State Policy and Fundamental Duties are sections of the Constitution of India that prescribe the fundamental obligations of the State to its citizens and the duties of the citizens to the State. These parts comprise a constitutional bill of rights for government policy-making and the behaviour and conduct of citizens. These parts are considered vital elements of the constitution, which was developed between 1947 and 1949 by the Constituent Assembly of India. The Fundamental Rights are defined as the basic human rights of all citizens. These rights, defined in Part III of the Constitution, apply irrespective of race, place of birth, religion, caste, creed or gender. They are enforceable by the courts, subject to specific restrictions.

The Directive Principles of State Policy are guidelines for the framing of laws by the government. These provisions-set out in Part IV of the Constitution-are not enforceable by the courts, but the principles on which they are based are fundamental guidelines for governance that the State is expected to apply in framing and passing laws.

The Fundamental Duties are defined as the moral obligations of all citizens to help promote a spirit of patriotism and to uphold the unity of India. These duties-set out in Part IV-A of the constitution-concern individuals and the nation. Like the Directive Principles, they are not legally enforceable.

The development of constitutional rights in India was inspired by historical documents such as England's Bill of Rights, the United States Bill of Rights and France's Declaration of the Rights of Man.

In 1928, an All Parties Conference of representatives from Indian political parties proposed constitutional reforms for India. This 11-member committee, led by Motilal Nehru, had been called into existence as a formal instrument to complement the widespread civil disobedience campaigns of the 1920s. These mass campaigns had originally been a response to the Rowlatt Acts, which in 1919 had given the British colonial government the powers of arrest and detention, conduction of searches and seizures without warrants, restriction of public gatherings and censorship of the press. Demanding dominion status and elections under universal suffrage, the committee called for guarantees of rights deemed fundamental, representation for religious and ethnic minorities and limitations on government powers.

In 1931, the Indian National Congress, at its Karachi session, adopted resolutions defining, as well as committing itself to the defence of fundamental civil rights, including socio-economic rights such as minimum wage, the abolition of untouchability and serfdom. Committing themselves to socialism in 1936, the leaders of the Congress party took examples from the Soviet constitution, which inspired the fundamental duties of citizens as a means of collective, patriotic responsibility.

The task of developing a constitution for an independent India was undertaken by the Constituent Assembly of India, which composed of elected representatives under the presidency of Rajendra Prasad. The assembly appointed a constitution drafting committee headed by Bhimrao Ramji Ambedkar. The process was influenced by the adoption of the Universal Declaration of Human Rights by the U.N. General Assembly on 10 December 1948. The declaration called upon all member States to adopt these rights in their constitutions. The Fundamental Rights and Directive Principles were included in the final draft of the constitution promulgated on

26 November 1949, while the Fundamental Duties were later added to the constitution by the 42nd Amendment Act in 1976. Changes in Fundamental Rights, Directive Principles and Fundamental Duties require a constitutional amendment, that must be passed by a two-thirds majority in both houses of Parliament. The Fundamental Rights — embodied in Part III of the constitution — guarantee civil liberties such that all Indians can lead their lives in peace as citizens of India. The six fundamental rights are right to equality, right to freedom, right against exploitation, right to freedom of religion, cultural and educational rights and right to constitutional remedies.

These include individual rights common to most liberal democracies, incorporated in the fundamental law of the land and are enforceable in a court of law. Violations of these rights result in punishments as prescribed in the Indian Penal Code, subject to discretion of the judiciary. These rights are neither absolute nor immune from constitutional amendments. They have been aimed at overturning the inequalities of pre-independence social practises. Specifically, they resulted in abolishment of untouchability and prohibit discrimination on the grounds of religion, race, caste, sex, or place of birth. They forbid human trafficking and unfree labour. They protect cultural and educational rights of ethnic and religious minorities by allowing them to preserve their languages and administer their own educational institutions.

All people, irrespective of race, religion, caste or sex, have the right to approach the High Courts or the Supreme Court for the enforcement of their fundamental rights. It is not necessary that the aggrieved party has to be the one to do so. In public interest, anyone can initiate litigation in the court on their behalf. This is known as "Public interest litigation". High Court and Supreme Court judges can also performance on their own on the basis of media reports. The Fundamental Rights emphasise equality by guaranteeing to all citizens the access and use of public institutions and protections, irrespective of their background. The rights to life and personal liberty apply for persons of any nationality, while others, such as the freedom of speech and expression are applicable only to the citizens of India (including non-resident Indian citizens). The right to equality in matters of public employment cannot be conferred to overseas citizens of India. Fundamental Rights primarily protect individuals from any arbitrary State actions, but some rights are enforceable against private individuals too. For instance, the constitution abolishes untouchability and prohibits *begar*. These provisions performance as a check both on State action and actions of private individuals.

Fundamental Rights are not absolute and are subject to reasonable restrictions as necessary for the protection of national interest. In the *Kesavananda Bharati vs. state of Kerala* case, the Supreme Court ruled that all provisions of the constitution, including Fundamental Rights can be amended. However, the Parliament cannot alter the basic structure of the constitution like secularism, democracy, federalism, separation of powers. Often called the "Basic structure doctrine", this decision is widely regarded as an important part of Indian history.

In the 1978 *Maneka Gandhi v. Union of India* case, the Supreme Court extended the doctrine's importance as superior to any parliamentary legislation. According to the verdict, no performance of parliament can be considered a law if it violated the basic structure of the constitution. This landmark guarantee of Fundamental Rights was regarded as a unique example of judicial independence in preserving the sanctity of Fundamental Rights. The Fundamental Rights can only be altered by a constitutional amendment, hence their inclusion is a check not only on the executive branch, but also on the Parliament and state legislatures. The imposition of a state of emergency may lead to a temporary suspension of the rights conferred by Article 19 (including freedoms of speech, assembly and movement, etc.) to preserve national security and public order. The President can, by order, suspend the right to constitutional remedies as well.

PERSONAL RIGHTS

The right to equality is one of the chief guarantees given in Articles 14, 15, 16, 17 and 18 of the constitution. It is the principal foundation of all other rights, guaranteeing equality of all citizens before law, social equality, equal access to public areas, equality in matters of public employment, the abolition of untouchability and of titles. However, reservations (i.e, quotas in jobs, education, etc.) can be made for women, children, scheduled castes and scheduled tribes.

The State cannot discriminate against anyone in the matters of employment except for the implementation of any mandated quotas, though exceptions can be made where specific knowledge is required. To preserve religious freedom, the holder of an office of any religious institution should be a person professing that particular religion. The right to equality in matters regarding public employment is not conferred to overseas citizens of India. The practise of untouchability has been declared an offence punishable by law.

The State cannot confer any titles and the citizens of India cannot accept titles from a foreign State. Indian aristocratic titles such as *Rai Bahadurs* and *Khan Bahadurs* have been abolished. However, military and academic distinctions can be conferred on the citizens of India. Awards such as the *Bharat Ratna* "cannot be used by the recipient as a title." A ruling by the Supreme Court on 15 December 1995 upheld the validity of such awards.

The Right to freedom is stated in Articles 19, 20, 21 and 22 with the view of guaranteeing individual rights that were considered vital by the framers of the constitution. The right to freedom encompasses the freedom of expression, the freedom to assemble peacefully without arms, the freedom to form associations and unions, the freedom to move freely and settle in any part of the territory of India and the freedom to practise any profession.

Restrictions can be imposed on all these rights in the interest of security, decency and morality. The constitution guarantees the right to life and personal liberty. Protection with respect to conviction for offences, protection of life and personal liberty and the rights of a person arrested under ordinary circumstances are laid down in the right to life and personal liberty. The Right to freedom of religion'—covered in Articles 25, 26, 27 and 28—provides religious freedom to all citizens and preserves the principle of secularism in India. According to the constitution, all religions are equal before the State. Citizens are free to preach, practise and propagate any religion of their choice. Several distinct and often controversial practises, such as the wearing and carrying of *kirpans* is included in the profession of Sikhism and protected under law. Religious communities can set up charitable institutions of their own, subject to certain restrictions in the interest of public order, morality and health. No person can be compelled to pay taxes for the promotion of a religion and a State-run institution cannot impart education that is associated with a particular religion.

ECONOMIC AND SOCIAL RIGHTS

The cultural and educational rights—given in Articles 29 and 30—are measures to protect the rights of ethnic and religious minorities. Any community that has a language and a script of its own has the right to conserve and develop them. No citizen can be discriminated against for admission in State or State-aided institutions.

All religious and ethno-linguistic communities can set up their own educational institutions in order to preserve and develop their own culture. In granting aid to institutions, the State cannot discriminate against any institution on the basis of the fact that it is administered by a minority institution. The right to education at elementary level has been made one of the Fundamental Rights under right to freedom by the 86th constitutional amendment of 2002.

The Right against exploitation, given in Articles 23 and 24 provides for the abolition of human trafficking, and the abolition of employment of children below the age of 14 years in dangerous jobs like factories and mines. Child labour is considered a violation of the spirit and provisions of the constitution. *Begar* (forced and unfree labour), practised in the past by landlords, has been declared a crime punishable by law. Trafficking in humans for the purpose of slave trade or prostitution is prohibited by law. An exception is made in employment without payment for services for public purposes, such as compulsory military conscription. The Right to constitutional remedies empowers the citizens to approach a court of law to appeal against denial of the Fundamental Rights. For instance, in case of imprisonment, the person can ask the court to see if it is in accordance with the provisions of the law of the country. If the court finds that it is not, the person will be released from custody. This procedure of asking the courts to preserve or safeguard the citizens' Fundamental Rights can be done in various ways. The courts can issue *writs*, namely *habeas corpus, mandamus, prohibition, quo warranto* and *certiorari*. When a national or state emergency is declared, this right is suspended by the central government.

The Right to property was a former Fundamental Right under Article 32 before it was revoked by the 44th Amendment Act of 1978. A new article, Article 300-A, was added to the constitution which provided that no person shall be deprived of his property, except by the authority of law. If a legislature makes a law depriving a person of his property, there would be no obligation on the part of the State to pay any compensation. The aggrieved person will have no right to move the court under Article 32. The right to property is no longer a fundamental right, though it is still a constitutional right. If the government appears to have acted unfairly, the action can be challenged in a court of law.

DIRECTIVE PRINCIPLES OF STATE POLICY

The Directive Principles of State Policy, embodied in Part IV of the constitution, are directions given to the central and state governments to guide the establishment of a just society in the country. According to the constitution, the government should keep them in mind while framing laws, even though they are non-justiciable in nature. Directive Principles are classified under the following categories: Gandhian, social, economic, political, administrative, legal, environmental, protection of monuments, peace and security. The Directive Principles performance as a check on the government; theorised as a yardstick in the hands of the people to measure the performance of the government. Article 31-C, added by the 25th Amendment Act of 1971, seeks to upgrade the Directive Principles. If laws are made to give effect to the Directive Principles over Fundamental Rights, they shall not be invalid on the grounds that they take away the Fundamental Rights. In case of a conflict between Fundamental Rights and Directive Principles, if the latter aim at promoting larger interest of the society, the courts will have to uphold the case in favour of Directive Principles.

The Directive Principles commit the State to promote the welfare of the people by affirming social, economic and political justice, as well as to fight economic inequality. The State must continually work towards providing an adequate means of livelihood for all citizens, equal pay for equal work for men and women, proper working conditions, protection against exploitation and reduce the concentration of wealth and means of production from the hands of a few.

The State must provide free legal aid to ensure that opportunities for securing justice are not denied to any citizen for reason of economic or other disabilities. The State should work for organisation of village panchayats, provide the right to work, education and public assistance in certain cases; as well as the provision of just and humane conditions of work and maternity relief. A living wage and safe working conditions for citizens must be ensured, as must their participation in the management of industries. The State is encouraged to secure a uniform civil code for all citizens, provide free and compulsory education to children, and to work for the economic uplift of scheduled castes, scheduled tribes and other backward classes.

The Directive Principles commit the State to raise the standard of living and improve public health. It should also organise agriculture and animal husbandry on modern and scientific lines by improving breeds and prohibiting slaughter of cows, calves, other milch and draught cattle. The State must safeguard the environment and wildlife of the country. The State must ensure the preservation of monuments and objects of national importance and separation of judiciary from executive in public services The State must also strive for the maintenance of international peace. The Directive Principles have been amended to meet definite objectives. Article 45, which ensures *Provision for free and compulsory education for children,* was added by the 86th Amendment Act, 2002. Article 48-A, which ensures *Protection of the environment and wildlife,* was added by the 42nd Amendment Act, 1976.

FUNDAMENTAL DUTIES

The Fundamental Duties of citizens were added by the 42nd Amendment Act in 1976. The ten Fundamental Duties—given in Article 51-A of the constitution—can be classified as either duties towards self, duties concerning the environment, duties towards the State and duties towards the nation. The 11th Fundamental Duty, which states that every citizen *"who is a parent or guardian, to provide opportunities for education to his child or, as the case may be, ward between the age of six and fourteen years"* was added by the 86th constitutional amendment in 2002. Citizens are morally obligated by the constitution to perform these duties.

However, these are non-justiciable, incorporated only with the purpose of promoting patriotism among citizens. These obligations extend not only to the citizens, but also to the State. There is reference to such duties in international instruments such as the Universal Declaration of Human Rights and International Covenant on Civil and Political Rights. The Fundamental Duties obligate all citizens to respect the national symbols of India (including the constitution), to cherish its heritage and assist in its defence. It aims to promote the equality of all individuals, protect the environment and public property, to develop scientific temper, to abjure violence, to strive towards excellence and to provide free and compulsory education.

The following are the Fundamental Duties prescribed by the Constitution of the nation under PART [IV-A] to its every citizen:

- To abide by the Constitution and respect its ideals and institutions, the National Flag and the National Anthem.

- To cherish and follow the noble ideals which inspired our national struggle for freedom.
- To uphold and protect the sovereignty, unity and integrity of India.
- To defend the country and render national service when called upon to do so.
- To promote harmony and the spirit of common brotherhood amongst all the people of India transcending religious, linguistic and regional or sectional diversities; to renounce practices derogatory to the dignity of women.
- To value and preserve the rich heritage of our composite culture.
- To protect and improve the natural environment including forests, lakes, rivers and wild life, and to have compassion for living creatures.
- To develop the scientific temper, humanism and the spirit of inquiry and reform.
- To safeguard public property and to abjure violence.
- To strive towards excellence in all spheres of individual and collective activity so that the nation constantly rises to higher levels of endeavor and achievement.

Criticism and Analysis

The Fundamental Rights have been criticised as inadequate in providing freedom and opportunity for all Indians. Many political groups have demanded that the right to work, the right to economic assistance in case of unemployment and similar socio-economic rights be enshrined as constitutional guarantees, that are presently listed in the directive principles of state policy. The right to freedom contains a number of limiting clauses and has been criticised for failing to check government powers such as provisions of preventive detention and suspension of fundamental rights in times of emergency. The phrases "security of State", "public order" and "morality" are unclear, having wide implication. The meaning of phrases like "reasonable restrictions" and "the interest of public order" have not been explicitly stated in the constitution, leading to frequent litigations. The *Maintenance of Internal Security Act* (1975) was strongly criticised for giving then-Prime Minister Indira Gandhi the authority to arrest opposition leaders following the declaration of emergency in 1975.

The *Prevention of Terrorism Act* (2002), now repealed, has been criticised as unfairly targeting the Muslim community. Initially, the Supreme Court provided extensive power to the State in its verdict to the *A. K. Gopalan vs. state of Madras* case in 1950. The Court held that howsoever unreasonable, a law was valid if made by a legislature competent to enact it. If Parliament validly enacted a law permitting the State to kill without any judicial process, this would amount to "procedure established by law" and such killings would not violate the guarantee contained in Article 21.2.

This interpretation was abandoned in a series of decisions starting from the 1970s and culminating in the judgement in 1978 *Maneka Gandhi v. Union of India*, which issued the *basic structure* doctrine. In *D. K. Basu vs. state of West Bengal* the Supreme Court ruled that the limiting clauses of the constitution as well as international human rights instruments do not come in the way of the Court's awarding of compensation in the cases of illegal arrest or detention, protecting the rights of citizens in spite of prevailing circumstances.

The freedom to assemble peaceably and without arms is allowed, but in many cases, these meetings are broken up by the police if they become disruptive. Freedom of press, meant to guarantee freedom of expression, has not been included in the constitution. Employment of child labour in hazardous environments has been reduced, but their employment in non-hazardous jobs, including their prevalent employment as domestic help violates the spirit of the constitution in the eyes of many critics and human rights advocates, as more than 16.5 million children are being used as labour. India was ranked 88 out of 159 countries in 2005, according to the degree to which corruption is perceived to exist among public officials and politicians.. The constitution is silent towards search and seizure.Rights against illegal search and seizure is a privilege under Indian penal code. Efforts to implement the Directive Principles include the Programme for the Universalisation of Elementary Education and the Five-Year Plans have accorded the highest priority in order to provide free education to all children up to the age of 14.

The 86th constitutional amendment of 2002 created Article 21-A, that seeks to provide free and compulsory education to all children aged 6 to 14 years. The State runs welfare programmes such as boys' and girls' hostels for scheduled castes and scheduled tribes' students. The year 1990–1991 was declared as the "Year of Social Justice" in the memory of B.R. Ambedkar.

The government provides free textbooks to students belonging to scheduled castes and tribes pursuing medicine and engineering courses. During 2002–2003, a sum of Rs. 4.77 crore (47.7 million) was released for this purpose. In order to protect scheduled castes and tribes from discrimination, the government enacted the *Prevention of Atrocities Act* in 1995, prescribing severe punishments for such actions.

Land reform legislations have been enacted several times to provide ownership rights to poor farmers. Up to September 2001, more than 20 million acres (81,000 km) of land had been distributed to scheduled castes, scheduled tribes and the landless poor. A core objective of the banking policy is to improve banking facilities in the rural areas. The *Minimum Wages Act* of 1948 empowers government to fix minimum wages for people working across the economic spectrum. The *Consumer Protection Act* of 1986 provides for the better protection of consumers.

The act is intended to provide simple, speedy and inexpensive redressal to the consumers' grievances, award relief and compensation wherever appropriate to the consumer. The *Equal Remuneration Act* of 1976 provides for equal pay for equal work for both men and women. The *Sampoorna Grameen Rozgar Yojana* (Universal Rural Employment Programme) was launched in 2001 to attain the objective of providing gainful employment for the rural poor. The programme was implemented through the Panchayati Raj institutions. A system of elected village councils, known as Panchayati Raj covers almost all states and territories of India. One-third of the total number of seats have been reserved for women in Panchayats at every level; and in the case of Bihar, half the seats have been reserved for women.

Legal aid at the expense of the State has been made compulsory in all cases pertaining to criminal law, if the accused does not have the means to engage a lawyer. The judiciary has been separated from the executive "in all the states and territories except Jammu and Kashmir and Nagaland." India's foreign policy has been influenced by the Directive Principles. India supported the United Nations in peace-keeping activities, with the Indian Army having participated in 37 UN peace-keeping operations.

The implementation of a uniform civil code for all citizens has not been achieved owing to widespread opposition from various religious groups and political parties. The Shah Bano case (1985–86) provoked a political firestorm in India when the Supreme Court ruled that Shah Bano, a Muslim woman who had been divorced by her husband in 1978 was entitled to receive alimony from her former husband under Indian law applicable for all Indian women.

This decision evoked outrage in the Muslim community, which sought the application of the Muslim personal law and in response the Parliament passed the Muslim Women (Protection of Rights on Divorce) Act, 1986 overturning the Supreme Court's verdict. This act provoked further outrage, as jurists, critics and politicians alleged that the fundamental right of equality for all citizens irrespective of religion or gender was being jettisoned to preserve the interests of distinct religious communities.

The verdict and the legislation remain a source of heated debate, with many citing the issue as a prime example of the poor implementation of Fundamental Rights. The Fundamental Duties have been criticised for being ambiguously worded, with the real meaning of phrases like "scientific temper" and "spirit of enquiry and reform" being debated. As the duties cannot be enforced through courts, their relevance to practical affairs is questioned. However, actions damaging public property and showing disrespect to the National Flag are offences punishable by law. Similarly, people may be called upon to defend the country by compulsorily recruitment to the armed forces of the country through conscription.

8

Rationale and Extent of State Intervention

The economy of India is the twelfth largest economy in the world by nominal value and the fourth largest by purchasing power parity (PPP). In the 1990s, following economic reform from the socialist-inspired economy of post-independence India, the country began to experience rapid economic growth, as markets opened for international competition and investment. In the 21st century, India is an emerging economic power with vast human and natural resources, and a huge knowledge base. Economists predict that by 2020, India will be among the leading economies of the world.

India was under social democratic-based policies from 1947 to 1991. The economy was characterised by extensive regulation, protectionism, and public ownership, leading to pervasive corruption and slow growth. Since 1991, continuing economic liberalisation has moved the economy towards a market-based system. A revival of economic reforms and better economic policy in 2000s accelerated India's economic growth rate. By 2008, India had established itself as the world's second-fastest growing major economy.

However, the year 2009 saw a significant slowdown in India's official GDP growth rate to 6.1% as well as the return of a large projected fiscal deficit of 10.3% of GDP which would be among the highest in the world. India's large service industry accounts for 62.6% of the country's GDP while the industrial and agricultural sector contribute 20% and 17.5%

respectively. Agriculture is the predominant occupation in India, accounting for about 52% of employment. The service sector makes up a further 34%, and industrial sector around 14%. The labour force totals half a billion workers.

Major agricultural products include rice, wheat, oilseed, cotton, jute, tea, sugarcane, potatoes, cattle, water buffalo, sheep, goats, poultry and fish. Major industries include telecommunications, textiles, chemicals, food processing, steel, transportation equipment, cement, mining, petroleum, machinery, information technology enabled services and software.

India's per capita income (nominal) is $1032, ranked 139th in the world, while its per capita (PPP) of US$2,932 is ranked 128th. India's trade has grown fast. India currently accounts for 1.5% of World trade as of 2007 according to the WTO. The World Trade Statistics of the WTO in 2006, India's total merchandise trade (counting exports and imports) was valued at $294 billion in 2006 and India's services trade inclusive of export and import was $143 billion. Thus, India's global economic engagement in 2006 covering both merchandise and services trade was of the order of $437 billion, up by a record 72% from a level of $253 billion in 2004. India's trade has reached a still relatively moderate share 24% of GDP in 2006, up from 6% in 1985.

Despite robust economic growth, India continues to face many major problems. The recent economic development has widened the economic inequality across the country. Despite sustained high economic growth rate, approximately 80% of its population lives on less than $2 a day (PPP). Even though the arrival of Green Revolution brought end to famines in India, 40% of children under the age of three are underweight and a third of all men and women suffer from chronic energy deficiency.

In the late 80s, the government led by Rajiv Gandhi eased restrictions on capacity expansion for incumbents, removed price controls and reduced corporate taxes. While this increased the rate of growth, it also led to high fiscal deficits and a worsening current account. The collapse of the Soviet

Union, which was India's major trading partner, and the first Gulf War, which caused a spike in oil prices, caused a major balance-of-payments crisis for India, which found itself facing the prospect of defaulting on its loans. India asked for a $1.8 billion bailout loan from IMF, which in return demanded reforms.

In response, Prime Minister Narasimha Rao along with his finance minister Manmohan Singh initiated the economic liberalisation of 1991. The reforms did away with the Licence Raj (investment, industrial and import licensing) and ended many public monopolies, allowing automatic approval of foreign direct investment in many sectors. Since then, the overall direction of liberalisation has remained the same, irrespective of the ruling party, although no party has tried to take on powerful lobbies such as the trade unions and farmers, or contentious issues such as reforming labour laws and reducing agricultural subsidies. Since 1990 India has emerged as one of the fastest-growing economies in the developing world; during this period, the economy has grown constantly, but with a few major setbacks. This has been accompanied by increases in life expectancy, literacy rates and food security.

While the credit rating of India was hit by its nuclear tests in 1998, it has been raised to investment level in 2007 by S&P and Moody's. In 2003, Goldman Sachs predicted that India's GDP in current prices will overtake France and Italy by 2020, Germany, UK and Russia by 2025 and Japan by 2035. By 2035, it was projected to be the third largest economy of the world, behind US and China.. In 2009 India purchased 200 Tons of Gold for $6.7 Billion from IMF as a total role reversal from 1991.

India ranks second worldwide in farm output. Agriculture and allied sectors like forestry, logging and fishing accounted for 16.6% of the GDP in 2007, employed 60% of the total workforce and despite a steady decline of its share in the GDP, is still the largest economic sector and plays a significant role in the overall socio-economic development of India. Yields per unit area of all crops have grown since 1950, due to the special emphasis placed on agriculture in the five-year plans and steady improvements in irrigation, technology, application of modern agricultural practices and provision of agricultural credit and subsidies since Green revolution in India. However, international comparisons reveal the average yield in India is generally 30% to 50% of the highest average yield in the world.

India is the largest producer in the world of milk, cashew nuts, coconuts, tea, ginger, turmeric and black pepper. It also has the world's largest cattle population: 193 million. It is the second largest producer of wheat, rice, sugar, cotton, silk, peanuts and inland fish. It is the third largest producer of tobacco. India is the largest fruit producer, accounting for 10% of the world fruit production. It is the leading producer of bananas, sapotas and mangoes.

India is the second largest producer and the largest consumer of silk in the world, with the majority of the 77 million kg (2005) production taking place in Karnataka State, particularly in Mysore and the North Bangalore regions of Muddenahalli, Kanivenarayanapura, and Doddaballapura, the upcoming sites of a INR 700 million "Silk City". Industry accounts for 54.6% of the GDP and employ 17% of the total workforce. However, about one-third of the industrial labour force is engaged in simple household manufacturing only. In absolute terms, India is 16th in the world in terms of nominal factory output. India's small industry makes up 5% of carbon dioxide emissions in the world.

Economic reforms brought foreign competition, led to privatisation of certain public sector industries, opened up sectors hitherto reserved for the public sector and led to an expansion in the production of fast-moving consumer goods. Post-liberalisation, the Indian private sector, which was usually run by oligopolies of old family firms and required political connections to prosper was faced with foreign competition, including the threat of cheaper Chinese imports. It has since handled the change by squeezing costs, revamping management, focusing on designing new products and relying on low labour costs and technology. Textile manufacturing is the second largest source for employment after agriculture and accounts for 26% of manufacturing output. Tirupur has gained universal recognition as the leading source of hosiery, knitted garments, casual wear and sportswear. Dharavi slum in Mumbai has gained fame for leather products. Tata Motors' Nano attempts to be the world's cheapest car.

India is fifteenth in services output. It provides employment to 23% of work force, and it is growing fast, growth rate 7.5% in 1991–2000 up from 4.5% in 1951–80. It has the largest share in the GDP, accounting for 55% in 2007 up from 15% in 1950. Business services are among the fastest growing sectors contributing to one third of the total output of services in 2000. The growth in the IT sector is attributed to increased specialization, and an availability of a large pool of low cost, but highly skilled, educated and fluent English-speaking workers, on the supply side, matched on the demand side by an increased demand from foreign consumers interested in India's service exports, or those looking to outsource their operations.

The share of India's IT industry to the country's GDP increased from 4.8% in 2005-06 to 7% in 2008. In 2009, seven Indian firms were listed among the top 15 technology outsourcing companies in the world. In March 2009, annual revenues from outsourcing operations in India amounted to US$60 billion and this is expected to increase to US$225 billion by 2020.

Organized retail such supermarkets accounts for 24% of the market as of 2008. Regulations prevent most foreign investment in retailing. Moreover, over thirty regulations such as "signboard licences" and "anti-hoarding measures" may have to be complied before a store can open doors. There are taxes for moving goods to states, from states, and even within states.

Tourism in India is relatively undeveloped, but growing at double digits. Some hospitals woo medical tourism. The Indian money market is classified into: the organised sector (comprising private, public and foreign owned commercial banks and cooperative banks, together known as *scheduled banks*); and the unorganised sector (comprising individual or family owned indigenous bankers or money lenders and non-banking financial companies (NBFCs)). The unorganised sector and microcredit are still preferred over traditional banks in rural and sub-urban areas, especially for non-productive purposes, like ceremonies and short duration loans.

Prime Minister Indira Gandhi nationalised 14 banks in 1969, followed by six others in 1980, and made it mandatory for banks to provide 40% of their net credit to priority sectors like agriculture, small-scale industry, retail trade, small businesses, etc. to ensure that the banks fulfill their social and developmental goals.

Since then, the number of bank branches has increased from 10,120 in 1969 to 98,910 in 2003 and the population covered by a branch decreased from 63,800 to 15,000 during the same period. The total deposits increased 32.6 times between 1971 to 1991 compared to 7 times between 1951 to 1971. Despite an increase of rural branches, from 1,860 or 22% of the total number of branches in 1969 to 32,270 or 48%, only 32,270 out of 5 lakh (500,000) villages are covered by a scheduled bank.

The public sector banks hold over 75% of total assets of the banking industry, with the private and foreign banks holding 18.2% and 6.5% respectively. Since liberalisation, the government has approved significant banking reforms. While some of these relate to nationalised banks (like encouraging mergers, reducing government interference and increasing profitability and competitiveness), other reforms have opened up the banking and insurance sectors to private and foreign players.

More than half of personal savings are invested in physical assets such as land, houses, cattle, and gold. India's total cultivable area is 1,269,219 km^2 (56.78% of total land area), which is decreasing due to constant pressure from an ever growing population and increased urbanisation. India has a total water surface area of 314,400 km^2 and receives an average annual rainfall of 1,100 mm. Irrigation accounts for 92% of the water utilisation, and comprised 380 km^2 in 1974, and is expected to rise to 1,050 km^2 by 2025, with the balance accounted for by industrial and domestic consumers. India's inland water resources comprising rivers, canals, ponds and lakes and marine resources comprising the east and west coasts of the Indian ocean and other gulfs and bays provide employment to nearly 6 million people in the fisheries sector. In 2008, India had the world's third largest fishing industry.

India's major mineral resources include coal, iron, manganese, mica, bauxite, titanium, chromite, limestone and thorium. India meets most of its domestic energy demand through its 92 billion tonnes of coal reserves (about 10% of world's coal reserves). Petronas takes key stake in Cairn before £3.6bn Indian float] India's huge thorium reserves — about 25% of world's reserves — is expected to fuel the country's ambitious nuclear energy programme in the long-run.

India's dwindling uranium reserves stagnated the growth of nuclear energy in the country for many years. However, the Indo-US nuclear deal has paved the way for India to import uranium from other countries. India is also believed to be rich in certain renewable sources of energy with significant future potential such as solar, wind and biofuels (jatropha, sugarcane). India has a self reliant Pharmaceuticals industry. Majority of it's medical consumables are produced domestically. Pharmaceutical Industry in India is dotted with companies like Ranbaxy Laboratories, Dr. Reddy's Laboratories, Cipla which have created a niche for themselves at world level.

Today, India is an exporter of countries like United States and Russia. In terms of the global market, India currently holds a modest 1-2% share, but it has been growing at approximately 10% per year. Indian Pharmaceutical Industry is often compared to Pharmaceutical Industry in the USA. India is one of the largest importers of crude oil. It has a strong domestic market for Petroleum products.

The petroleum industry in India mostly consists of public sector companies such as Oil and Natural Gas Corporation Limited (ONGC), Hindustan Petroleum Corporation Limited (HPCL), Indian Petrochemicals Corporation Limited (IPCL), but there are also private sector players like Reliance Petroleum Limited of Mukesh Ambani's Reliance Industries Limited

(RIL). Recently, oil and natural gas exploration has begun taking place in India. India's oil reserves, found in Bombay High off the coast of Maharashtra, Gujarat, Rajasthan and in eastern Assam meet 25% of the country's domestic oil demand. India's total proven oil reserves stand at 11 billion barrels, of which Bombay High is believed to hold 6.1 billion barrels and Mangala Area in Rajasthan an additional 3.6 billion barrels.

India's economy is mostly dependent on its large internal market with external trade accounting for just 20% of the country's GDP. In 2008, India accounted for 1.45% of global merchandise trade and 2.8% of global commercial services export. Until the liberalization of 1991, India was largely and intentionally isolated from the world markets, to protect its economy and to achieve self-reliance.

Foreign trade was subject to import tariffs, export taxes and quantitative restrictions, while foreign direct investment (FDI) was restricted by upper-limit equity participation, restrictions on technology transfer, export obligations and government approvals; these approvals were needed for nearly 60% of new FDI in the industrial sector. The restrictions ensured that FDI averaged only around US$200 million annually between 1985 and 1991; a large percentage of the capital flows consisted of foreign aid, commercial borrowing and deposits of non-resident Indians.

India's exports were stagnant for the first 15 years after independence, due to the predominance of tea, jute and cotton manufactures, demand for which was generally inelastic. Imports in the same period consisted predominantly of machinery, equipment and raw materials, due to nascent industrialization. Since liberalization, the value of India's international trade has become more broad-based and has risen to Rs. 63,080,109 crores in 2003–04 from Rs.1,250 crores in 1950–51.

India's major trading partners are China, the US, the UAE, the UK, Japan and the EU. The exports during April 2007 were $12.31 billion up by 16% and import were $17.68 billion with an increase of 18.06% over the previous year. In 2006-07, major export commodities included engineering goods, petroleum products, chemicals and pharmaceuticals, gems and jewellery, textiles and garments, agricultural products, iron ore and other minerals. Major import commodities included crude oil and related products, machinery, electronic goods, gold and silver.

India is a founding-member of General Agreement on Tariffs and Trade (GATT) since 1947 and its successor, the WTO. While participating actively in its general council meetings, India has been crucial in voicing the concerns of the developing world. For instance, India has continued its opposition to the inclusion of such matters as labour and environment issues and other *non-tariff barriers* into the WTO policies.

Since independence, India's balance of payments on its current account has been negative. Since liberalisation in the 1990s (precipitated by a balance of payment crisis), India's exports have been consistently rising, covering 80.3% of its imports in 2002–03, up from 66.2% in 1990–91. India's growing oil import bill is seen as the main driver behind the large current account deficit. In 2007-08, India imported 120.1 million tonnes of crude oil, more than 3/4th of the domestic demand, at a cost of $61.72 billion.

Although India is still a net importer, since 1996–97 its overall balance of payments (i.e., including the capital account balance) has been positive, largely on account of increased foreign direct investment and deposits from non-resident Indians; until this time, the overall balance was only occasionally positive on account of external assistance and commercial borrowings. As a result, India's foreign currency reserves stood at $285 billion in 2008.

Due to the global late-2000s recession, both Indian exports and imports declined by 29.2% and 39.2% respectively in June 2009. The steep decline was because countries hit hardest by the global recession, such as United States and members of the European Union, account for more than 60% of Indian exports. However, since the decline in imports was much sharper compared to the decline in exports, India's trade deficit reduced to $252.5 billion. India's reliance on external assistance and commercial borrowings has decreased since 1991–92, and since 2002–03, it has gradually been repaying these debts. Declining interest rates and reduced borrowings decreased India's debt service ratio to 4.5% in 2007. In India, External Commercial Borrowings (ECBs) are being permitted by the Government for providing an additional source of funds to Indian corporates. The Ministry of Finance monitors and regulates these borrowings (ECBs) through ECB policy guidelines.

FOREIGN DIRECT INVESTMENT IN INDIA

As the fourth-largest economy in the world in PPP terms, India is a preferred destination for foreign direct investments (FDI); India has strengths in telecommunication, information technology and other significant areas such as auto components, chemicals, apparels, pharmaceuticals, and jewellery. Despite a surge in foreign investments, rigid FDI policies resulted in a significant hindrance. However, due to some positive economic reforms aimed at deregulating the economy and stimulating foreign investment, India has positioned itself as one of the front-runners of the rapidly growing Asia Pacific Region. India has a large pool of skilled managerial and technical expertise. The size of the middle-class population stands at 300 million and represents a growing consumer market.

The inordinately high investment from Mauritius is due to routing of international funds through the country given significant capital gains tax advantages; double taxation is avoided due to a tax treaty between India and Mauritius, and Mauriitus is a capital gains tax haven, effectively creating a zero-taxation FDI channel.

India's recently liberalized FDI policy (2005) allows up to a 100% FDI stake in ventures. Industrial policy reforms have substantially reduced industrial licensing requirements, removed restrictions on expansion and facilitated easy access to foreign technology and foreign direct investment FDI. The upward moving growth curve of the real-estate sector owes some credit to a booming economy and liberalized FDI regime. In March 2005, the government amended the rules to allow

100 per cent FDI in the construction business. This automatic route has been permitted in townships, housing, built-up infrastructure and construction development projects including housing, commercial premises, hotels, resorts, hospitals, educational institutions, recreational facilities, and city- and regional-level infrastructure.

A number of changes were approved on the FDI policy to remove the caps in most sectors. Fields which require relaxation in FDI restrictions include civil aviation, construction development, industrial parks, petroleum and natural gas, commodity exchanges, credit-information services and mining. But this still leaves an unfinished agenda of permitting greater foreign investment in politically sensitive areas such as insurance and retailing.

FDI inflows into India reached a record $19.5 billion in fiscal year 2006-07 (April-March), according to the government's Secretariat for Industrial Assistance. This was more than double the total of US$7.8bn in the previous fiscal year. The FDI inflow for 2007-08 has been reported as $24 billion and for 2008-09, it is expected to be above $35 billion. A critical factor in determining India's continued economic growth and realizing the potential to be an economic superpower is going to depend on how the government can create incentives for FDI flow across a large number of sectors in India.

The Indian rupee is the only legal tender accepted in India. The exchange rate as on 1 February 2010 is 46.18 INR the USD, 64.03 to a EUR, and 73.82 to a GBP. The Indian rupee is accepted as legal tender in the neighbouring Nepal and Bhutan, both of which peg their currency to that of the Indian rupee. The rupee is divided into 100 paise. The highest-denomination banknote is the 1,000 rupee note; the lowest-denomination coin in circulation is the 25 paise coin (it earlier had 1, 2, 5, 10 and 20 paise coins which have been discontinued by the Reserve Bank of India).

The Rupee hit a record low during early 2009 on account of global recession. However, due to a strong domestic market, India managed to bounce back sooner than the western countries. Since September 2009 there has been a constant appreciation in Rupee versus most Tier 1 currencies. On 11 January 2010 Rupee went as high as 45.50 to a United states dollar and on 10 January 2010 as high as Rupee 73.93 to a British Pound. A rising rupee also prompted Government of India to buy 200 tonnes of Gold from IMF.

The RBI, the country's central bank was established on 1 April 1935. It serves as the nation's monetary authority, regulator and supervisor of the financial system, manager of exchange control and as an issuer of currency. The RBI is governed by a central board, headed by a governor who is appointed by the Central government of India. Percentage of population living under the poverty line of $1 (PPP) a day, currently 356.35 rupees a month in rural areas (around $7.4 a month).

As of 2005:

- 77.7% of the population lives on less than $2.50 (PPP) a day, down from 92.5% in 1981. This compares with 80.5% in Sub-Saharan Africa.
- 65.6% of the population lives on less than $2 a day (PPP), which is around 20 rupees or $0.5 a day in nominal terms. It was down from 86.6% and compares with 73.0% in Sub-Saharan Africa.
- 24.3% of the population earned less than $1 (PPP, around $0.25 in nominal terms) a day in 2005, down from 42.1% in 1981.
- 41.6% of its population is living below the new international poverty line of $1.25 (PPP) per day, down from 59.8% in 1981. The World Bank further estimates that a third of the global poor now reside in India.

Today, more people can afford a bicycle than ever before. Some 40% of Indian households owns a bicycle, with ownership rates ranging from around 30% to 70% at state level. Housing is modest. Times of India, "a majority of Indians have per capita space equivalent to or less than a 10 feet x 10 feet room for their living, sleeping, cooking, washing and toilet needs." and "one in every three urban Indians lives in homes too cramped to exceed even the minimum requirements of a prison cell in the US." The average is 103 sq ft (9.6 m) per person in rural areas and 117 sq ft (10.9 m) per person in urban areas.

Around half of Indian children are malnourished. The proportion of underweight children is nearly double that of Sub-Saharan Africa. However, India has not had famines since the Green Revolution in the early 1970s. While poverty in India has reduced significantly, official figures estimate that 27.5% of Indians still lived below the national poverty line of $1 (PPP, around 10 rupees in nominal terms) a day in 2004-2005. A 2007 report by the state-run National Commission for Enterprises in the Unorganised Sector (NCEUS) found that 65% of Indians, or 750 million people, lived on less than 20 rupees per day with most working in "informal labour sector with no job or social security, living in abject poverty."

Since the early 1950s, successive governments have implemented various plans, under planning, to alleviate poverty, that have met with partial success. All these programmes have relied upon the strategies of the *Food for work* programme and *National Rural Employment Programme* of the 1980s, which attempted to use the unemployed to generate productive assets and build rural infrastructure. In August 2005, the Indian parliament passed the *Rural Employment Guarantee Bill,* the largest programme of this type in terms of cost and coverage, which promises 100 days of minimum wage employment to every rural household in all the India's 600 districts. The question of whether economic reforms have reduced poverty or not has fuelled debates without generating any clear cut answers and has also put political pressure on further economic reforms, especially those involving the downsizing of labour and cutting agricultural subsidies.

Agricultural and allied sectors accounted for about 60% of the total workforce in 2003 same as in 1993–94. While agriculture has faced stagnation in growth, services have seen a steady growth. Of the total workforce, 8% is in the organised sector, two-thirds of which are in the public sector. The NSSO survey estimated that in 1999–2000, 106 million, nearly 10%

of the population were unemployed and the overall unemployment rate was 7.3%, with rural areas doing marginally better (7.2%) than urban areas (7.7%). India's labour force is growing by 2.5% annually, but employment only at 2.3% a year.

Official unemployment exceeds 9%. Regulation and other obstacles have discouraged the emergence of formal businesses and jobs. Almost 30% of workers are casual workers who work only when they are able to get jobs and remain unpaid for the rest of the time. Only 10% of the workforce is in regular employment. India's labour regulations are heavy even by developing country standards and analysts have urged the government to abolish them.

Unemployment in India is characterized by chronic underemployment or disguised unemployment. Government plans that target eradication of both poverty and unemployment (which in recent decades has sent millions of poor and unskilled people into urban areas in search of livelihoods) attempt to solve the problem, by providing financial assistance for setting up businesses, skill honing, setting up public sector enterprises, reservations in governments, etc. The decreased role of the public sector after liberalization has further underlined the need for focusing on better education and has also put political pressure on further reforms.

Child labour is a complex problem that is basically rooted in poverty. The Indian government is implementing the world's largest child labour elimination programme, with primary education targeted for ~250 million. Numerous non-governmental and voluntary organizations are also involved. Special investigation cells have been set up in states to enforce existing laws banning employment of children (under 14) in hazardous industries. The allocation of the Government of India for the eradication of child labour was $10 million in 1995-96 and $16 million in 1996-97. The allocation for 2007 is $21 million. In 2006, remittances from Indian migrants overseas made up $27 billion or about 3% of India's GDP. Based on increased and sustaining growth, more inflows into foreign direct investment, Goldman Sachs predicts that "from 2007 to 2020, India's GDP per capita in US$ terms will quadruple", and that the Indian economy will surpass the United States (in US$) by 2043.

In spite of the high growth rate, the report stated that India would continue to remain a low-income country for decades to come but could be a "motor for the world economy" if it fulfills its growth potential. Goldman Sachs has outlined 10 things that it needs to do in order to achieve its potential and grow 40 times by 2050.

These are:

- Improve governance
- Raise educational achievement
- Increase quality and quantity of universities
- Control inflation
- Introduce a credible fiscal policy
- Liberalize financial markets
- Increase trade with neighbours
- Increase agricultural productivity
- Improve infrastructure and
- Improve environmental quality.

Slow agricultural growth is a concern for policymakers as some two-thirds of India's people depend on rural employment for a living. Current agricultural practices are neither economically nor environmentally sustainable and India's yields for many agricultural commodities are low. Poorly maintained irrigation systems and almost universal lack of good extension services are among the factors responsible. Farmers' access to markets is hampered by poor roads, rudimentary market infrastructure, and excessive regulation. – *World Bank: "India Country Overview 2008"*

The low productivity in India is a result of the following factors:

- *According to "India*: Priorities for Agriculture and Rural Development" by World Bank, India's large agricultural subsidies are hampering productivity-enhancing investment. Overregulation of agriculture has increased costs, price risks and uncertainty. Government interventions in labour, land, and credit markets are hurting the market. Infrastructure and services are inadequate.

- Illiteracy, slow progress in implementing land reforms and inadequate or inefficient finance and marketing services for farm produce.
- The average size of land holdings is very small (less than 20,000 m^2) and is subject to fragmentation, due to land ceiling acts and in some cases, family disputes. Such small holdings are often over-manned, resulting in disguised unemployment and low productivity of labour.
- Adoption of modern agricultural practices and use of technology is inadequate, hampered by ignorance of such practices, high costs and impracticality in the case of small land holdings.
- World Bank says that the allocation of water is inefficient, unsustainable and inequitable. The irrigation infrastructure is deteriorating. Irrigation facilities are inadequate, as revealed by the fact that only 52.6% of the land was irrigated in 2003–04, which result in farmers still being dependent on rainfall, specifically the Monsoon season. A good monsoon results in a robust growth for the economy as a whole, while a poor monsoon leads to a sluggish growth. Farm credit is regulated by NABARD, which is the statutory apex agent for rural development in the subcontinent.

India has many farm insurance companies that insure wheat, fruit, rice and rubber farmers in the event of natural disasters or catastrophic crop failure, under the supervision of the Ministry of Agriculture. One notable company that provides all of these insurance policies is Agriculture Insurance Company of India and it alone insures almost 20 million farmers.

India's population is growing faster than its ability to produce rice and wheat. The most important structural reform for self-sufficiency is the ITC Limited plan to connect 20,000 villages to the Internet by 2013. This will provide farmers with up to date crop prices for the first time, which should minimise losses incurred from neighbouring producers selling early and in turn facilitate investment in rural areas.

Corruption has been one of the pervasive problems affecting India. The economic reforms of 1991 reduced the red tape, bureaucracy and the *Licence Raj* that had strangled private enterprise and was blamed by Chakravarthi Rajagopalachari for the corruption and inefficiencies. Yet, a 2005 study by Transparency International (TI) India found that more than half of those surveyed had firsthand experience of paying bribe or peddling influence to get a job done in a public office.

The Right to Information Act (2005) and equivalent acts in the Indian states, that require government officials to furnish information requested by citizens or face punitive action, computerisation of services and various central and state government acts that established vigilance commissions have considerably reduced corruption or at least have opened up avenues to redress grievances. The 2009 report by Transparency International ranks India at 84th place and states that significant improvements were made by India in reducing corruption.

The number of people employed in non-agricultural occupations in the public and private sectors. Totals are rounded. Private sector data relates to non-agriculture establishments with 10 or more employees. The current government has concluded that most spending fails to reach its intended recipients.

Lant Pritchett calls India's public sector "one of the world's top ten biggest problems — of the order of AIDS and climate change". The Economist's article about Indian civil service (2008) says that Indian central government employs around 3 million people and states another 7 million, including "vast armies of paper-shuffling peons". Million dollar bureaucracies can be run without a single computer in the management. At local level, administration can be worse. It is not unheard of that most state assembly seats are held by convicted criminals. One study found out that 25% of public sector teachers and 40% of public sector medical workers could not be found at the workplace. India's absence rates are one of the worst in the world. The Reserve Bank of India has warned that India's public-debt to GDP ratio is over 70%. The government of India is highly indebted and its former investment-grade status has deteriorated near junk status. India's current public-debt to GDP ratio is 58.2% (US has 60.8%).

India has made huge progress in terms of increasing primary education attendance rate and expanding literacy to approximately two thirds of the population. The right to education at elementary level has been made one of the fundamental rights under the Eighty-Sixth Amendment of 2002. However, education is still far behind developing countries such as China and continues to face challenges. Despite growing investment in education, 40% of the population is illiterate and only 15% of the students reach high school.

An optimistic estimate is that only one in five job-seekers in India has ever had any sort of vocational training. Development of infrastructure was completely in the hands of the public sector and was plagued by corruption, bureaucratic inefficiencies, urban-bias and an inability to scale investment. India's low spending on power, construction, transportation, telecommunications and real estate, at $31 billion or 6% of GDP in 2002 had prevented India from sustaining higher growth rates.

This has prompted the government to partially open up infrastructure to the private sector allowing foreign investment which has helped in a sustained growth rate of close to 9% for the past six quarters. Some 600 million Indians have no mains electricity at all. While 80% of Indian villages have at least an electricity line, just 44% of rural households have access to electricity.

A sample of 97,882 households in 2002, electricity was the main source of lighting for 53% of rural households compared to 36% in 1993. Some half of the electricity is stolen, compared with 3% in China. The stolen electricity amounts to 1.5% of

GDP. Almost all of the electricity in India is produced by the public sector. Power outages are common. Many buy their own power generators to ensure electricity supply. As of 2005 the electricity production was at 661.6 billion kWh with oil production standing at 785,000 bbl/day.

In 2007, electricity demand exceeded supply by 15%. Multi Commodity Exchange has tried to get a permit to offer electricity future markets. Indian Road Network is developing. Trucking goods from Gurgaon to the port in Mumbai can take up to 10 days. India has the world's third largest road network. Container traffic is growing at 15% a year. Some 60% of India's container traffic is handled by the Jawaharlal Nehru Port Trust in Mumbai.

Internet use is rare; there were only 7.57 million broadband lines in India in November 2009, however it is still growing at slower rate and is expected to boom after the launch of 3G and wimax services. Most urban cities have good water supply water 24 hours a day, while some smaller cities face water shortages in summer season. A World Bank report says it is an institutional problem in water agencies, or "how the agency is embedded in the relationships between politics and the citizens who are the consumers."

India's labour regulations – among the most restrictive and complex in the world – have constrained the growth of the formal manufacturing sector where these laws have their widest application. Better designed labour regulations can attract more labour- intensive investment and create jobs for India's unemployed millions and those trapped in poor quality jobs. Given the country's momentum of growth, the window of opportunity must not be lost for improving the job prospects for the 80 million new entrants who are expected to join the work force over the next decade. – *World Bank: India Country Overview 2008.*

India's restrictive labour regulations hamper the large-scale creation of formal industrial jobs. A recent report highlights a growing labour unrest all over India which is hampering the industrial output. India ranked 133th on the Ease of Doing Business Index 2010, behind countries such as

China (89th), Pakistan (85th), and Nigeria (125th). Lagging states need to bring more jobs to their people by creating an attractive investment destination. Reforming cumbersome regulatory procedures, improving rural connectivity, establishing law and order, creating a stable platform for natural resource investment that balances business interests with social concerns, and providing rural finance are important. – *World Bank: India Country Overview 2008*

One of the critical problems facing India's economy is the sharp and growing regional variations among India's different states and territories in terms of per capita income, poverty, availability of infrastructure and socio-economic development. Seven low-income states - Bihar, Chhattisgarh, Jharkhand, Madhya Pradesh, Orissa, Rajasthan, and Uttar Pradesh - are home to more than half of India's population.

Between 1999 and 2008, the annualized growth rates for Maharashtra (9%), Gujarat (8.8%), Haryana (8.7%), or Delhi (7.4%) were much higher than for Bihar (5.1%), Uttar Pradesh (4.4%), or Madhya Pradesh (3.5%). Poverty rates in rural Orissa (43%) and rural Bihar (40%) are some of the worst in the world. On the other hand, rural Haryana (5.7%) and rural Punjab (2.4%) compare well with middle-income countries.

The five-year plans have attempted to reduce regional disparities by encouraging industrial development in the interior regions, but industries still tend to concentrate around urban areas and port cities After liberalization, the more advanced states are better placed to benefit from them, with infrastructure like well developed ports, urbanisation and an educated and skilled workforce which attract manufacturing and service sectors.

The union and state governments of backward regions are trying to reduce the disparities by offering tax holidays, cheap land, etc., and focusing more on sectors like tourism, which although being geographically and historically determined, can become a source of growth and is faster to develop than other sectors.

9

Legal Environment

In India there are several Acts and legislations enacted by the Government of India for regulation of industries in the country. These enactments play a very important role in the country's overall progress and economic development. These legislations are amended from time to time in accordance with the changing circumstances and environment. The most important Act is the Companies Act, 1956 which relates to setting up and operation of companies in India. It empowers the Central Government to regulate the formation, financing, functioning and winding up of companies. It contains the mechanism regarding organisational, financial, managerial and all the relevant aspects of a company.

In order to provide the Central Government with the means to implement its industrial policies, several legislations have been enacted. The most important being the Industries (Development and Regulation) Act, 1951 (IDRA). The main objectives of the Act is to empower the Government to take necessary steps for the development of industries; to regulate the pattern and direction of industrial development; and to control the activities, performance and results of industrial undertakings in the public interest.

The bulk of the transactions in trade, commerce and industry are based on contracts. In India, the Indian Contract Act,1872 is the governing legislation for contracts, which lays down the general principles relating to formation, performance and enforceability of contracts and the rules relating to certain special types of contracts like Indemnity and Guarantee; Bailment and Pledge; as well as Agency. Another important aspect of legislations is the industrial relations, which involves various aspects of interactions between the employer and the employees; among the employees as well as between the employers. In such relations whenever there is a clash of interest, it may result in dissatisfaction for either of the parties involved and hence lead to industrial disputes or conflicts.

The Industrial Disputes Act, 1947 is the main legislation for investigation and settlement of all industrial disputes. The Act enumerates the contingencies when a strike or lock-out can be lawfully resorted to, when they can be declared illegal or unlawful, conditions for laying off, retrenching, discharging or dismissing a workman, circumstances under which an industrial unit can be closed down and several other matters related to industrial employees and employers.

Trade unions are also an important part of an industrial set up. The legislation regulating these trade unions is the Indian Trade Unions Act, 1926. The Act deals with the registration of trade unions, their rights, their liabilities and responsibilities as well as ensures that their funds are utilised properly.

It gives legal and corporate status to the registered trade unions. It also seeks to protect them from civil or criminal prosecution so that they could carry on their legitimate activities for the benefit of the working class.

MRTP, FEMA, EXIM IN LIGHT OF LIBERALIZATION POLICIES

Economic development can only result from state-led policies designed to address the numerous production failures and bottlenecks that characterize the economies of underdeveloped countries. SEZ is one such state led policy.

SEZs are benefited, apart from general fiscal and non fiscal concessions to firms, from the following:

- Location-specific advantage.
- Modern and efficient infrastructure.
- Better governance due to single window facilities to ensure corruption and red tape free business environment.

SEZs thus make up for infrastructural deficiencies and procedural complexities that characterize developing countries and offer a more conducive investment climate. Trade related infrastructure and institutional framework are generally deficient in developing countries. Besides, too many windows in the administrative set up, bureaucratic hassles and barriers raised by monetary, trade, fiscal, taxation, tariff and labour policies further increase production and transaction costs of exports. Since country-wide development of infrastructure is expensive and implementation of structural reforms require time due to socio-economic and political realities, Special Economic Zones SEZs or Export Processing Zones (EPZs) are considered an strategic tool for the promotion of exports in developing economies such as those of India, China, Bangladesh etc. The SEZ offers quality infrastructure and hassle free business environment permitting an economy to promote and diversify exports and develop a competitive industrial base.

However, given the limited technological and marketing capabilities of developing countries, the zones may not affect exports substantially unless they attract FDI also. Due to easy access to proprietary technology of their parents and international marketing network, MNCs affiliates are likely to be more competitive in international markets. Furthermore, in this era of globalization, MNCs restructuring their operations to avail economies of scale and scope by internalizing the economies of specialization through the integration of assets, production and marketing activities across countries to advance the core competencies in the global markets. The vision of SEZs/ EPZs in an export oriented regime is to establish a viable internationally competitive platform that is capable of attracting export oriented FDI to promote exports.

SEZs are industrial clusters of companies that are concentrated in a geographic region. These companies share economic infrastructure, a pool of skilled human capital, and governmental and other institutions that provide education, specialized training, information and technical support. Also, these companies may co-operate to create joint companies, distribution agreement, technology transfer agreements and common manufacturing agreements. External economies of scale and other advantages of the cluster help the operating firms in reducing costs, acquiring competitive advantages and attracting foreign direct investment.

To sum up, SEZs play a crucial initiating role in the development of national industrial capacity by: 1) offering a platform for internationally mobile productive units, 2) creating an environment conducive to promote investment and exports, 3) initiating a shift in the orientation of the domestic private sector towards export activities, 4) leading government to adapt a more proactive and responsive attitude towards private sector's requirements of regulatory and administrative efficiency.

Evolution

India initiated the process of industrial growth in 1948 (immediately after the political independence), when it announced its first Industrial Policy Resolution, IPR 1948. The strategy adopted was one of import-substitution industrialization across all sectors. Export promotion had also been a concern of the government. Thus, attempts to promote the EPZ as an export platform on the basis of economic incentives, such as the provision of better infrastructure and tax holidays became a feature of Indian development. The first zone was set up in 1965 at Kandla, Gujarat. The country has had four phases in the evolution of the EPZ policy since then. Following is a brief overview of the evolution of the EPZ policy in India through these four phases.

Initial Phase: 1965-1985

The first zone was set up in Kandla in a highly backward region of Kutch in Gujarat as early as in 1965. It was followed by the Santacruz export processing zone in Mumbai which came into operation in 1973. There was however no clarity of objectives that the government wanted to achieve. Kandla and Santacruz EPZs were set up with different sets of objectives. Operationally, an overall inward looking trade policy with umpteen controls and regulations influenced the EPZ policy also. The policies were rigid and the package of incentives and facilities was not attractive. Zone authorities had limited powers. There was no single window facility within the zone. Entrepreneurs had to acquire individual clearances from various state government and central government departments. Day-to-day operations were subjected to rigorous controls. Custom procedures for bonding, bank guarantees and movement of goods were rigid. FDI policy was also highly restrictive.

The business environment rating index which rated investment climate in 43 countries on the basis of 18 independent factors, Indian, zones were placed at the bottom for FDI (TCS 1976). In 1980 the government introduced the Export Oriented Units Plan (EOU). This plan facilitates the setting up of EOUs beyond the boundaries of EPZs. The responsibility of administering these units was also entrusted with the zone administration.

Expansionary Phase: 1985-1991

Towards the end of the 1970s, India's failure to step up significantly the volume of her manufactured exports in the background of the Second Oil Price Shock began to worry the policy makers. To provide fillip to exports, the government decided to establish four more zones in 1984. These were at Noida (Uttar Pradesh), Falta (West Bengal) Cochin (Kerala) and Chennai (Tamil Nadu).

Thereafter, Visakhapatnam EPZ in Andhra Pradesh was established in 1989, though it could not become operational before 1994. All these zones with the exception of Chennai were set up in industrially backward regions. The primary objectives of the zones were still not specified and there were no significant changes in other laws and procedures pertaining to the EPZs.

Consolidating Phase: 1991-2000

In 1991, a massive dose of liberalization was administered in the Indian economy. In this context, wide-ranging measures were initiated by the government for revamping and restructuring EPZs also. This phase was thus marked by progressive liberalization of policy provisions and relaxation in the severity of controls and simplification of procedures. The focus had been on delegating powers to zone authorities, providing additional fiscal incentives, simplifying policy provisions and providing greater facilities. The scope and coverage of the EPZ/EOU plan was enlarged in 1992 by permitting the agriculture, horticulture and aqua culture sector unit also. In 1994, trading, re-engineering and re-conditioning units were also permitted to be set up.

Emergence Phase: 2000 Onwards

This period has witnessed a major shift in direction, thrust and approach. The EXIM Policy (1997-2002) has introduced a new plan from April 1, 2000 for establishment of the Special Economic Zones (SEZs) in different parts of the country. SEZ is an almost self contained area with high class infrastructure for commercial as well as residential inhabitation. SEZs are permitted to be set up in the public, private, joint sector or by the State Governments with a minimum size of not less than 1000 hectares.

The number of incentives both fiscal and non fiscal has also been extended to the units operating in SEZs. Several measures have been adopted to improve the quality of governance of the zones. These include relaxation in the conditions for approval process and simplifying custom rules. More recently, Development Commissioners are given the labour commissioner's powers. SEZ policy is thus the most significant thrust towards ensuring the success of export processing zones.

From November 1, 2000 the Export Processing Zones at Kandla, Santa Cruz (Mumbai), Cochin and Surat have been converted into SEZs. In 2003, other existing EPZs namely, Noida, Falta, Chennai, Vizag were also converted into SEZs. In addition, approval has been given for the setting up of SEZs in various parts of the country in the private/ joint sectors or by the state.

SEZ POLICY

Section 5 of SEZ Act, 2005 specifies objectives of setting up of SEZs. The Central Government, while notifying any area as a Special Economic Zone or an additional area to be included in the Special Economic Zone in the Special Economic Zone and discharging its functions under this Act, shall be guided by the following, namely:

- Generation of additional economic activity;
- Promotion of exports of goods and services;
- Promotion of investment from domestic and foreign sources;
- Creation of employment opportunities;
- Development of infrastructure facilities;
- Maintenance of sovereignty and integrity of India, the security of the State and friendly relations with foreign States.

The salient features of SEZ Act, 2005 are as follows:

- An SEZ can be established either jointly or severally by the Central Government or any person for manufacture of goods or rendering services or for both or as an FTWZ.
- Any person who intends to set up can make a proposal to the State Government concerned which in turn sends the proposal to Board of Approvals
- First time the option has been given to the developers to make a proposal directly to BOA also.
- Central Government can set up the SEZ suo moto after consulting the State Government concerned.
- Central Government may prescribe the minimum area of land.
- Central Government has also been empowered to prescribe different minimum area of land for a class or classes of SEZs.
- Central Government is empowered to approve more than one developer in an SEZ in cases where one developer does not have in his possession the minimum area of contiguous land.
- SEZ developers have been given full freedom to levy

user charges on agreed terms and can allocate space or built up area.

Exemptions from Taxes, Duties or Cess

Any goods or services exported out of or imported into or procured from the DTA by:

- A unit in SEZ; or
- A developer

Shall be exempt from payment of taxes, duties or cess under all enactments specified in the First Schedule.

- First Schedule includes 21 Enactments
- This list includes the Agriculture Produce Cess Act, the Coffee Act, the Rubber Act, the Tea Act, the Mica Act, the Textile Committee Act, the MPEDA Act, the Agriculture & Processed Food Export Cess Act, the Spices Act, etc.

Special Provisions for SEZs

- Duty free goods for development of SEZ as well as for SEZ units
- Supply from DTA to SEZ treated as physical export.
- Exemption from Service Tax.
- Exemption from CST.
- Exemption from securities transaction tax.
- Exemption from Income Tax to SEZ units for 15 years (100% exemption for first 5 years, 50% of income exempted for the next 5 years and then in the next 5 years the 50% of the profits which are ploughed back in the capital investment would be exempted).
- Existing SEZ unit to get income tax exemption for the balance period. No income tax exemption if 10 years IT benefit already availed.
- IT exemption extended to export of services which would include trading as well.
- SEZ developers given IT exemption for 10 consecutive assessment years out of first 15 years of its operations.
- OBU entitled for IT exemption for 10 years (100% exemption for first 5 years and next 5 years 50% exemption).

- Unit of an International Financial Service Centre entitled for IT exemption fro a period of 10 years (100% exemption for first 5 years
- For the purpose of IT exemption manufacture shall have the same meaning as assigned in the SEZ Act.
- Exemption from capital gains in case of transfer of undertaking from an urban/ rural area of SEZ.
- Sale in the DTA on payment of full applicable duty.
- Exemption from MAT to SEZ developers and SEZ units.
- SEZ units and developers exempted from Dividend Distribution Tax.
- Exemption of interest income of NRI in respect of deposits in OBUs.

Miscellaneous:

- The Central Government may by notification direct any of the provisions of any other central act or any rules or regulations made there under or nay notification or orders issued or directions give there under shall not apply to an SEZ or a class of SEZ or all SEZs.
- State Governments may notify policies for developers and units and take suitable steps for enactment of any law.
  - Granting exemption from the state taxes, levies and duties to the developers or the entrepreneurs
  - Delegating the power conferred upon any person or authority under any state act, to the Development Commissioner.
- The provisions of this Act shall have affect not withstanding anything inconsistent therewith contained in any other law for the time being enforced.
- An SEZ shall be deemed to be a Port, Airport, ICD, Land Station and Land Customs Station, as the case may be, under Section 7 of the Customs Act.
- Central Government empowered to carry out amendment in Insurance Act, 1938, Banking Regulation Act, 1949 and Indian Stamp Act, 1989.

Other Non-fiscal Incentives in SEZs:

- Exemption from industrial licensing for manufacture of items reserved for SSIs.
- 100 per cent FDI investment through automatic route to manufacturing SEZ units (barring a handful of sensitive industries).
- Facility to retain 100% foreign exchange receipts in EEFC Account.
- Facility to realise and repatriate export proceeds within 12 months.
- No cap on foreign investment for SSI reserved items.
- Re-export of imported goods found defective, goods imported from foreign supplies on loan basis etc., without G.R. Waiver under intimation to the Development Commissioner.
- "Write-off" of unrealised export bills up to 5 per cent.
- Commodity hedging by SEZ units permitted.
- Capitalization of import payables.
- Profits allowed to be repatriated freely without any dividend balancing requirement.
- No fixed wastage norms.
- Full freedom for subcontracting including subcontracting abroad.
- Subcontracting facility available to jewellery units.
- Duty free goods to be utilized in 5 years.

Administrative Set up

Special Economic zones in India have a three-tier management structure. At the apex level is the SEZ section within the Ministry of Commerce headed by the Commerce Secretary, which considers policy issues and periodically reviews the working of zones. At the next level is the Board of Approval, which is responsible for examining proposals for setting up enterprises in the sectors. It is headed by a person of the Additional Secretary level.

At the third tier is the: Development Commissioner who is the chief executive of the SEZ. He is responsible for the day-to-day administration, approves investment proposals under the automatic route and enforces various regulatory provisions. Recently, powers of Labour Commissioners are also delegated to him. He is assisted by a Joint Development Commissioner, four Deputy Development Commissioners, two Assistant Commissioners of Customs, security officer and other ministerial staff. Furthermore, Government delegated more powers to Development Commissioners of the Special Economic Zones (SEZs). Development Commissioners (DCs) of Special Economic Zones were now authorised to exercise the administrative powers in capacity expansion, broad banding and export import permissions5.

Besides, DCs were also allowed to authorise the change in name of the company or the implementing agency, to permit change of location from the place mentioned in the Letter of Approval/ Letter of Intent to another, to extend the validity period of Letter of Intent/Letter of Permission/Letter of Approval, to revise the Value Addition upward or downward upto the minimum Value Addition percentage as prescribed for the item of manufacture under the Policy and to permit disposal of obsolete capital goods, in DTA, on payment of applicable duties, without any restrictions.

Procedures for sourcing indigenous capital goods and raw materials were simplified. Multiple bonds for import clearance were replaced by a single bond. In 1998, custom procedures were further simplified when a common bond for imports, exports, job work and repair was introduced. It was in 2000 that path breaking reforms were introduced in the zone governance. Conditions for automatic approvals are relaxed considerably.

Now the Development Commissioners (DCs) may accord automatic approval to all projects where the activity proposed does not attract compulsory licensing. All proposals which do not meet any or all of the parameters for automatic approval are considered and approved by the Board of Approval of SEZ set up in the Department of Commerce. These include all services related proposals. The Board of Approval now is a larger body and quite broadbased to provide a single interface to those keen on setting up units. It has representatives of various Ministries like Small-Scale Industries, Environment and Forests, Science & Technology as members of the board. It has been broad based to include a representative of the Central Board of Direct Taxes and state government representatives also.

All proposals for FDI/NRI/OCB investments in EPZ units qualify for approval through automatic route subject to sectoral norms. Proposals not covered under the automatic route are considered and approved by FIPB. Thus the process of approval has been relaxed considerably and important powers have been delegated to the Development Commissioners only after 2000. The approval process now takes 7-10 days. The other formalities that need to be completed however include, Legal undertaking, Custom bonding, Factory registration, Building approval, Sales tax registration, Labour and environment certifications.

Our survey of the SEZ units revealed that units have to deal with as many as 15 authorities at the time of entry. These include, DC, municipal body, ESI, PF, Income tax, sales tax, factory registration, labour, pollution and excise. They have to deal with many of them in day-to-day operations as well. The zone acts as a facilitator in providing many of these services. The role of the administration here is to invite the government officials from various departments and arrange meetings with entrepreneurs.

However, around 40% of the respondents felt that the zones are not effective in providing single window services. Besides, most entrepreneurs complained that there were delays in decision making by the Ministry of Commerce and that there was lack of flexibility and sensitivity. Most of the firms located in SEZ is of the opinion that in order to improve the quality of governance, more powers should be delegated to Development Commissioners.

INFRASTRUCTURE

One of the basic elements critical for any export activity is adequate infrastructure especially physical infrastructure (transport system such as port, airport, water, electricity and communication facilities). Infrastructure within SEZs is generally considered superior to that available in the wider economy.

Foreign Investment

Foreign investment is the key to success of EPZs/ SEZs. With substantially liberalized EXIM policies, most of the East Asian countries attracted huge foreign investment in the initial stages of their opening up. EPZs in India have been largely dominated by domestically owned enterprises or joint ventures.

Table. Types of Investments in Indian Epzs (as on 31st March 1998) (rs. Crore)

Zone	Nri	Foreign	Domestic	Total
KAFTZ	2.6	0.6	82.4	85.6
SEEPZ	13.8	21.7	222.9	258.4
MEPZ	6.6	45.3	68.2	120.2
CEPZ	18	25	217	260
FEPZ	5	5.7	178.3	189.1
NEPZ	34.5	54	341	429.5
TOTL	80.6	152.4	1,109.9	1,342.9

Low level of foreign investment in Indian SEZs is attributed to regulatory policies, excessive controls and unattractive package of incentives for FDI. As a result of this situation, Indian advantage in terms of low labour cost, availability of trained manpower and existence of vast domestic market remained unexploited. Until July 1991, out of 325 operating units in EPZs, 70 were joint ventures and 26 fully foreign owned.

These two categories represented 30 per cent of the total units in EPZs. Between July 1991 and March 1998, 200 units were added to the EPZs. Of these units, 74 were joint ventures and 15 were fully foreign owned. After the liberalization of Indian economy, the proportion of joint ventures/ foreign owned units in the EPZs has gone up to 45 per cent. This reflected comparatively larger involvement of joint ventures in Indian EPZs/ SEZs. With overall restructuring of trade related policies and continuation of economic reforms, investment climate in the Indian SEZs will improve further.

Offshore Banking

Offshore banking units (OBUs) are permitted in the SEZs. These banks virtually are the foreign branches of banks, but located in India. OBUs are exempted from Cash Reserve Ratio (CRR) and statutory liquidity ratio (SLR) and make available finance to SEZ units and SEZ developers at international rates.

Technology Transfer

Transfer of foreign technology in the Indian SEZs has been insignificant. This is mainly due to excessive involvement of domestic units in the SEZs and their greater pre-occupation in the manufacture of low technology items like garments and electronics which do not require great skill. Nearly 60 per cent of exports from SEZs comprise gems and jewellery which are based on local skill and indigenous know-how.

Unless foreign investment in Indian SEZs increases, the transfer of technology in these clusters will remain low. So far the transfer of skills and know-how in the SEZs has been confined to study tours and training of workers for production of simple and labour intensive items. Transfer of product and process technology in the SEZs is limited.

Employment

Unlike smaller countries, employment is not a major objective for establishment of SEZs in India. An ILO study has pointed out that while the impact of MNCs on generation of employment in the SEZs has been very high in Singapore and Malaysia and significant in Korea and Hong Kong, it is negligible in India. Considering the level of activities in SEZs, the incremental effect of foreign units on employment generation in Indian SEZs is satisfactory.

Total employment increased constantly from 70 workers in 1966 to nearly 88,977 workers in 2002. Employment per zone also spurted from 70 to over 12,000 during the period. The average annual growth rate in employment, however, declined continuously despite setting up of 5 additional zones – 4 in the late 1980s and VSEZ in 1995. This shows that Indian SEZs could not maintain the rate of growth after the initial phase of rapid expansion. Among Indian SEZs, SEEPZ is the largest followed by MSEZ. Though variations exist, overall male/ female sex ratio is 57:43 and lowest in NSEZ at 25 per cent. Female workers are mainly involved in electronics and garments.

Linkages

Linkages of SEZs with the domestic economy are governed by the policies/ procedures for sale and sub-contracting in DTA. Due to high rate of duty, domestic sale of SEZ item has been very small (3% of production in 1997-98). Sourcing of raw material is limited as inputs for garments, electronics and gems and jewellery are imported. Sub-contracting was marginal due to restrictive policies and cumbersome procedures.

Net Foreign Exchange

NFE earning of EPZs have been quite significant: Exports from Indian SEZs were to the extent of Rs. 18,655 crore (US$ 4.14 bn) in the year 2004-05. however, with the establishment of new SEZs, exports, employment, FDI and value addition in the country in the expected to increase phenomenally in the coming years. SEZ is certainly going to become a main instrument in export promotion and employment generation.

Exports

Staring with a few lakh in 1966, exports of EPZs/ SEZs have touched Rs. 18,655 crore (US$ 4.14 bn) in 2004 –05. Although exports of EPZs/SEZs have registered a spectacular growth over the years, their share in all India exports has remained insignificant.

This is largely attributed to smaller number of these zones and their limited size of operation in relation to huge Indian economy. Zone-specific problems in terms of location, infrastructure, etc., have also affected export performance of

EPZs/ SEZs. Further, no EPZ was established after 1991. Interest for setting up these Zones has revived after introduction of SEZ policy in 2000. Post SEZ policy announcement, three SEZs set up at Manikanchan, Jaipur and Indore showed an export performance of Rs.156.23 crore during 2004-05. This development gives a positive signal for future growth of exports of EPZs/ SEZs.

Of the traditionally operating SEZs, only three enclaves – SEEPZ SEZ, NOIDA SEZ and MSEZ – have faired well and their forex earnings account for nearly û th of the total exports of SEZs. Variations existing in the export performance of these zones are directly related to their internal problems and order bookings of individual units. SEEPZ SEZ which accounts for over 50 per cent of export of these zones is ideally located, infrastructurally well developed and have pioneering entrepreneurs.

This zone picked up substantial growth with the addition of Gems & Jewellery complex in 1986 and liberalization of EXIM Policy after 1991. Gems & Jewellery accounts for more than 50 per cent of SEEPZ SEZ exports. Area of this zone is small and it has no scope for further expansion. Location of NSEZ and MSEZ is equally good. NSEZ is closer to national capital and international airport. MSEZ has the advantage of being nearer to a port as well as airport.

Both these zones provide relatively developed infrastructure and have easy access to skilled and unskilled workers. KASEZ was set up 40 years ago and has not yet been fully occupied. Falta SEZ is far away from Kolkata and Haldia ports. Falta also lacks in markets, housing colonies and vending facilities. Transport facilities are inadequate and the approach road is in a bad shape. As pointed out earlier, major problem of the Indian SEZs is their small sized operations. Excepting a few large units, most of the operators in SEZs are small and lack financial muscle and managerial strength to withstand competition.

This is evident by the fact that a small number of units have a highly disproportionate share in exports and employment. Nearly û th of exports from the EPZs/ SEZs are confined to items like gems & jewellery, computer software, textiles, electronics and pharmaceuticals. Barring electronics and gems & jewellery, export of most of the items from EPZs fluctuated significantly over the years.

This is followed by 11.9 to 20.0 per cent by engineering and software, 11.2 to 19.7 per cent by engineering and hardware, 7.3 to 10.1 per cent by textiles, 3.6 to 5.6 per cent by engineering goods, 4.9 to 6.3 per cent by pharmaceuticals & chemicals and the balance by plastics & leather products, food and agro products and trading.

Table. Sectoral Performance of Zones of Indian Sez In Selected Years

Year	Drug	Electronics	Engineer	Gems	Textiles	Others
1985	24.1	19.3	39	0	14.2	3.4
1990	26.4	24.6	27.4	10.6	8.8	2.1
1995	5.2	30.3	27.9	25.1	6.8	4.7
2000	5.0	39.8	5.6	35.2	8.2	6.2
2001	6.2	33.6	4.7	35.2	10.2	10.1
2002	6.2	33.6	4.8	42.3	7.2	5.9

Expansion in Zone Investment and Employment

India had a very slow expansion in the initial phases of EPZ policy. Expansion in the zones started picking up in the 1980s in terms of employment but total investment remained abysmally small till the late 1980s. In the 1990s, investment also started increasing. Growth rates in employment slowed down considerably in the late 1990s but in terms of investment growth rate India outperformed Sri Lanka. Thus, while India started the EPZ programme in the mid sixties, expansion in EPZs started taking place in the 1980s.

In contrast, SEZs in India continue to be dominated by domestic investment. This was despite its edge in terms of labour costs, availability of trained manpower and a stable macroeconomic environment. The share of FDI in total investment increased slowly from 12% in 1989 to slightly over 18% in 2000. During 2000-2003, however, FDI inflows increased faster. By 2003, its share in total investment had increased to 25%. Under the SEZ plan, therefore, FDI is expected to assume a much larger role.

Of the three South Asian countries, zone investment and employment levels remain the lowest in India. Though Kandla, is the biggest zone in South Asia having the size of 700 acres, it ranks the lowest in terms of investment. Vizag and Noida have comparable size as Dhaka but in terms of investment and employment they cannot be compared with the latter. Santacruz which is the smallest in size (104 acres) in India has the highest employment. Chennai and Noida are the other zones that have employment exceeding 10,000. All other zones, Cochin (103 acres), Falta (280 acres), Vizag (360 acres) have very small employment and investment. Surat which became operational in the late 1990s also appears to be amongst the slowest growing new zones of South Asia.

It shows that FDI accounts for substantial investment in Chennai and Vizag EPZs in India. Cochin and Noida follow them with FDI accounting for around one-fifth of their total. Though Santacruz has expanded very fast, FDI participation is very small in the zone. Kandla and Falta also continue to perform poorly in attracting FDI. Indian zones exhibited the lowest growth rates in employment and investment for a long period of time. It was in the late 1990s that investment levels increased rapidly in the zones. India thus could not take advantage of being an early mover.

EXPORT PERFORMANCE

The share of SEZs in a country's exports is an index of their relative role amongst various other instruments of export promotion. In India, the share of SEZs in total manufactured exports was 0.14% in 1973. In the next 5 years, by 1979, the share of SEZs in manufactured exports increased to 0.59%. It moved slowly to touch the figure of slightly over 5% by 2002-03 i.e. in 23 years.

In the mid 1980s, engineering sector accounted for the largest share of exports followed by drugs, electronics and textiles in that order. By the late 1980s, the share of engineering goods started declining. Currently it is around 5% of total exports. The share of drugs also started declining in 1989 and fell from over 25% in the mid 1980s to around 5% by 1991. Decline in textile had been slow but steady. It declined from 15% in 1984 steadily to about 7% in 2002. In contrast, exports of gems and jewellery rose rapidly. In 2002, they accounted for 42% of the total EPZ exports. Electronics exports also grew faster than the overall zone exports. As a consequence, their share almost doubled from 20% in 1984 to 40% in 1997. Thereafter, it fluctuated and in 2002 stood at 33%. Exports of other products, including leather products did not show any perceptible rise. Currently, only two sectors, electronics and gems and jewellery account for three fourths of the total zone exports. In the electronics sector, over 50% of total exports are currently accounted for by software.

Zone-wise sectoral distribution of exports shows unmistakable trends of increasing specialisation. Cochin tends to specialise in electronics (in particular hardware), Falta in textiles, Kandla in pharmaceuticals and Vizag in gems and jewellery. Santacruz is allowed to have only electronics and gems and jewellery units. The share of the latter has been increasing in the zones. Noida is also specializing in gems and jewellery while Chennai has electronics, engineering and textile units.

Variation in the Zone Performance

SEZs are benefited usually from better location, modern and efficient infrastructure, general fiscal and non fiscal concessions to firms and single window facilities to ensure corruption and red tape free business environment. These factors ensure good investment climate. This in turn helps in reducing the costs of exporting and, hence enhances competitive advantages of firms in the zones.

Good investment climate may also be crucial for attracting FDI in the zones. In practice, export oriented FDI in developing countries is cost efficiency seeking and remains essentially labour/resource intensive. Export oriented FDI in these countries may also take the form of relocation of some of the production facilities. MNCs seek locations where they can combine their mobile resources most efficiently with the immobile resources they need to produce goods and services The location of investment then becomes more responsive to the factors that ensure lower costs of production and the availability of complimentary factors of production. Since zones provide the platform for low cost production, they are expected to be successful in attracting FDI.

Securing lower production base was the most important motive for their investing in the zones. Thus, the zones' performance in attracting investment and promoting export competitiveness seems to be directly related with the location, infrastructure facilities, quality of governance and the incentive package. Zone specific characteristics such as the size and level of diversification may also affect the performance of the individual zones.

Five sets of determinants are known for zones' success:

- Location specific factors
- Quality of infrastructure
- Quality of governance
- Incentive package
- Zone specific characteristics.

Location Specific Factors

Early proponents of EPZs considered them as potential hubs for non urban, decentralized industrial development. They favoured placing SEZs away from urban and industrial centres. International experience however suggests that if SEZs are located in backward areas with poor social and economic infrastructure and lack of industrial culture their performance is likely to be below expectation. For instance, it is argued that the growth in Hainan SEZ in China was rather slow due to its location in backwardness region. Bataan zone in Phillipines, Puertio Limone zone in Costa Rica and Franche d'Inga zone in Zaire and Dakar EPZ are also examples of poor location. All these zones failed to achieve success. Locating SEZs near or in industrial/urban areas is also likely to be an important factor critical to their success. This satisfies the labour needs of the zone firms, ensures more accessible and uninterrupted utilities, better services and allows for more spillover effects. Furthermore, if EPZs are located near ports or airports they are expected to be more attractive than other industrial sites and are likely to show better export performance.

Finally, country specific factors such as the level of development of the country, availability of cheap labour and raw materials and overall policy regime also confer locational advantages on producing firms. The level of development reflects the investment climate in a country and may be crucial in determining the success of the zone. Efficiency seeking or export oriented investments may be influenced by the availability of cheap labour also.

- *Region specific location factors:* Development of the region in which zone is located and Industrial culture in the region.
- *Strategic Location specific factors:* Proximity of the zone to ports, and airports and proximity to a bigger city.
- *Country specific location factors*: development of the country, Labour cost, availability of raw materials, Policy Regime.

Quality of Infrastructure

The term 'infrastructure' includes physical infrastructure within the zone, physical infrastructure external to the zone and social infrastructure within the zone.

Physical infrastructure within the zone includes: water, electricity, warehousing, transport within the zone, telecommunication, police station, fire station and banks while physical infrastructure external to the zone includes: transport facilities for the zones, roads leading to the zones and port facilities. Social infrastructure within the zone comprises of residential complexes, schools, hospitals and recreation facilities.

Availability of good quality infrastructure improves the business climate by reducing the costs of operations and hence raising rates of returns. The effect of physical infrastructure on the zone's ability to attract FDI and export performance would be positive. The presence of housing, schools, hospital and recreation facilities are also likely to influence the level of investment and economic performance of the zone's performance significantly. Variables representing three types of infrastructure namely, economic infrastructure within the zone, infrastructure external to the zone in the rest of the economy, and social infrastructure.

Quality of Governance

A streamlined, prompt and efficient bureaucracy and custom controls in all stages of the creation and running of an SEZ is crucial to its performance. It greatly influences the attractiveness of a zone to foreign investors and its eventual performance.

The provision of efficient bureaucratic and economic services, a clear and transparent legal and regulatory structure and an unfettered and stable policy framework ensure the success of the zones. The units need to interact not only with the zone administration but also with the government departments outside the zones.

Policy Concessions

A major preferential treatment is given to SEZ units by granting them the government policy concessions. Governments offer a multitude of fiscal and non fiscal concessions. Fiscal concessions include duty free imports of raw and intermediate inputs and capital goods and income tax exemptions. Non fiscal incentives vary widely across countries. These include, relaxation from industrial laws including labour laws. The theory behind these incentives is that liberalising the rules and tax commitments lowers direct and indirect costs.

Fiscal incentives have direct bearing on the cost. These incentives may help in directly reducing the costs of producing and exporting. Non fiscal incentives affect costs indirectly. These concessions expedite the decision making, and streamline day to day operations. Investor friendly custom regime for instance implies that the entrepreneurs are free from routine inspections of import- export cargo. Relaxations in labour market help in reducing labour market rigidities and may affect the labour productivity. In a distorted economy these concessions are used to offset anti export bias. Zones are termed 'international laboratories' in which developing countries liberalising their economies can experiment with highly liberal trade and industrial policies while changes in national policies may be slow. Governments can therefore play a crucial role in putting into place an export-friendly 'enabling environment'. Therefore the more attractive is the incentive package, the better will be the performance of the zones.

Zone Specific Characteristics

Size: Generally, it is believed that only a large sized zone can generate economic activity on some reasonable scale. In a small zone, the requisite infrastructure and services cannot be provided nor can multiple economic activities be promoted. Size of the zone therefore is expected to be positively related with the performance of the zone.

Concentration of economic activities: Cluster approach suggests that highly concentrated zones are more likely to succeed. External economies of scale and other advantages of the cluster help the operating firms in reducing costs and acquiring competitive advantages. Thus the lower the extent of diversification of the zones in a country, the greater may be the advantages that firms reap from the clusters. However, there is also another view, which suggests that diversification of economic activities in a zone may act as a hedge against the risk of fall in the international demand for a specific product. Furthermore, it also implies diversification of countries to which exports may be directed.

Capital intensity of the zone: In labour- abundant South Asian countries, zones are likely to attract labour intensive investment. Sectoral decomposition of zones' exports suggests that these countries have been attracting labour intensive production in the zones. In such a scenario, capital intensity may vary largely due to different techniques of production or the scale of production. High capital intensity may imply the use of relatively more sophisticated technology, better quality control (Wells 1973, Keddie 1976) or larger scales of production. Capital intensity may, therefore, be related positively with the export performance of zones.

Infrastructure

Of the three categories of infrastructure, physical infrastructure within the zone and that external to the zone are equally important. It is not the internal infrastructure only that needs to be taken care of but rather; infrastructure connecting the zone to the wider economy should also be developed for the export competitiveness. Social infrastructure on the other hand such as schools, hospitals, recreation centres etc also plays a vital role.

Location

Location of the zones along with the effect of the country specific factors influences the attractiveness of the zones. Zones should be close to bigger cities. It is not important that they should be located in developed region. It was argued for instance that Chittagong was located in an underdeveloped region near a well Noida was also located in a backward region but its proximity with Delhi benefited the zone. The presence of government offices, better residential and banking facilities and cosmopolitan nature of the city attract foreign investors to the zones near bigger cities. Presence of other industrial clusters within the regions is also likely to benefit the zone units in terms of support services and labour availability. Thus the spill over effects of the bigger city is stated to have a significant impact on the zone attractiveness.

While the strategic location of the zones and proximity to the ports and airports is also equally important. If ports/ airports are not in the proximity of the zone, then roads and transport facilities linking the zones with the ports and airports should be developed. This is simply because much of the trade is routed through ports. Availability of cheap raw material is an important location specific factor. Availability of cheap labour and lower real estate and overhead costs are also some of the most important factors among factor availability factors. Availability of cheap raw materials was considered desirable but not very/most important. This because many units were importing raw materials. Better law and order conditions are stated to be very important for better zone performance. The prevalence of industrial peace influences the investment climate adversely. The zones provide them secured business environment.

Sometimes it is argued that companies are not attracted by incentives per se and that good infrastructure and cheap labour availability are important. However, it has been found that fiscal incentives are considered very important in determining the attractiveness of the zones. For many of the units tax benefits are much more important than subsidies or grants. In India, on the contrary, a highly restrictive package was offered to zone units at the time when tax rates and protective barriers were very high in the rest of the country. Even FDI norms were also not relaxed for the zones. This perhaps contributed to the failure of the zones in attracting FDI. Later, when policy barriers were relaxed in the rest of the economy, zones were also given benefits of liberalization but this might not have ensured higher relative advantage to the zone units vis-â-vis the rest of the economy. Exemption from other industrial laws is also considered very important However; exemption from labour laws was considered a very crucial factor.

Governance

Good quality governance is another factor that emerged crucial in determining the success of the zones. Single window clearances (pre entry, and post entry) and custom clearance facilities, attitude of the officials, work culture of the department etc.Among other governance related matters such as simple rules and accessibility to rules are most important. Two things may be observed. One, all the four sets of factors namely better location, infrastructure, governance and an attractive incentive package are rated almost equally important in determining the attractiveness of the zones. It is the package of all these complementary services that ensures success of the zones. Two, various aspects of location, facilities and incentives are rated differently.

The study can be summarized as follows:

- Traditionally, EPZs/ SEZs were created as open market within an economy that was dominated by distortionary trade, macro and exchange regulation and other regulatory governmental controls. However, new theories developed since the 1980s posit that EPZs/ SEZs play a crucial initiating role in the development of national industrial capacity by creating an environment conducive to promote investment and exports. As a result, many developing countries have been reverting to them in the early stages of their industrial development with the expectation that they provide the engine of growth to propel their economies into industrialization.
- Evolution of EPZs/ SEZs in India is associated with the traditional view to develop a platform for building industrial and export capabilities at the early stages of industrial development. However, promoting SEZs/ EPZs programme are much more vigourously done now than in the initial phases of their evolution.
- Bangladesh and Sri Lanka both created an elaborate institutional framework to govern the EPZs in the initial stages. Their vision was clear and resolutely pro-business. They enacted legislation, created a focused administrative infrastructure to govern EPZs, offered highly attractive incentives and located zones in the best possible locations. In India on the other hand, EPZs policy suffered from a lack of vision. The first zone was established as early as in1965 with multiple objectives in a highly backward region. The second zone was set up in Santacruz with a different set of objectives. The management and operation of the zone was affected by the overall policy regime. Wide-ranging measures were initiated by the

government for revamping and restructuring EPZs as late as in the 1990s. The SEZ policy announced in 2000 is the most significant thrust towards ensuring the success of export processing zones in India.

- Zone units in Bangladesh are enjoying huge relative benefits compared to the domestic units in terms of incentive package, infrastructure facilities and the quality of governance. Sri Lanka also offers a highly focused administrative set up for the development of the zones and highly developed infrastructure facilities like Bangladesh. Besides, Sri Lanka also offered several incentives to the units in the initial phase of the evolution of the zones. However, since the late 1990s, the government is cutting down the incentives offered to the units. In India, EPZs/ SEZs are managed by the government department till recently. At the zone level, there is no fine tuning of the division of responsibilities along the lines that is seen in other two countries. However, one distinguishing feature of the Indian system is with regard to the custom services. In India, these services are directly under the jurisprudence of the zone administration. In Sri Lanka and Bangladesh, on the contrary, custom departments are controlled by the government. The incentive package had been highly restrictive till recently but now the government has announced a substantially improved set of incentives and facilities. Infrastructure facilities provided by the zones in India are comparable with Sri Lanka. However Bangladesh appears to have an edge here also due to direct interference of the EPZ authorities in providing major infrastructure facilities (water, electricity and telecommunication) to the zone units.
- Clarity in vision and concerted efforts finally reflected in the expansion of the zones and participation by FDI in Sri Lanka and Bangladesh. In terms of over all export growth also the two countries scored over India. However, in terms of productive efficiency

(Exports per unit of labour) India appears to have excelled. Even after controlling the effect of capital intensity, India's productive efficiency turned out to be the highest in the 1990s. During 2000- 2003 however, Sri Lanka out performed India.

- Countries wishing to take advantage of the opportunities provided by zones will have to put together a co-ordinated package of incentives, infrastructure and good governance. Some aspects of location, facilities and incentives are more important than the others. Tax benefits are more sought after than subsidies, relaxation in labour laws is stated to be more important than relaxation in other laws, locating the zones near bigger cities/ports is considered more important.
- Our empirical analysis reveals that the relative advantages enjoyed by the EPZs/ SEZs units (in terms of incentives, infrastructure and governance) vis-â-vis the rest of the economy attract investment in the zones while overall governance and infrastructure facilities in a country determine the export competitiveness of its zones. Furthermore, location of a zone in a development region and/ or near strategic positions such as bigger cities, ports and airports affect both the investment and export competitiveness. Composition of economic activities in the zones such as clustering and capital intensity also affects the export competitiveness.

Four major policy implications are:

- The establishment of a successful EPZ/ SEZ programme does not require removing one or two obstacle; it requires removing all of them simultaneously. This is because EPZs offer a package of services simultaneously. In short, EPZs/ SEZs have a much higher probability of success when there is vision in the design, establishment and operations of the EPZ.
- Overall investment climate (infrastructure, governance) in a country matters in the success of

its zones in terms of competitiveness. Generally, it is argued that the EPZs/ SEZs concept is attractive because it is much easier to resolve the problems of infrastructure and governance on a limited geographical area than it is to resolve them countrywide. Zones may attract investment due to relative advantages that the units enjoy here but they may not be efficient in terms of productivity. Zones cannot be insulated from the broader institutional and economic context of the country and that they cannot be treated as an economy within the economy. Zones are a part of the economy and require overall improvement in the investment climate to ensure success in the long run. They should not therefore be viewed as alternative to the overall development model. This is perhaps the reason why EPZs failed to fulfill the role of engines of industrialization in most countries on a sustainable basis.

- Zones tend to specialise in terms of economic activities depending on the availability of human capital, resources and infrastructure in the region. They thus tend to transform into horizontally-integrated industrial clusters, which includes industries that might share a common market for the end products, use a common technology or labour force skills, or require similar natural resources. It seems therefore that it would be desirable to develop zones as industrial clusters of specific products. This may encourage downstream industries also.
- Finally, zones in the long run, need to give way to industrial clusters of horizontally and vertically integrated industries in general, high tech industries in particular. This would not only help in jump-start the manufacturing processes but would also improve export competitiveness with greater return.

SEZ BILL AND ESSENCE

The EXIM policy, 1997-2002, effective 1-4-2000 had seen the announcement of a plan of Special Economic Zones (SEZs).

The EXIM Policy, 2002-2007 made effective from 1-4-2003 gives a stimulus to the plan by providing more incentives and procedural relaxation. It also serves to emphasize that the SEZs plan is visualized by the Government as its most important export incentive plan. The SEZ has been defined as a specifically delineated area wherein units may be set up for specified purposes for export. The units are eligible for duty free import/procurement of required raw materials, inputs etc. The idea is that the incentives granted, fiscal and non-fiscal, attract investment, both foreign and domestic, and the export will be facilitated. At first look it may appear that there does little or no difference between the then exist EPZs and the new SEZ. Both are enclaved duty free areas wherein the units avail hose of fiscal and other concessions with the objective of facilitating their exports. However, a closer look reveals the critical differences between the two.

The essential underlying principle governing the policy on SEZs is the two. The essential underlying principle governing the policy on SEZs is that these are treated as foreign territories... much more that tin the case of the EOUs/ EPZs. Thus, whereas the fiscal incentives in terms of duty exemptions are available both to SEZ and EOUs, additionally other legislation such as Labour Law is sought to be relaxed to a large extent in the case of the former. It is also the intention that the units shall avail 'single window' clearance, whether the matter releases to the Central or the State Government. As regards the operationalization of the SEZ plan, with effect from 1-11-2000 the FTZs/ EPZs at Kandla, Kochi, Surat and Mumbai stand converted to SEZs. The EPZs at Noida, Falta, Vishakapatnam and Chennai were likewise converted to SEZs with effect from 1-1-2003. Thus, as on date there are no EPZs. Further, the policy is t o set up only SEZs shall be done by the State Governments or Private Sector or as joint Sector venture between these two.

Exim Policy Provisions for Sezs

Paragraphs 7.1 to 7.23 of the EXIM Policy, 2002-2007 detail the SEZ plan. As provided therein, the SEZs are envisaged as duty free enclaves deemed to be foreign territories for the purposes of trade operations, duties and tariffs. In other worlds, all activities within the SEZs will be as if being done outside India. Naturally, the units therein may import/ procure the required raw materials, inputs, capital goods etc. duty free. Also, their clearances to the DTA will be treated as imports into India.

The said Policy provisions are briefly summed up, as follows:

- SEZ units are permitted to be set up fro the purpose of manufacture of goods and rendering of services. The SEZ itself may have areas demarcated as processing areas wherein units will be set up and non-processing areas wherein other facilities may be provided.
- SEZs may be set up in the public, joint sector or by State Governments, as notified by the Ministry of Commerce and Industry.
- SEZ units are allowed to import. procure free of duty (including from bonded warehouses in the DTA and from International Exhibitions held in India) all their requirement of inputs, raw materials, capital goods (including second had capital goods) etc. Goods may also be got free of cost or on loan from the clients. Goods required for making capital goods for use in the unit may be imported. However, good which are prohibited items of import in the ITC (HS) are not allowed.
- The Unit Approval Committee is the competent authority for approval of units under the plan, if they satisfy the specified conditions. IF not, approval will be given by Development Commissioner after clearance of BOA. Any change in approved activity or undertaking of any new activity is to be intimated to the Development Commissioner.
- A SEZ unit is required to execute a legal undertaking with the Development Commissioner to fulfil its obligation to achieve positive NFE.
- A SEZ unit is required to be a positive Net Foreign

Exchange Earner (NFE), calculated cumulatively over a five year period.

- DTA sale facility is available to SEZ units, including service/ trading units, subject to payment of full duty (not concessional duty, as in the case of EOUs) and meeting the requirement of the EXIM policy.
- The units including gem and jewellery units may sub-contract a part of their product or production process in the DTA or through other SEZ/ EOU/ EHTP/ STP units with permission of customs. Further, the units, other than gem and jewellery units are allowed to undertake job work on behalf of the DTA units for direct export. Sub-contracting of part of their production process may also be got done abroad, with approval of BOA.
- The transfer of goods imported. Procured or manufactured by a SEZ unit to another SEZ/ EOU/ EHTP/ STP unit is allowed subject to maintenance of proper records.
- The units may carry out all activities, unless otherwise specified, on the basis of self-certification, subject to monitoring by a Committee headed by the Development Commissioner and including the customs.
- Gems and Jewellery units may participate in exhibitions in India and abroad.
- Specified supplies by SEZ unit in DTA such as supplies to other SEZ/EOU/EHTP/STP units; supplies to bonded warehouses in DTA; supplies against special entitlement of duty free import of goods; supplies to defence and internal security forces, foreign missions/ diplomats of (if exempted from duty) etc., will be counted towards fulfilment of its NFE.
- A SEZ unit is allowed to export through merchant exporter/ status holder or other SEZ/ EOU/ EHTP/ STP unit.
- A SEZ unit may supply/ sell samples in DTA for

display/ market promotion and also transfer the goods to DTA for repair/ replacement, testing or calibration, quality testing and R & D purposes, on the basis of records maintained and on prior intimation to the customs authorities.

- Supplies by DTA units to SEZ units will qualify as 'deemed exports', eligible for the specified benefits.
- Duty free imported/ procured goods may be disposed in DTA on payment of duty and subject to import license, as applicable or exported or destroyed.
- Imported/procured goods or parts thereof found defective maybe brought back for repair/ replacement.
- A SEZ unit may replace the goods or parts therefore found defective or otherwise unfit for use or which become damaged or defective may be returned or destroyed and replacement thereof or the same goods after repairs thereof may be imported or procured from the authorized suppliers in India/ domestic suppliers.
- A SEZ unit may exit from the plan after approval of the Development Commissioner as per the specified conditions including payment of applicable customs and central excise duties. Such unit may also be permitted, as a one-time option, to debond and enter the EPCG plan.
- Developer of SEZs in Private/ Joint/ State sector may import/ procure the specified goods without payment of duty for the development, operation and maintenance of SEZs.

Therefore, the policy provisions in respect of the SEZ units are similar to those for the EOU/ EHTP/ STP units.

This is to be expected since, as in the case of the erstwhile EPZ units, the SEZ plan also envisages like duty free enclave for the units along with necessary fiscal and other incentives such as the duty free procurement/ import of goods. Yet there are certain critical differences, which make the SEZ plan an improvement.

Eligibility And Approval Under The Plan

Paragraph 7.1. of the EXIM policy defines a SEZ as a delineated duty free enclave deemed to be a foreign territory for purposes of trade operations and duties and tariffs. Further, goods and services going to SEZ are treated as exports and the reverse is treated as imports. The areas of activity for which the SEZ units may avail the facility of duty free import/ procurement of goods are the manufacture of goods and rendering of services. This is an exhaustive list and practically every activity is covered. Thus, units undertaking the said activities are eligible under the plan.

Whereas the eligibility for units under the SEZ plan is seen in the context of the proposed activity, other important eligibility criterion are the viability of the project, the projected turnover, and whether it would satisfy the condition of positive NFE. In terms of paragraph 7.7 of the EXIM policy read the Hand book of Procedures 3 copies of the application in the prescribed proforma are to be submitted to the Development Commissioner of the SEZ concerned.

Completed application entitled ' Application Form for setting up units in SEZ must be accompanied by a crossed bank draft for Rs.5000/- in favour of the Pay and Accounts officer, Department of industrial Policy and Promotion, Ministry of Industry, payable at Central Bank of India, Udyog Bhawan Branch, New Delhi. The Development Commissioner will acknowledge the receipt of the application and a reference number will be given.

With few exceptions the Unit Approval Committee is the competent authority for approval of units under the SEZ plan. It is also provided that the units shall inform the Committee/ Development Commissioner in case of any change in approved activity or undertaking of any new activity. This shall specify the conditions/ parameters and also obligations and conditions under which the unit shall work. If the application does not satisfy the conditions of automatic approval (it requires an industrial licence or is in service sector (other than software, IT, trading etc.) or it is a case of conversion of EOUT into SEZ unit) it shall be remitted to the SEZ, BOA, and Department of Industrial Policy and Promotion and after its clearance the Development Commissioner will grant the approval within 45 days.

Once the application for setting up a unit under the SEZ plan is approved/ rejected, the Letters of Permission/ Intent (LOP/ LOI) or letters of concerned. The LOP/LOI shall specify the item(s) of manufacture/ service activity; annual capacity; projected annual export performance for the first five years in dollar terms; Net foreign exchange earnings as a percentage of exports (NFE) to be achieved; limitation, if any, regarding sale of finished goods, by-products and rejects in the DTA; and such other matter as necessary.

It shall also impose such conditions as necessary. Further, in case of any change in the approved activity, or if the unit undertakes a new activity, the Development Commissioner is required to issue an amended LOP within 6 days of the receipt of intimation. The LOP shall be construed as a license for all purposes under the plan, including for the procurement of raw materials and consumables either directly or through designated canalising agency. It is valid for 3 years from its date of issue during which the time the unit should commence commercial production.

The LOP shall automatically lapse if an application for the extension of its validity is not make before the end of the said period. Each LOP/ LOI shall have separate earmarked premises. The LOP/ LOI is valid for 5 years once the unit commences production. The approval may be further renewed for another 5 years.

It is also provided that the Importer-Exporter code numbers for SEZ unit's hall is allotted by the Development Commissioner concerned. This is issued after the execution of the legal undertaking.

Note:

- As a policy it has been decided not to allow polluting industrial units (agro-chemicals, dyes, solvents etc) and socially obnoxious items (liquor etc.) and strategically important items of defence in the SEZ.

Units engaged in re-cycling of ferrous and non-ferrous metals will not allowed under they make ingots.

- In terms of the Handbook of Procedures failure to abide by any of the conditions of the LOP/ LOI shall render the unit liable to penal action under the Foreign Trade (Development and Regulation) Act, 1992 and the Rules and Orders made thereunder without prejudice to any other action under any other law/ rules and cancellations or revocation of LOP/ LOI/ IL]

The registering authority for the SEZ unit will be the Development Commissioner concerned. A separate registration cum membership certificate shall not be required, as provided for the paragraph 2.44of the EXIM Policy. It is also provided that the Importer-Exporter code numbers for SEZ units shall be allotted by the Development Commissioner concerned.

The SEZ units are also entitled to automatic issue of the Green Card by the Development Commissioner after the execution of the legal undertaking.

The identified criteria for approval of SEZ units by Unit Approval Committee are:

- The project is not included in Schedule I or II of the Notification No. 447 (E), dated 25-7-1991 issued under the Industries (Development and Regulation) Act, 1951. In other words, the item of manufacture does not require an Industrial Licence under the said Act.
- The project is located in area within a SEZ for which availability of space and conformity with environmental and other standards is satisfied.
- The project undertakes to achieve positive NFE.
- The foreign technology agreement, if any entered into by the unit, is as per the RBI regulations i.e. restricted to a lump sum payment of US $ 2 million or 8% royalty (net of taxes), over the period of 5 years from the commencement of production.

General Conditions of Approval Of Units

The several terms and conditions of governing a unit approved under the SEZ plan are summed up, as follows:

- The approval period shall be 5 years, renewable for further 5 years at a time.
- The LOP will be valid for 3 years from the date of its issue within which period the unit shall implement the project and commence commercial production.
- Unit shall export its production of goods and services as per the EXIM Policy for the approval period of 5 years with option to bedond thereafter or continue further under the plan. Export of Special Chemicals, Organisms, Materials, Equipment and Technologies (SCOMET) shall be subject to fulfilment of conditions in the ITC (HS).
- Possession of allotted plot/SDF is to be taken within 3 months of issue of LOA and construction/ implementation of project started within next 6 months.
- The unit is required to confirm the acceptance of the terms and conditions mentioned in the LOP within a period of 45 days to the Development Commissioner.
- The start of commercial production/ business is to be intimated to the Development Commissioner.
- The entire operations shall be in a customs bonded premises.
- The unit shall be required to execute a legal undertaking with the Development Commissioner for meeting the conditions of approval including the export obligation.
- The achievement of positive NFE shall be necessary. Duty free raw materials procured from an EOU/SEZ/ EHTP/STP unit shall be treated as imports for the purpose of computing the net foreign exchange earnings.

- Duty free import of capital goods, components, raw materials and consumables, spares, material handling equipment etc. shall be permitted. Items in the Prohibited list of imports in the ITC (HS) will not be allowed. Services may be procured from DTA free of Service Tax.
- Indigenous available capital goods, components, raw materials etc. will be allowed without payment of central excise duty.
- If an industrial enterprise is operating both as domestic unit and as SEZ unit, it shall have two distinct identities with separate accounts including separate bank accounts. It is however not necessary for them to be two separate legal entity. It should be possible to distinguish the import or export or supplies effected by the SEZ unit from those made by the other (domestic) units of the enterprise.
- Normally raw material tie-ups will not be insisted upon.
- No export benefits like cash assistance, replenishment licenses would be admissible on the exports.
- The exit of the unit from the plan upon completion of the export obligation shall mean the physical vacation of the premises in the SEZ. Thereafter, the permission to the unit to produce the domestic market (when located in DTA) shall be decided in the light of the industrial policy in force at that time in relation to production of the items reserved for small scale sector.
- On exit from the plan duties of customs and central excise, as applicable shall be levied on the finished goods, raw materials capital goods etc.
- An application for industrial license to the SIA shall be treated as an application under the MRTP Act, 1969.
- If an approved unit fails to fulfil its export obligation, the future course of action will be decided by the Monitoring Committee.

- There shall be exemption from taxes on finished products, when exported. Export duties shall be leviable unless specifically exempted.
- Supplies to SEZ units by domestic units will be treated as deemed exports with accompanying benefits.

  Note: Finance Act, 2002-2003 has amended the Central Excise Act, 1944 and Customs Act, 1962 with the objective that the good sent from the DTA to the SEZ would be treated as exports with all attendant benefits.
- SEZ unit can sell its products to domestic projects under Global Tender conditions.
- Adequate steps shall be taken to prevent air, water and soil pollution and the standards of the State Pollution Board in this regard must be satisfied. Further, adequate steps will be taken to the satisfaction o the State Government in regard to the process hazards for ensuring safety in plants for manufacture of chemicals, fertilizer and pharmaceuticals.
- The external commercial borrowing, if any, shall be subject to approval of RBI in terms of Foreign Exchange Management Act, 1999 as per guidelines of the ECB Division, Department of Economic Affairs, Ministry of Finance. Generally, loan agreements may be entered into for raising fresh ECB with average maturity of not less than 3 years for an mount of US$ 50 million and for refinancing an existing ECB without prior approval.
- Repatriation of dividend/ profits and foreign travel expense etc. is freely allowed.
- 100% NRI holding in the undertaking is allowed.
- Foreign collaboration would be permitted. Engagement of foreign technicians and payment thereof shall be as per Government policy in force.
- The condition of foreign equity as stipulated in the Department of Economic Affairs Press Note of 19-2-1972 will not be enforced.

- Royalty will be calculated on the basis of the net ex-factory sale price of the product, exclusive of the excise duty minus the cost of the standard bought out components and the landed cost of the imported components, irrespective of the source of procurement, including ocean freight, insurance, customs duty etc.

SEZ POLICY

The Government of India through the SEZ Policy has made available a basket of Incentives, Exemptions, Concessions and Privileges (IECP) to the SEZ. Developers and the SEZ Units. Some of the major IECPs available to the Developer and Unit are:

The benefits available under the SEZ Policy essentially translate into:

- Reduced Cost of Infrastructure
- Reduced Cost of Utilities
- Reduced Cost of Raw Material
- Reduced Cost of Capital
- Reduced Cost of Manpower
- Operational Ease

These Baskets of Benefits available to the Developer and the Units are aimed at enabling Global competitiveness

BENEFITS – SEZ DEVELOPER

The Developer is an entity who develops, operates and maintains any infrastructure facility in an SEZ. The benefits available to the Developer have now been made available to Co Developers of the SEZ as well.

Some of the benefits available to SEZ Developer are:

- Developer of a SEZ may import/procure goods from DTA without payment of duty for the development, operation and maintenance of any Infrastructure, Utility, Facility or Service.
- Income tax exemption for a block of 10 years in 15 years from the date of operations at the option of developer

- Income Tax exemption to Investors in SEZs.
- Investment made by individuals etc. in the SEZ Company is also eligible for exemption u/s 88 of IT Act.
- Exemption from Service Tax
- Exemption from Central Sales Tax on Sales made from Domestic Area to SEZ Developer
- Full authority to provide services like water, electricity, security, restaurants, recreation centres etc. on commercial lines.
- Generation, Transmission and Distribution of Power in SEZs allowed.
- Foreign investment permitted to develop township within the SEZ with residential areas, markets, play grounds, clubs, recreation centres etc.
- Freedom in allocation of developed plots to approved SEZ units on purely commercial basis

Benefits – Sez Unit

The Policy provides a basket of Incentives, Exemptions, Concessions & Privileges to the SEZ Unit. It is aimed at making SEZ Exports more competitive and gives an advantage to SEZ Exporters.

Some of the benefits available to the SEZ Units are:

Customs and Excise:

- SEZ units may import or procure from the domestic sources, all their requirements of capital goods, raw materials, consumables, spares, packing materials, office equipment, DG sets etc. in the Zone without any license or specific approval.
- Exemption from Customs duty on import of capital goods, raw materials, consumables, spares etc.
- Exemption from Central Excise duty on procurement of capital goods, raw materials, consumables, spares etc. from the Domestic Market
- Goods imported/procured locally duty free could be utilized over a period of 5 years.
- Domestic Sales on payment of applicable duty.

Taxes:

- 100% Income Tax exemption (Sec. 10A) for first 5 years and 50% for 5 years thereafter. Reinvestment allowance to the extent of 50% of ploughed back profits for the next 5 years.
- Exemption from Service Tax
- Physical export benefit to DTA units for goods supplied to SEZ units

Foreign Direct Investment:

- 100% foreign direct investment under the automatic route is allowed in manufacturing sector in SEZ units.
- No cap on foreign investments for SSI reserved items.

Banking & Finance:

- Setting up Off-shore Banking Units (OBUs) allowed in SEZs. Thus SEZ units can avail of financing at International rates.
- OBU's allowed 100% Income Tax exemption on profit for 5 years and 50% for next 5 years.
- External commercial borrowings by units up to $ 500 million a year allowed without any maturity restrictions.
- Flexibility to keep 100% of export proceeds in EEFC account with freedom to make overseas investment from it.
- Commodity hedging permitted.
- Exemption from interest rate surcharge on import finance.
- Facility to realise and repatriate export proceeds within 12 months.
- SEZ units allowed to 'write-off' unrealised export bills up to 5%.

Operational:

- Performance Monitoring on Self Certification basis.
- No routine examination by Customs of export and Import cargo

Gujarat SEZ Act, 2004

In addition to the benefits made available by the Central

Government, the Government of Gujarat has committed to make available the following benefits by passing the Gujarat SEZ Act.

Fiscal Benefits:

- All sales and transactions within the processing area of the Zone shall be exempt from all taxes, cess, duties, fees or any other levies under any State law to the extent specified below:
  - Stamp duty and registration fees payable on transfer of land
  - Levy of Stamp duty and registration fees on loan agreement, credit deeds and mortgages.
  - Sales Tax, Purchase Tax, Motor Spirit Tax, Luxury Tax, Entertainment Tax and other taxes and cess payable on sales and transactions.
- Exemption from electricity duty under the Bombay Electricity Duty Act, 1958 for a period of 10 years from the date of production or supply of services as the case may be.
- Inputs (goods and services) made to Zone Units from Domestic Tariff Area shall be exempted from sales tax and other taxes under the State laws.

Relaxations in Labour Laws:

- The power, duties and functions conferred on the Commissioner of Labour shall vest with the Development Commissioner of the SEZ.
- The Units in the Zone to furnish Consolidated Annual Report to the Development Commissioner instead of periodical returns under the following *Acts, namely*:
  - The Workmen's Compensation Act, 1923;
  - The Payment of Wages Act, 1936;
  - The Factories Act, 1948;
  - The Minimum Wages Act, 1948;
  - The Maternity Bene fit Act, 1961;
  - The Payment of Bonus Act, 1965;
  - The Contract Labour (Regulation and Abolition) Act, 1970;

Modifications in various labour laws:

- The provisions of Bombay Industrial Relations Act, 1946 shall not apply to units set up in the SEZ
- The State Government authorized to vary the time limit laid down in section 66(1)(b) of the Factories Act, 1948 (pertaining to work timings of women worker).
- Industry or establishment set up in the special economic zone granted the status of Public Utility under Industrial Disputes Act, 1947.
- SEZs excluded from the definition of establishment under The Contract Labour (Regulation and Abolition) Act, 1970.
- All the office bearers of the registered trade unions of the industrial establishments situated in the SEZ shall be persons actually engaged or employed in an industry with which trade union is connected – benefit granted under Trade Unions Act, 1926.

All requisite approvals and permissions will be through "Single Window Mechanism" ensuring "hassle free operations".

Cost advantage of sez units compared to dtas:

- Land Acquisition Stage
- No Stamp duty & Registration Fee
- Land through Mundra SEZ Ltd.
- Project Planning Stage
- No Service Tax on Consultancy Services availed
- Financing Stage
- Various exemptions bring down the project cost by about 15-20%
- Foreign Currency funding through OBUs
- Rupee funding at lower rates – no CRR, SLR & Priority lending.
- Construction Stage
- No duties on imports or goods sourced locally for capital goods.
- No State & Local levies like Sales Tax, Turnover tax, Purchase Tax, Mandi Tax etc.

- Operations & Maintenance Stage
- No duties on consumables & spares.
- Development commissioner "Single Window" for all approvals and clearances
- "Single Window" for all infrastructure, Utilities, Facilities & Services
- Reduced Transportation Cost & Reduced Transit Time.

INDIAN SEZS- ARE WE REPLICATING THE CHINESE SEZS?

SEZs in China have been extremely successful with a 40% share of exports, compared to the 4% of Indian SEZs. SEZs were the key drivers of the growth of the Chinese economy in the last two decades. India has much to learn from the Chinese SEZ model. The SEZ bill, which is a part of the foreign trade policy 2004-2009, is poised to make India a favourable destination for investment.

SEZs have been the growth engines for exports, FDI and Industrial growth across many countries in Asia. SEZs have become laboratories for the economic reforms in the past two decades. In the late 1970s, the Indian and Chinese economies were comparable. But, in the 1980s and 1990s China cruised ahead of India, and today it finds itself at the top in all sectors against India except in software and knowledge-based products. This growth in the Chinese economy is mainly due to the fact that the Special Economic Zones (SEZs) were a part of their open door policy.

In India, SEZs were first planned in the Exim Policy in 2001 to boost exports. The Indian Government has converted all in the 1990s, into SEZs because they failed to increase the exports. EPZs are small industrial estates, whereas the SEZs are industrial townships offering more facilities and incentives. The intentions of the SEZs are much larger than mere endorsement of export processing zones. After studying the Chinese SEZ model, the Indian authorities have decided to start the SEZs in strategic locations close to port cities and economic centres. The developments of Greenfield SEZs have already started in the country. The incentives offered by the Indian SEZs are more or less the same as those offered by the Chinese SEZs, but they are failing to attract both the FDI and the domestic investments.

Lessons From Chiense Sezs

China started four SEZs in 1979 and the fifth one was set up in 1988. Cities along the sea coast, including Shanghai, were 'opened up' for foreign investments and given a status comparable to SEZs. In the late 1980s, almost every city in China had its own science and technology development zone, where conditions were more or less similar to the SEZs. There are many distinctive features that have contributed to the success of Chinese SEZs. The include large size, FDI from the non-resident Chinese, attractive incentives, flexible laws, liberal customs procedures and decentralization of power to the local authorities.

The SEZs in China are located on the coasting near Hong Kong and Taiwan which are major economic centres in the region. A large chunk of the FDI was contributed by the non-resident Chinese from Hong Kong and Taiwan. They invested in the labour intensive industries. Later, the MNCs also started investing in technology-oriented industries by bring modern technology to China. If we ignore the phenomenon of non-resident Chinese for a while, and assume that they were not there then reality is that the SEZs in China did not see much success for a long time. FDI received during 1979-2004 was about $ 400 billion, which are primarily capital intensive. Almost 80-90% of FDI in China has gone into SEZs located on the eastern coast, particularly in southern china's Hainan and Guangdong provinces and in the greater Shanghai and Beijing areas.

The size of the SEZs has been an important factor in the success of China's reforms process. China has now declared the entire region or province as an SEZ. The area occupied by the Chinese SEZs is very large; these townships provide almost every facility like housing, transportation, telecommunication, power generation etc. Every SEZ in China is spread over thousands of square kilometres. For foreign investors, it is the labour policy in China's SEZs that is the biggest attraction. The hire and fire policy has attracted foreing investors to invest in China's SEZs. All the jobs are on a contract, which can either be meant for one particular job or be flexible enough for all kinds of jobs.

Decentralization of power to the local authorities is another major reason for the success of SEZs in China. Local authorities have the necessary powers to frame their own policies to improve the SEZs and attract foreign and domestic investors. They can approve FDI proposals up to $ 30 million. Most foreign investments can be approved locally and require virtually no central clearance.

A strong domestic market has played an important role in the success of China's SEZs. SEZs in China benefited from linkages with domestic economy. This promoted local purchases and technology transfers. China focuses on unsophisticated labour intensive products such as clothing and footwear.

Marketing has another factor in attracting foreign investment to the SEZs. The thrust of the SEZs in China was to attract FDI and technology. The SEZ authorities in China persuaded investors aggressively and provinces and local authorities competed with each other to attract FDI.

ADVOCACY FOR INDIA

Indian, receiving $ 4 billion a year as FDI in skill-intensive. Most of the FDI in India is concentrated in the IT sector and only a small portion of it is invested in SEZs. India's SEZs are lacking in NRI investments, which was not the case with China. "But they have their distinct roles in terms of transfer of knowledge, skill, software and experiences.

India cannot compete with China in the unsophisticated, labour intensive products such as clothing and footwear. Alternatively, India has got strength in biotechnology, electronics and knowledge-based products with the assistance of NRIs. Concentrating on those industries in which we expertise and management skills will help benefit the Indian

SEZs. So, the thrust should be on sector-specific SEZs. Indian SEZs are small in size and these zones are built in very limited space. In India, the average size of a SEZ is 1 – 3 sq. km. It is a difficult to develop, the requisite infrastructure in such small areas. Multiple economic activities are also difficult to perform. Acquiring land in the proposed SEZ locations region is the key to building large SEZs.

Indian SEZs are small in size and these zones are built in very limited is 1-3 sq. km. It is difficult to develop the requisite infrastructure in such small areas. Multiple economic activities are also difficult to perform. Acquiring land in the proposed SEZ locations region is the key to building large SEZs. Labour laws are very inflexible and trade unions seem to be strong in India. This can impact productivity and delay exports. Flexibility in labour laws is one important step for improving the exports from the SEZs.

The state governments or public/ private/ joint sector can set up SEZs. The power of approving the FDI proposals is with the development commissioner appointed by the Central Government. This causes the delay in the approvals. Decentralize the powers to the local authorities and state governments for the quicker approvals of the investment proposals. A single window clearance perhaps is the best policy for attracting investments.

India has big domestic market like China, but the SEZs, even after paying high import duties, are not allowed to sell more than 50% of the exports. These are policy barriers to sales in domestic market. The objectives of the SEZs in China and India also differ. While China concentrates on FDI and technology, India concentrates only on the exports. India needs to update the skills level over time to match biotechnology, electronics and knowledge-based industries.

Proper balance needs to be maintained among the following investors: 100% foreign owned, joint ventures with foreign companies, and 100% domestic companies. This will encourage the private profit to be spent in India for re-investment. The higher the linkages of SEZs higher will be the benefits to the economy. Indian SEZs policy allows sales in the domestic market on the payment of current indirect taxes and not on the existing high import duties. India, like China should also concentrate on FDI and technology for the SEZs. India should send its officials and development commissioners for SEZs for foreign countries to attract prospective investors. If India wants foreign investments, then it should market and promote its SEZs.

Manufacturing bases are shifting from the developed countries to the developing countries primarily due to cheap labour prices and proximity to new markets. The potential for attracting FDI is the SEZs in manufacturing is high, if India provides a hassle free environment for the investors and all necessary fiscal incentives. Linking the SEZs and domestic markets will also be beneficial for the economy. Once the obstacles of investing in the SEZs are removed, then India can replicate China's success.

MERITS AND DEMERITS OF SPECIAL ECONOMIC ZONE

Limitation of sezs:

(A) *Sezs as panoply against poverty*:

- *Women*: It is argued that Special Economic Zones would provide gainful employment to large numbers of people who hitherto would not be able to find jobs. The bogey of poverty removal through employment is therefore bandied about with much aplomb by the proponents of SEZs.

As in other countries, where Special Economic Zones attract a large number of women workers, India too has many women workers in the SEZs and in future, more women are likely to be employed in them. While women workers usually earn salaries that they would not be able to earn outside the zone and also, the difference between men and women workers' wage would not be too different, a number of problems are endemic to the SEZ cause:

Multinational corporations that set up their factories in these special zones employ thousands of women but their work is mostly repetitive in nature like knitting, sewing or fixing small parts. As a result, women often suffer from chronic illnesses because of the monotony and repetitive nature of their jobs and the highly restricted spaces in which they are confined to during work hours. They suffer from various problems related to night shifts and close monitoring by tyrannical supervisors. They are also not given proper contracts and are hired and fired easily. No health benefits are usually given to women workers and with marriage or pregnancy, their contracts are often terminated.

- *Infrastructure*: For India to attract anywhere near the quanta of investment from multi-national corporations that China does it would have to beef up its infrastructure. In general the state of India's infrastructure is nowhere near China's. While Special Economic Zones are meant to be export generation zones the grim fact remains that the majority of the SEZs in India lack international connectivity. Indeed, SEZs at Kandla, Mundra, Indore and Jaipur have no international airports and do not have maritime access.
- *Competition*: Most countries in South Asia-Nepal, Bangladesh, Sri Lanka and Pakistan have all tried to promote their exports and also create employment by establishing these special economic zones. Since all are highly populous countries, they are heavily into exports of goods requiring cheap labour. In fact they are all competing with each other in almost the same products-garments, sports goods, knitted garments, textiles, gems and jewellery. Bangladesh and Sri Lanka have really done well in garment exports and 90 per cent of the workers in Bangladesh's garment sector, are women. Employment of women in SEZs in Bangladesh is epitomized by the fact that women are paid considerably lower than men.
- *Precipitous Movement of Multinational Corporations*:

One of the major predicaments that face SEZs is the fact that multi-national corporations that are being wooed with a missionary zeal by India and her neighbouring countries would jump ship the moment they realise they'll get a better deal in other countries.

At the moment, multinational companies are being offered opportunities on terms that are on par with those existing in all of India's neighbouring countries. China has by far the most attractive terms and conditions. In this intense competition, there has been a tendency for the multinational companies to keep changing their locations whenever they see a slight cost advantage. This can result in sudden closure of factories and resulting unemployment.

- Do the Numbers stack up: An estimated only 50,000 additional jobs can be created in the Special Economic Zones as compared to the big monetary and fiscal concessions given to them, the best course would be to have a few really well functioning special economic zones that are properly and efficiently run.
- *Bandwagon Effect*: Copying the Chinese model entirely may not be beneficial to India as Chinese SEZs are much larger in magnitude, and in addition to export processing they promote activities such as commerce, tourism, housing, agriculture and industrial production. The scope of Indian SEZs is limited

(B) SEZs and India's Energy Security: Tax arbitrage possibilities in special economic zones and excessive protection for refining are combining to harm India's energy security. Global oil majors are keen to set up shop in India's special economic zones in order to take advantages of the reduced duties on petroleum products which guarantee steep, world-beating refinery margins.

Even domestic oil majors such as upstream crude oil specialist ONGC have chalked out big plans to foray downstream, into refining. The issue that arises is that oil companies would tend to take advantage of the duty differential and would give the prospect of investing in oil exploration a goby. Given that India is already one of the largest consumers of crude oil, upstream investment is a crucial facet in India's energy security.

Value adds-The Lack of it: Value added in refining is modest, normally in the single digits. India's very high duty differential between crude and products translates as effective protection of almost 50%. This is the reason why gross refinery margins (GRMs) in India have traditionally been way above global levels and gives rise to the fact that India has a thoroughly high-cost oil economy, now a big and fast-growing chunk of its GDP.

ONGC, India's most valuable company, does need to become wholly integrated oil major, as is standard practice abroad. But its investment intentions belie a balanced approach. The plan is for ONGC to boost its crude output by just about 10% to 30 million tonnes by 2009-10, but shore up refining capacity to over 40 million tonnes well beforehand.

ONGC is of the opinion that its reserves and assets are best leveraged by increasing refining capability, and the assured cash-flow that goes with it. However, there is no reason for policy to encourage such a trend, given that refinery projects are hugely capital-intensive but result in minimal value addition. And the fact is that there are huge tax benefits and outright write-offs on offer for refining projects in the SEZs, where ONGC plans much of its downstream investments. Such generous tax breaks would thoroughly distort resource allocation.

The logic behind propping capital-intensive refinery projects with a smorgasbord of tax breaks seems farfetched. Limited tax benefits and other incentives might be justified for labour intensive textile projects with much scope for value addition. Besides, the steeply higher import duty on refined products compared to that on crude further distorts the investment regime.

It makes it worth the while to rev up refining capacity and simply cash in on the almost 50% effective tariff protection on hand. Meanwhile, for 2004-05, ONGC has failed to make a single oil discovery although it reportedly drilled nine wells and invested $416 million. It may well be that its planned cash-flows downstream would ultimately help ONGC step up high-risk upstream investments. But it's clearly all the more reason to eschew tax breaks for refinery SEZs and high relative oil duties.

(C) *An idea whose time has lapsed*: The idea of SEZ came to value addition, employment generation and all such remnants of the control regime. Now, the sole purpose of the SEZs is to export goods and services and earn foreign exchange. And to make it easier, an SEZ developer and enterprise can export goods or services or, simply, trade. The word 'processing' that bound 'export' and 'zone' is now unnecessary. Small wonder then, the Commerce ministry is flooded with applications from domestic and foreign companies.

So what do blue chip Indian and foreign companies hope to get when they apply to the Commerce Ministry for an SEZ? The SEZ Act provides tax exemptions to SEZ units and SEZ developers from all indirect taxes including basic customs duty, countervailing duty education cess and, direct taxes. As the Act lays emphasis on providing good infrastructure at low cost for SEZ units and developers, basic inputs needed to achieve that end will attract lower duties.

The act is also mindful of the need for uninterrupted and cheap power. So power plants can be imported or procured from domestic producers without attracting any duty. Transaction costs, the nightmare of every enterprise, will also be minimised for the SEZ participants by the single window clearance at the zone level via the good offices of the Development Commissioner.

SEZs, like the EPZs before them, are supposed to develop backward and forward linkages. Presumably, the means ripple effects on job work and technology transfer of non-SEZs areas, the hinterland. But one of the prominently highlighted attractions is the complete freedom to subcontract, even abroad. An unlike the EPZs of the caution and control era, SEZs today can engage in manufacturing, trading or service activities. Foreign investors will be permitted to develop townships within the SEZs with residential areas, markets play-grounds, clubs, recreation spaces and the like. In China, the idea was a runaway success, though only parts of it – the SEZs reaped benefits. The rest of the country became all the more poor in comparison with the self-perpetuating wealth creators of the eastern provinces. Will it work for India? In 2000 when the SEZ took roots, India was being liberalised with goal being to make economic activity more efficient, cost effective and profitable. Data on economic growth bear testimony to the success of policy, half-baked, reluctant or even accidental at it may have been.

With two successive quarters posting 8 per cent growth in GDP, and a strong export growth despite sluggish G7 growth rates, what magic can the SEZs pull off that the rest of the economy, without those special order privileges? A look at the share of EPZs/ SEZs exports in total manufactured exports presents a different picture. The average annual growth rates of SEZ exports declined continuously over the years, falling steeply over the period from 77 per cent in the first phase (1966-1980) to 7 per cent by 2001- 2003, the fourth phase.

Employment, as a measure of expansion, grew absolutely. But the average annual growth rate shrank continuously. This was despite the fact that four new EPZs became operational in the late 1980s and another EPZ at Vizag came up in 1994" So, after an initial expansion the momentum slowed. Foreign exchange earnings – the most important benefits to be expected from SEZs. In absolute terms the export earnings look very impressive.

It is when you look at the rate of growth that the picture gets bleaker with the figure actually declining. But the true picture is that the value addition, the ratio of net foreign exchange to exports, did not record any appreciable increase.

The rest of the country has always done better than EPZs/ SEZs without the privileges that the zones enjoyed.

(D) *SEZs – A Problem Of Plenty*: It may become a problem of plenty. Too many SEZs in the state have left the state government worrying about the implications it might have on the state revenue collections, especially sales tax.

The centre cleared nine SEZs in Gujarat in addition to the two in Kandla and Surat, which had already got the nod. Two more proposals by Adani's in Dholera and Essar in Hazira are taking the tally of approved and proposed SEZs in the state to 13.Officials in the sales tax department as well as the finance and industries departments have been discussing the issue of quite some time now. It came up as a major issue when Reliance' Jamnagar SEZ was taken up for clearance but the revenue department's observations were overruled. Experts believe that if the sales are not integrated with DTA properly, it can spell huge losses for the state government.

While transactions within the SEZ shall be exempted from all states taxes including sales tax, VAT, motor spirit tax, luxury tax and entertainment tax, purchase tax and other state taxes " inputs (goods and services) made to SEZ units from Domestic Tariff Area (DTA) will be exempt from sales tax and other state taxes.

Virtues or Reasons To Promote Sez

(A) SEZs enhance competitive efficiency

- Liberalisation forced industry into a drive for internal efficiency thereby stimulating exports and GDP; but domestic external inefficiency has to be tackled for further sharpening export competitiveness. The special economic zone (SEZ) is the strategic answer both to overcome transactional inefficiencies and to take advantage of globally reduced tariff levels under the WTO.
- The SEZ would be specially earmarked geographical zones, which can be developed by private sector or public sector developer or in a PPP mode. Approved industrial units, banks, insurance, etc, can be located here. A state can

have more than one SEZ with freedom to the manufacturing unit to establish in any SEZ in any state. State governments will have to attract industry by framing bold policies and providing world-class external infrastructure to the zone.

- Cost of the infrastructure has been reduced by about 20% by exempting all materials and services, purchased by the SEZ developer, from Customs, excise duty, service tax, central sales tax and many states already have a policy of exemption from state taxes. The services provided by the developer are free from services tax and income tax. The dividend payment by the developer or service provider would also be free in the hands of payer and payee. Stamp duty exemption has been provided for the SEZ estate transactions.
- Power plants can be set up within the SEZ for supply to SEZ approved units with the above duty exemptions on capital equipment as well as raw materials and will become a source of efficient, quality power at competitive prices. As there is no customs duty on power imported from abroad these units can perhaps supply power to units in the domestic area (DTA) outside the SEZ also very competitively without high countervailing duties.
- A strategy for reducing cost of finance has also been developed. Offshore banking units (OBU), international financing centres (IFC) and insurance units can be set up in SEZ. Such OBU and IFC will be exempted from tax deducted at source from NRIs. SLR investments or SLR deposits with the RBI will not be required thereby increasing the proportion of deployable funds and reducing cross subsidisation by borrowers. The profits of the OBU relating to SEZ units financing would also be exempted

from tax for 10 years. These measures would sharply reduce the OBU's cost of credit for the SEZ approved units. OBUs should be authorised to fund export activities of export units wherever they may be located, i.e. within or outside the SEZ. OBUs would be under RBI rules.

- The SEZ Act (2005) Second schedule ushers in a wide-ranging tax holiday plan. No excise duty, customs, service or sales tax or state taxes (subject to specific state legislation) would be payable on inputs of raw materials, components or services; also on capital equipment.
- The SEZ Act has adopted a one window approach to cut down on time consumed by bureaucratic processes. The Act envisages a board of approvals at the central level. Application for approvals of SEZs has to be made either directly to the board; or through the state government. In the former case, after the board approval, it has to be submitted to the state government. A development commissioner (DC) is to be appointed by Central Government for each SEZ. All powers for approval under 21 laws as per Schedule 1 of SEZ are delegated to this DC except those of approvals by the RBI. The state government are also expected to similarly delegate powers to him and to grant exemption from some laws.
- A proposed business unit in the SEZ has to apply for approval to the board of approvals initially and with appointment of DC, only to the DC. All formalities of customs, excise and other taxes would thereafter be complied with on a self-certification and self-regulation basis by the approved unit, with all filings to the DC office. These measures will hugely simplify compliances and cut down on time. The State Government can consider giving flexibility in some of the

labour laws as in IT industry; but large-scale exemption has not been provided for.

- The approved unit must have positive net foreign earnings in five years. For this purpose Forex cost of asset is to be recovered as per Schedule of Depreciation over five years. Forex cost of know-how, plant depreciation, royalty, and production inputs must be so covered by forex sales earnings. SEZ units are allowed to sell to DTA units on payment of relevant customs duty; and sale to other SEZ units or units under EPCG, EOU, etc, are counted on export. The Act also provides for transfer of ownership of financially weak units with the DC approval and for the tax holiday for the balance period to be available to the new owner.
- To enable existing export activity to get a fillip, EOUs & EPCG units are allowed to move to SEZ; however, their profits would be tax free only for the remaining period of their tax holiday under the currently applicable tax holiday. Industry now has a challenging opportunity to stimulate export based units in a conducive environment without abusing the system.

(B) *Ways to make sezs privately run cities*: SEZs should be viewed as a vehicle for introducing policy and institutional reform that are difficult to introduce more generally but could be feasible in these limited areas. Thus, Indian SEZs have been successful in streamlining the customs procedures and keeping corruption levels low. Lack of single window clearance facilities, centralized governance, stringent labour laws and poor investment climate in SEZs.

The incomplete success of SEZs can been seen from the fact that the share of these zones in the total exports is just around 4.5% when compared to 64% for Mauritius, 40% for Mexico and 20% each for Bangladesh and Sri Lanka. India could introduce laws allowing private companies to own and manage SEZs as a possible solution. With say 10 such zones focusing on exports, India could aim to double its exports every five years. SEZs can become privately run cities. China's Shenzen, for example, has become a city with 10 million people in two decades. If India were to start with 10 new privately run SEZs they could perhaps accommodate 100 million people in two decades.

Indian SEZs have so far seen a lopsided growth in exports, with gems and jewellery being the single largest contributor (as high as 49.87% of the total exports from Noida SEZ), followed by electronics and software. Heavy manufacturing is absent, given that Indian SEZs have a focus on "low volume high value" products. Heavy manufacturing industries are not encouraged to set up their plant in these SEZs because of the relatively small size o these zones.

The large size of the Chinese SEZs is critically important for bringing greater economies of scale, a diversified activity mix and social infrastructure other zone, and attracting private entrepreneurs to China. Indian SEZs need to spread to larger areas. Industrial Dispute Act and Factory Act should be reviewed for the zones. In China, labour contracts are signed between the employer and employees, which regulate the labour relationships. This system provides flexibility to SEZs in labour relationships. This system provides flexibility to SEZs in labour retrenchment during a business downturn.

Providing export credit at cheaper interest rates will also help. Chinese SEZs get export credit at about 4%.

(C) Endorse modern sezs in india: Indian authorities should promote the modern version of SEZs - free ports, and encourage setting up of growth poles and clusters. This is what countries like Korea, Japan, Malayasia, Hong Kong, Taiwan and Singapore did. China has also moved in that direction to promote a Freeport in Pudong, and growth poles and clusters in the Shanghai-Suzhou region. In both versions of SEZs, and growth poles and clusters, an important role was played by the diasporas. The first four Chnese zones were in close proximity to Hong Kong and Taiwan, and were thus able to attract investment and technology from overseas Chinese. The diaspora's role in the development of growth ples and clusters in Eat Asia is also acknowledged. This aspect will probably be ignored in the SEZ legislation.

The traditional version of SEZs cannot succeed in India because there will be too much government control. The commerce ministry will decide who heads the zones, and the same customs officials with a control mindset will operate there. Not to speak of a host of public authorities involved with the implementation of SEZ policies, adding to the confusion. Bureaucratic approval will be time consuming, especially if tax incentives and other sops are to be provided.

We should move towards the modern version of SEZs-free ports. It is a much broader concept than the earlier Chinese SEZs and appropriate for an economy moving towards becoming a developed country. It replicates a First World environment with minimal restrictions, streamlined procedures, sound infrastructure and easy access through world class ports and airports. All activities are eligible, with no export requirements. Sales to domestic tariff areas are allowed, subject to payment of national duties. Permanent Visas are allowed to qualified investors. The process should be demand-driven, with a bulk of investments coming from the private sector - domestic and foreign. Singapore, Hong Kong, Gibraltar and Jebel Ali in Dubai are well known free ports.

(D) *The SEZ bounty*: Among the developers of the approved zones are such prominent corporate names as Reliance, Bajaj Auto, Mahindra & Mahindra, TCS, Wipro and Ranbaxy, as well as others known for their strategic orientation and long term commitments. Their participation provides a great deal of credibility of the process and reinforces the expectations of proponents of the whole programme.

Before going into the merits of those expectations, one would have to concede that both history and the current policy regime run somewhat counter to them. Over the years that we have had various generations of the concept in place - free trade zones or export processing zones or any other their collective share of the country's total exports has not risen above 5 per cent. This sluggishness was evident even while the growth rate of aggregate exports was quite buoyant, leading to the inescapable cease that these mechanisms simply did not offer a large enough advantage for exporters to locate their facilities in them.

What ever impeded the competitiveness of domestic producers outside the zones apparently had an influence inside them as well. The direct fiscal incentives were obviously not strong enough to offset those advantages. The developer: Private or in partnership with a public agency - will have enough control over the infrastructure and services within the zone to provide his clients with a high degree of assurance with respect to their quality and reliability. The zones tht we have had so far have been managed by public agencies, who, as we all know, cannot usually offer that kind of comfort.

What the developers are essentially banking on is a huge pent up demand for high-quality facilities, the absence of which is deterring a range of investment activity. There is a perception that a lot of investment that would otherwise take place isn't because the infrastructure situation is a huge deterrent. If this problem is solved within the frame work of the SEZ, a substantial part of this potential would be realised.

The commercial interest in SEZ development, is this interest aligned with the country's economic objectives? From the macroeconomic standpoint, it would be a tragedy if the performance of the economy did not stimulate a high level of investment, which would then complete the virtuous circle by itself reinforcing the growth momentum. To the extent that the zones bring about an improvement in the investment climate and thereby contribute to increasing levels of investment in the economy, their impact will be unambiguously positive.

Given the average size of the bigger zones, the developers should be able to offer extremely attractive prices for high-quality services, sweetened by the fiscal benefits they will receive. Although the policy objective is oriented towards exports, it does not prohibit producers from selling in the domestic market, provided they pay all the duties that exports are exempt from, including customs duties on imports to the country. The critical question is: are the zones "investment creating" – attracting investment that wouldn't otherwise take place or "investment –diverting" – inducing relocation from existing facilities? Either way, the business proposition remains intact, but, quite obviously, the macroeconomic interest is best served by the former. Which way will the pendulum swing?

Two factors will determine the direction. The first is the signal that state governments send on allowing de facto labour market flexibility. If they fight shy, producers who already have workers on their rolls will shift in order to take advantage of the infrastructure, while losing nothing on the labour front. However, new business will continue to have a problem with the prospect of a permanent labour force. The second is the degree of dependence on infrastructure outside the zone, which will, almost be definition, not match up to its counterpart within. Again, the logic of relocation is clear, while the logic of start-ups is not.

In short, in the current policy framework the zones undoubtedly offer a great business proposition to the developers. Their overall economic impact, however, depends not only on the zone policy itself but also on the situation with respect to several other issues.

A broad brush picture of epzs/ sezs experiences:

- Under propitious circumstances and good management, EPZs generally achieve the two basic goals of creating employment (especially non-traditional employment and income opportunities for women) and increasing foreign earnings. For instance, Mauritius EPZs boasted 71 per cent of the nation's gross exports in 1994 and employed 16.6 per cent of the work force.
- However, some argue that the net foreign earnings may not constitute a large enough sum to warrant the investments undertaken by the country to

accommodate a zone. The opportunity costs of such public investments should be considered more closely.

- Furthermore, there are potential revenue losses from concessions on income taxes and tariffs.
- EPZs/ SEZs are sensitive to the national economic environment. They will perform better when the country pursues sound macroeconomic and realistic exchange rate policies.
- Zones may contribute to the building of national human capital in two ways. Previously unskilled workers have benefited from EPZ presence. Their productivity has increased via job training and learning by doing. The benefits of this skill acquisition is limited however, as most production processes are low-skill and low-tech. The most valuable aspect of this type of employment, aside from the income earned, may be the workers' learning of industrial work discipline and routine.
- Training has also occurred at the supervisory and managerial level, with local employees becoming privy to new organizational and managerial methods, negotiation and marketing skills, general business know-how, foreign contacts and entrepreneurship.
- In addition, a successful zone, per se, is an efficient and competitive industrial infrastructure. As such it provides the country in which it operates an industrial set-up which it may lack. Most African nations would fit this profile.
- There are many cases of catalyst and demonstration effects on the host economy. These effects, together with the labour training, may be the zone's lasting contributions to the country in which it operates.
- Creation of backward linkages seems largely conditional on the industrial base of the nation. In countries which did not already enjoy a solid industrial base and which adopted EPZs/ SEZs to encourage these linkages and foster a domestic industrial base, some linkage occurred, though it was

spotty and inconsistent, with firm zones complaining of the poor quality or the incompatibility of local inputs.

- In countries where a solid industrial base existed prior to the establishment of the EPZs/ SEZs e.g. Taiwan and S. Korea- linkages have occurred. The transfer of know-how and technology was facilitated by the existing technological sophistication and highly educated labour force. In these cases, EPZs/ SEZs fostered economic growth through export promotion. Even at the height of their influence, EPZs/ SEZs never acquired a prominent role either in terms of exports value or employment creation in S. Korea or Taiwan.
- Wages in most EPZs/ SEZs are equal or higher than average wages outside the zones. Labour work safety and health laws in many zones have raised concerns with regards to workers' welfare. The size, nationality and corporate policy of the firm, the type of industrial production, labour market conditions and the country's institutions and regulations play a determining role in establishing the wage rate, workers' rights and work environment in EPZs/ SEZs.
- Overall, the EPZs/ SEZs did not universally fulfill the role of "engines of industrialization and growth" as some proponents had anticipated. They have been an engine —among others – in the economy, when they have been given their proper place as a policy tool, and where proper perspective is taken as to the ultimate achievements and costs. EPZs/ SEZs' greatest contribution seems to be job creation and income generation. Their lasting legacy can be three fold. They can contribute to building human capital, and through their demonstration and catalyst effects on the country entrepreneur pool. Also, an efficient, competitive zone is an industrial infrastructure that many countries lack.

- EPZs/ SEZs face new challenges in the increasingly global economy. Rapid changes in consumption preferences and the resulting competitive pressures to meet this demand can affect the locational choices of investors. Furthermore, increased product sharing is changing the reducing the need for country specific technical expertise. This phenomenon has a differential impact on industries as a function of their technical sophistication.
- Exclusion of a country from a preferential trade/ integration arrangement seems to impact EPZ/ SEZ firms which operate there. These firms may or may not flourish from the membership of their host country in preferential trade arrangements. The EPZs/ SEZs firms' initial product mix, market orientation, technological sophistication, strategic business planning and adaptability to the new competitive conditions will have influence on their continued success and contributions to the country in which they operate.

SEZ DRIVE IN GUJARAT

What is clear however is that the successful development strategies of some countries/regions cannot produce the same salubrious results when implemented in other national settings? When China opened some coastal pockets for foreign direct investment, these SEZs quickly blossomed into vibrant export platforms and created backward linkages with the immediate hinterland. Whereas, when landlocked Mongolia turned the entire country into a free trade and investment zone in the late 1990s, the inflow of foreign capital was a mere trickle compared to China's experience. This case is that the time-tested effective growth policy package for a coastal economy, and minor modifications of it, are unlikely to work for an interior economy. Gujarat being a coastal state where a number of prerequisites for attaining and sustaining high growth are already in place is a very strong candidate for following an outward-oriented growth strategy.

China's boom has come in three main ways:

- First, agriculture boomed as soon as the commune system was dismantled, and peasant farming resumed on the basis of household plots of land.
- Second, rural industry was greatly liberalized after 1978, especially in the form of TVEs (Township & Village Enterprises)
- Third, urban export-oriented enterprises were encouraged by the designation of a growing number of SEZs, coastal open cities, and economic and technological development zones (EDTZs), all designed to encourage manufacturing exports.

These special areas received various kinds of favourable tax and regulatory treatment, such as tax holidays, duty-free access to imported inputs and capital goods needed for export production. Thus, the SEZs and other special areas were akin to the export processing zones that had been used in other parts of Asia as part of their initial export-led growth.

SEZs in the manufacturing sector can play a major role in the overall growth strategy of the state. Virtually all of the East Asian countries have utilized SEZs to help attract foreign investment and to initiate the process of manufacturing export-led growth. SEZs have attempted to carve out a geographical zone in which export businesses can conduct profitable export-oriented activities, exempt from costly regulations, tax laws, and labour standards that apply more generally within the country. In general, the relatively successful industrial policies have had a few common characteristics:

- They have aimed to promote exports, rather than to protect the domestic market;
- They have provided subsidies on the basis of successful performance (e.g. the growth of exports) rather than to cover losses;
- They have given temporary rather than permanent subsidies (e.g. a five-year tax holiday for new export firms).

At the centre of China's export strategy were the special economic zones in which favourable export conditions were assured. These SEZs, along China's coastline, were designed to give foreign investors and domestic enterprises favourable conditions for rapid export promotion. All key aspects of the export environment were secured. Exporters, for example, were allowed to import intermediate products and capital goods duty free. They were given generous tax holidays. The exporters were assured decent physical infrastructure, often through the provision of land, power, physical security, and transport to the ports, within specially created industrial parks.

The Open Door Policy had five major goals:

- Import of foreign Capital
- Import of advanced technology
- Import of western management know-how
- Export promotion and import substitution.
- Employment generation and improvement of skills for the Chinese labour force

FDI inflows did not respond immediately in large volumes to the establishment of the SEZs in southern China (1979 in Guangdong, and 1980 in Fujian), partly because out of caution and partly because the liberal regulatory framework began to be introduced only in 1982. FDI flows started pouring in only from 1984 onward (when it doubled from US$0.6 billion in 1983 to US$1.3 billion in 1984). This jump in total FDI in 1984 was not simply due to the opening of 14 Open Coastal Cities and 10 Economic and Technological Development Zones that year, but because there was an enormous rise in FDI into the existing SEZs. FDI into Guangdong increased from US$245 million in 1983 to US$ 542 million in 1984.

As far as FDI is concerned, Gujarat is not rated as one of the most attractive destinations for FDI in India, perhaps ranked around 5th or 6th out of total States and Union Territories. It is interesting to note that while Gujarat is perhaps next only to Maharashtra as far as attracting domestic private investment is concerned; it does not score as well when it comes to foreign direct investment. This issue needs to be looked at from several different angles, for instance is the State doing enough on the marketing front, not just in the U.S., but also in other parts of the westerns world; have there been any exercises undertaken to understand what could be the issues and concerns of MNCs when it comes to investing in Gujarat; are the investment incentives offered by the State in line with others, such as Maharashtra or Tamil Nadu? Perhaps, a strategy focusing on the comparative advantages of Gujarat, relative to its other competitor states in India needs to be put in place that highlights for MNCs why they should consider Gujarat ONLY if investments are planned in X, Y, or Z sectors.

Coastal, urban-based industry can serve both the internal market and the international market, and can more readily make logistical links with foreign suppliers and customers than can interior-based enterprises. New export-oriented units are therefore heavily concentrated on the coast. As China's experience demonstrates, trade liberalization in a low-wage, surplus-labour environment permits a rapid expansion of export-oriented industry, which can absorb large numbers of workers to provide goods for the world market in real, significant foreign exchange earning private sector activity.

The concentration of FDI in the coastal provinces of China and especially in five of them has been increasing over time: from 1992 to 2002, coastal provinces received 80 per cent of FDI (against 70% in 1979-1991). Foreign trade was even more concentrated in coastal provinces which were responsible for more than 90 per cent of foreign trade (88% in 1992). Thus these coastal provinces showed a close relationship between FDI and foreign trade and this relationship has strongly influenced the economic openness of the coastal Chinese regions vis-â-vis the inward regions.

At the end of the nineties, non-coastal provinces were still closed economies, as evidenced by the ratio of foreign trade and FDI in GDP, whereas several areas of Eastern China were becoming internationalized economies (Guangdong, Fujian, Tianjin, and Shanghai). The rapid expansion of export oriented industries based on imported inputs had accelerated the integration of coastal economies in international trade and production networks, but this had possibly been achieved at the expense of backward and forward linkages with the rest of the economy and especially at the expenses of inland economies. Regional breakdown of FDI shows a dividing line between coastal provinces and inland provinces in attracting foreign capital. Since 1992, four fifths of FDI have been concentrated in coastal provinces and more precisely in five of them; Guangdong, Jiangsu, Fujian, Shanghai municipality and Shandong received more than 60 per cent of total FDI. The private money inland has moved to the coast, with net capital flows moving from the lagging West to the prosperous Eastern belt, where earnings are much higher.

Thus the coastal regions have grown extraordinarily rich and other regions do not have a share in their growth. Unemployment in other regions is rising and includes those leaving farms and others retrenched by state-owned enterprises (SOEs). To make matters worse, the inland region has suffered a brain drain, as skilled and entrepreneurial youth migrate east for higher salaries and better living conditions. Some 115 million migrant workers are seeking jobs as migrants in booming cities along the coast.

As most of FDI in China is export-motivated, FDI would prefer provinces that provide easier access to sea transportation. Unlike policy, however, geography has another key growth mechanism beside FDI, and that second growth mechanism (which is more important) is rural enterprises. Since a large (and growing) proportion of China's exports are produced by rural enterprises, it has been natural for these export-oriented rural enterprises to be established in the coastal provinces. Our view is that these rural enterprises had generated agglomeration effects that induced new rural enterprises (not necessarily export-oriented) to locate themselves in the same localities.

The prediction of this agglomeration effects hypothesis is that the positive impulse from export would create a vibrant rural industrial sector that would make the coastal region a major growth pole. The SEZs have allowed for the transfer of management know-how from abroad. This is important to India/ Gujarat as it expands its experiment with market based economic policies and tries to compete in the global marketplace. There is enough evidence to show that the SEZs have resulted in true export creation, not just diversion. Restrictions on exports and imports have also been liberalized, compared with pre-1979 levels.

The domestic resource cost ratio, a measure of the financial benefit that an enterprise can generate from its exports, is significantly lower in the market oriented cities in China than elsewhere in the country. This shows also that these enterprises are operating as profit maximizers and are not being state-subsidized. Designation as an SEZ contributes significantly to developing infrastructure in the province in question. A case in point is Guangdong which lagged behind Shanghai significantly in terms of infrastructure. Now it has become one of the foremost developed areas in this respect.

Enterprises in the SEZs are offered preferential treatment in terms of taxation, import licensing, and tariffs. The most important difference between the SEZs and the rest of China is that investment decisions are made autonomously, not subject to central planning. Local authorities can implement policies to attract investment and to develop local infrastructure as long as they can raise the funds to do so. This has created a climate that is very conducive to foreign investment. Enterprises in the zones are both state-owned and non-state owned. Non-state owned enterprises can be fully foreign-funded and owned, equity joint ventures, or contractual joint ventures.

Additionally, SEZs enjoy considerable autonomy in investment, pricing, housing, and labour and land management policies. There has been a dramatic impact on employment generation in the SEZ provinces, and this has had favourable spillover effects on the rest of the country. Much of this is employment generation, not simply diversion. There is some concern that the jobs are primarily low-skill and low-paying.

However, there is no question that labour is being released from the less productive agricultural sector to a more 'modern' sector with higher returns. This has stimulated the growth of light industry and service activities. The open door policies further helped because small-scale enterprises set up initially to meet domestic demand can expand by exporting labour intensive manufactured goods. Thus the huge potential gains from specialization and trade have been effectively exploited, and significant amounts of employment have been generated through the zones.

Consistent with the experience of other East Asian countries such as the Republic of Korea, Singapore, Taiwan, and Thailand – is that exports are key to high GDP growth rates. Successful export expansion in turn depends on a policy package which conveys a clear message that the country will give priority to export-oriented firms rather than sheltering import-competing industries. China has benefited greatly from the clear direction its reforms have taken, in spite of occasional bumps along the way.

Focussed sectors in gujarat sez for competitive advantages:

Kandla:

- Engineering
- Chemical and allied products
- RMG
- Plastic Units
- Packaging industries
- Trading Units

Mundra:

- Light & Heavy Engineering.
- Auto & Component
- Textile & Apparel
- Agro & Food Processing
- Drugs & Pharma
- Chemical & Fertilizer

Surat:

- Diamond
- Gems & Jewellery
- Pharmaceuticals
- Chemicals
- RMG
- Light Engineering
- IT Hardware
- Tobacco

SEZ IN GUJARAT – ENTREPRENEURS' PERSPECTIVE

(A) *Quality of Governance*: We attempted to analyse the entrepreneurs' perspective on the quality of governance across the selected zones in Gujarat through the units to understand and analyse.

- First, the quality of governance in general is above the average in almost all the cases.
- Second, the factor of 'simplified rules' suggesting that the rules in these zones are complex and that this leads to increase in delays in bureaucratic decisions, holds true for Kandla Zone.
- Third, custom clearance powers are delegated to the zonal authorities. Moreover the government has implemented the plan of self certification. This might have helped in reducing the level of rent seeking.

Note: If provision of amenities such as on-site canteens, day cares and health services enhances the employees' work and living standard and improves their productivity while reducing absenteeism and labour turn-over. Privately run, high-end zones tend to fulfill these services better than public SEZs. The government should apply uniform regulations to all zones.

(B) *Incentives*: Sometimes it is argued that companies are not attracted by incentives per se and that good infrastructure and cheap labour availability are important (ICIR, 1992). To understand more, wc checked with the units in these zones to know: 'how important it is to offer fiscal incentives for attracting investment in the zones?' The fiscal incentives are considered very important in determining the attractiveness of the zones. Over 85 per cent of the respondents in India regarded them as very important. It is therefore important to analyse the incentive package offered by these zones to the zone units.

Prior to 1981, income tax concession plans were not given to the zone units. Tax holidays of 5 years were extended to the units only in 1981. Besides, there were no standardized procedures for exemption from excise duties. In Kandla, on the other hand, all inputs were entitled to excise exemptions. There was no state sales tax exemption for Kandla until 1974. Central sales tax was not exempted until 1978. Domestic tariff area sale was permitted only against import licenses and the rates of duty were exorbitant. Subcontracting of production was not allowed.

Some favourable policy changes were introduced in the incentive package during the 1980s. The condition of import license for DTA sale was waived in 1987. Subcontracting for job work in DTA was allowed with the approval of Assistant Commissioner of customs. Sub contracting procedures relating to indemnity bonds and revolving bank guarantees were simplified and in 1986, reimbursement of CST was granted to EPZ units. There were no significant changes in other laws and procedures pertaining to EPZs.

During the 1990s, when the government undertook to simplify and rationalize the tax structure and major tax cuts were being introduced in the rest of the economy, incentive package was made more attractive for the zone units also. Though there was no change in the tax holiday, duty on DTA sales was reduced to 50% of custom duty in 1991 and the rate of duty on sale of rejects was reduced to 50% of the applicable duty. Besides, DTA sales entitlement for agro based EPZ units was raised in 1992 to 50% of production.

EPZ units were given option in 1995 to switch over to export promotion capital goods (EPCG) plan. In the EXIM policy for 1997-02, additional DTA sale was allowed to units based on indigenous raw materials, provided they fulfilled the export obligation. Electronic hardware units were allowed to sell upto 50% of production in the domestic market on payment of applicable duties. Software units were permitted to effect online DTA sales. An attractive package of incentives was offered to SEZ units in 2000 and thereafter both in Fiscal and Non Fiscal.

Note: Unless domestic firms benefit from such tax (income, trade) privileges, bestowing them on SEZ firms discriminate against the domestic firms excluded from the zone. The special treatment acts as a barrier to connect with the host economy. More specifically, if domestic firms do not benefit from functional drawback policies, the tariff free inputs for the firms in the zone acts as import subsidies competing against domestic input production and discouraging creation of backward linkages. If countries do not allow domestic sales of SEZ products, the potential for forward linkages vanishes as well.

(C) *Infrastructure Facilities by the Zones*: The analysis of the infrastructure facilities directly provided by the zone authorities in the three zones. No exclusive arrangements have been made for water, electricity or telecommunications by the zone authorities in Gujarat except Mundra which plans to have its own thermal power plant and water supply in the near future. The units have to depend on the state boards for electricity supply. Units may arrange water from outside the zones. Zones are providing, financial infrastructure such as banks, ATMs and post offices but the units can use banks outside the zones also. Some of the zones are providing other trade related infrastructure such as warehousing facilities, ICD, transport facilities and other physical infrastructure such as water purifiers and effluent treatment plant etc.

The firms or units in the SEZ, were asked to comment about the quality of infrastructure and found that water and electricity are two most important aspects of infrastructure. The satisfaction level of entrepreneurs in respect of these infrastructures facilities available/ provided in SEZ. Water is not equally important for all the firms but essential in Pharmaceuticals, FMCG, Dyeing and Bleaching industries but in rest of the industries, it is required primarily for the drinking purpose. Some of the units in Kandla had shown their concern on the quality of water provided in the SEZ, as they have to depend on water tankers and further water treatment required for their usage. This results in more wastage of their resources and adds to their cost.

Table. Evaluation of the Factor Availability and Factor Cost

Sr. No.	Factors
1	Lower real estate cost
2	Lower wages
3	Availability of skilled labour
4	Domestically manufactured parts and components
5	Availability of concessional finance
6	Availability of cheap raw materials

Evalutaion of governance:

1	Single window clearance
2	Custom clearance
3	Easy information on zones
4	Accessibilty to rules
5	Simplified rules

Evaluation of the factors crucial for the success of the zones: Investor's perspective in descending order.

Sr. No.	Factors
1	Tax Concessions
2	Physical Infrastructure within zone
3	Infrastructure external to the zone
4	Proximity to port, airport and bigger cities
5	Governance of the Zone
6	Exemption from other industrial laws
7	Regional development
8	Availability of raw materials
9	Social Infrastructure
10	Subsidies

- *Power*: Power availability is rated satisfactory in major zones. Power cuts are very frequent outside the zones especially in Kutch. Many firms however have installed their own power generators. This was mainly due to fluctuation in power supply or to meet power failures. The major concern for the units in these zones is cost of power available to them than the rest of the country. The charges are the highest in the country. Drastic steps to reduce the power cost are taken by the SEZs to make these units more competitive. For e.g. In Mundra SEZ, apart from the power supply from State Board, Adani Group is planning to set up its own thermal power plant in the SEZ. This will not only ensure continuous power supply but also will bring down the cost from Rs. 4.5 per unit to Rs. 2/- per unit.

Transport: Transport facilities are also considered important and vital as it relates not only to the prosperity of the region but also plays a vital role in their logistics cost and time duration. Transport facilities within the zones are almost non existent in all the three zones and hence are below average. From Gandhidham to Mundra transport for the zones and road conditions are considered to be below average and pathetic.

In most of the zones except Surat, transport facilities for the zones are average. Poor and congested roads sharply increase the time for transporting the containers as well as movement of people to and from the Port/ SEZ. This also results in time loss for the labours working in these zones. If these zones provide company buses to carry labour to the zones it will be of great help in saving time and availability of perennial labour supply and also to avoid heavy rush and traffic jams in the morning and evening hours. Rail transport system is not well developed either in Kandla or Mundra except for containers. Thus the outside road infrastructure connecting the zones with port, airport and other social utilities is poor in these zones. Port facilities are rated best at Mundra and Kandla when compared with the rest of the ports of the country but it has to travel a long way to match the standards of some its immediate neighbours such as Colombo or Singapore.

- *Port*: The port in Western part of Gujarat has the deepest draft of the country and is sufficiently deep for large international vessels. Feeder ships connect the country with Singapore or other countries from where these are loaded in larger vessels. This increases time and cost of transportation. Besides, cargo handling facilities are also stated to be poor when compared to Hong Kong or Singapore but far better than available in some of the Indian ports. Non availability of port near Surat SEZ has proven to be a great disadvantage as it has to depend on JNPT or Navi Mumbai for transportation of goods and generally these ports remain congested all through out the year. Indian ports are also stated to be characterized by delays and inefficiencies. Cost of Indian goods can be brought down if proper and timely handlings of goods are carried out at ports.
- *Airport*: Lack of international airports at Surat or Kandla/ Mundra may also have an adverse effect on the progress of these SEZs. For instance, Gems and Jewellery business being a high value added item requires air connectivity. This can be one of the main reasons for SEEPZ benefiting from the Gem and Jewellery industry irrespective of Surat being the major centre for processing, due to its proximity to both port and international airport. The same can be said for Kandla/ Mundra, as foreign investors find it difficult to reach these places as it requires 4 to 5 hours of road travel, which can be taxing on these investors.

Note: Early proponents of EPZs considered them as potential hubs for non-urban, decentralized industrial development. They favoured placing EPZs away from urban and populated centres to encourage job creation and economic development in rural areas and to reduce the rural-urban migration. It soon became clear that EPZs would not flourish in such an environment unless they were fitted with easy access to sea ports or airports, energy and water sources, good roads, above average (by country standards) communication facilities and available and adequately skilled workers. The Bataan Zone in the Philippines, located in a mountainous area some 160 km from Manila, is a prime example of a poor locational choice.

Despite the government spending nearly $200 million in 1973 on building the zone (Warr, 1985), it failed to reach its goals due to it isolation from the country's industrial centre and poor infrastructure. The same occurred to the Puerto Limon zone on Costa Rica's Atlantic/Caribbean cost (Ryan, et. al., 1993).

The Zone Franche d'Inga in Zaire is a third example of this miscalculation. It was located in a remote area of the country, with poor infrastructure to service it and few workers with adequate skills to satisfy its labour demands. The new philosophy highlights the importance of locating EPZs near or in industrial/urban areas. This satisfies the labour needs of the zone firms and allows for more spillover effects. Such a locational choice also ensures more accessible and uninterrupted utilities, better infrastructure and services, and proximity to airports and sea ports.

- *Communication*: Communication facilities are considered to be the most satisfactory of all the infrastructure facilities. Given the information revolution taking place these zones, have benefited a lot. But still more can be done by providing facilities such as broadband connectivity etc.

Apparently, overall quality of infrastructure in the zones is considered above average when compared to rest of the zones in the country. However, infrastructure external to the zones such as roads and ports are not found to be adequate in general. When compared to the zones of South East Asian countries or Middle East infrastructure needs a major thrust.

(D) *State-run sezs lose out to private competitors*: Despite the hype generated by the Government over its Special Economic Zone (SEZ) lack of infrastructure are turning many big business houses away from the state SEZ.

Though the government is of the opinion that SEZ policy would lead employment generation, the lack of enough land required for setting up huge units, lack of clarity over the labour laws in a SEZ are turning big entrepreneurs away from the se SEZs.

Many point that out that state SEZ lack social infrastructure, such as educational institutions, entertainment centres, accommodation for employees etc. Even the tax sops are not acting in impetus. But when the state SEZ lack these, private players such as Adani Group under the banner of Mundra SEZ Ltd., Reliance Industries Ltd., and Seaking Infrastructure Ltd., are planning to take the state-run SEZs head-on by offering the social infrastructure within their proposed SEZs along with hughe lands devoted to the industries with the offer for providing them flexibility to expand their units in future if required.

While the Adanis have already initiated civil work for its mega-SEZ project to be spread over 10,000 hectares of land at Mundra in Kutch and have finalized plans for setting up health facilities with Apollo Group, discussions are on between Adanis and various educational institutions to set up schools/ colleges within the proposed SEZ. Reliance also finalized its plan to setup its port-based SEZ in the Jamnagar coast with an investment ranging between Rs. 12,000-15,000 crore which according to sources also would be armed with various facilities for the family members of the employees working in the industrial units to be setup in the SEZ. Reliance is also planning to setup a technical and management school within its proposed SEZ and a school till 12th Standard on the line of its Kokilaben Ambani School at Vadianar may be setup within the SEZ campus or adjoining areas.

Reliance like the Ambanis is expected to spread its SEZ on over 10,000 hectares of land thus offering flexibility for future expansion for the industries to operate from within its SEZ. However, the state run SEZs such as Kandla feel that they could have hiked up their business in several multiplications provided they could have offered required infrastructure and social infrastructure to the industries which are already in and these SEZs could have also attracted bigger industry players. As far as Kandla Special Economic Zone (KASEZ) is concerned, it is the most spacious of all the Special Economic Zone Export Processing Zones of India.

Though authorities have termed it as "The Paradise for free enterprise" industry representatives are not happy with the infrastructure at Kandla. Lack of flights discourages foreigners and high power and water charges push up input costs. Lack of servicing globally had caused despair to international customers. There are no flights to Kandla and clients have to drive from Bhuj to the unit in the Kandla SEZ.

While power was available at Rs. 2 per unit in Indore, Madhya Pradesh SEZ, at Kandla SEZ it cost Rs. 5 per unit. Also water supplies are irregular, for which the units had to buy water tankers at huge cost.

In the current global scenario, it is possible for Gujarat to achieve very dynamic growth based upon labour-intensive manufacturing that combines the vast supply of its labour, including skilled managerial and engineering labour, with foreign capital, technology, and markets. On this basis, the East Asian economies have achieved growth rates consistently above 6 per cent per year up until their financial crisis, and China has managed growth in excess of 10 per cent per year in the 1990s.

Traditional textiles and apparel, electronics and other labour-intensive operations remains an area where India in general and Gujarat in particular could do a lot more than in the past. Gujarat has the resource base, it has the entrepreneurship, has the access to the sea coast, a vast labour force, it has everything that coastal China has had except the interest of the bureaucrats which neglected this for a long time and which even today underemphasizes the role of industrial facilities, underemphasizes the role of infrastructure, of land area, of effective port facilities that one needs to sustain high rates of growth.

But it is, a place where one could find tens of millions of jobs over the next few years in real, significant foreign exchange earning private sector activity. This would require a change of attitude, a real promotion of these sectors both at the state and central government levels. The reform process in India has so far mainly concentrated at the federal level. India has yet to free up its state governments sufficiently so that they can add much greater dynamism to the reforms. Greater freedom to the states will help foster greater competition among themselves.

The state governments in India need to be viewed as potential agents of rapid and salutary change. While some healthy competition is evident in India among the three southern states of Andhra Pradesh, Karnataka, and Tamil Nadu, and the two western states of Gujarat and Maharashtra, however, much of the rest of Indian states are yet to begin competing with each other. Brazil, China, and Russia are examples where regional governments have taken the lead in pushing reforms and prompting further actions by the central government.

Decentralization has been crucial in making the SEZs attractive to investment. Special policies that allow a greater portion of firms' profits to be retained instead of being transferred to the Centre are notable. China's economic system is highly decentralized and policy implementation is now largely under the control of provincial authorities. Hence in fast growing provinces, provincial and local officials have been deeply involved in the development process in general and export promotion in particular. Besides their role in facilitating foreign investment, there are a number of ways in which local governments promote exports.

The central government sets mandatory targets or export quotas for only a limited number of items or by volume. But in some provinces, like Jiangsu, the export quota system is far more elaborate. Moreover, taking advantage of their monophony power, TCs are able to buy goods at prices well below domestic prices, making their output competitive in the world market. Operating within central government guidelines, provincial governments have been expanding Direct Export Rights to enterprises, but the criteria for doing so are very stringent. As a result only 5 per cent of China's exports are produced by enterprises with Direct Export Rights. Also within central government guidelines, local authorities decide the allocation of imported raw materials by sharing locally retained foreign exchange earnings among enterprises, collectives, and town and village enterprises in different sectors.

Provinces and cities also indirectly subsidize exports by providing critical inputs like electric power to export-oriented enterprises. Additional incentives are provided in the form of higher bonuses for managers and employees awarded on the basis of export performance. Finally, local authorities establish joint ventures between FTCs and enterprises to promote exports.

The success of Gujarat lies in the factor that export growth should be diversified away from traditional sectors, especially raw materials, into non-traditional sectors, especially manufactured goods. Gujarat may lack in the technology by itself to be competitive in manufactured goods. Therefore, it has to invite foreign direct investors to provide the capital and the expertise to achieve export competitiveness in a wide range of sectors, including electronics, apparel, plastic goods, ceramics, and many other labour-intensive sectors.

In each sector, the key is to link foreign investor capital and expertise with a large and low-cost labour force. The foreign investors should bring in the product design, specialized machine tools and capital goods, key intermediate products, and knowledge of world marketing channels. The State Government should assure these foreign investors certain key conditions for profitability, such as low taxes, reliable infrastructure, physical security, adequate power, decent logistics for the import and export of goods, and so forth.

At the centre of State's export strategy should be SEZs in which favourable export conditions should be assured. These SEZs, along Gujarat's coastline, should be designed to give foreign investors and domestic enterprises favourable conditions for rapid export promotion. All key aspects of the export environment should be secured. Exporters, apart from being allowed to import intermediate products and capital goods duty free along with generous tax holidays should also be provided with decent physical infrastructure, often through the provision of land, power, physical security, and transport to the ports, within specially created industrial parks.

State's export environment suffers from several institutional weaknesses. Vast majority of India's employment is informal, in small, tax-evading, inefficient enterprises. Equally remarkably, India's legislation continues to restrict the entry of large firms, or the growth of small firms into large firms, in several areas of potential comparative advantage. Thus, garments, toys, shoes and leather products continue to be reserved, to a varying extent, for small-scale producers. Such restrictions virtually assure China's dominance in these sectors compared with India. India's tax and tariff structures similarly remain anti-export biased. India's high overall tariff rates, especially tariffs on intermediate products that are used by exporters, impose a heavy indirect tax on export competitiveness.

Deregulation of the private sector is perhaps one of the most critical areas in the context of India's reforms. Since almost 90-plus per cent of the workforce is in the informal sector, it is of utmost importance to deregulate the private sector so as to get the unorganized sector workforce in the mainstream. Workers in large firms in the formal sector have a virtual guarantee of continued employment according to the Industrial Disputes Act. For firms of 100 employees or more, reductions in the workforce must be upon the permission of state government, which is almost never granted. Remarkably, loss-making firms are also not allowed to close their operations without government consent.

Indeed with a more open and deregulated economy, and a positive and prompt decision making State Government, Gujarat may well be in a position to perform as China has done over the last two decades. The proper elements of a revised growth strategy - rapid export-growth- should now be clear. Both the hardware and software of export-led growth need revamping. On the hardware side, the development of industrial parks for exports should be greatly intensified and enhanced. Private developers need the freedom to acquire urban and peri-urban land and to develop privately financed infrastructure in support of exports.

The government must take urgent measures to reduce export costs, including private-sector provision of port services; zero tariff ratings on capital and intermediate goods imports used for export (based on an effective duty exemption plan); enhanced export-oriented infrastructure, especially roads to the ports and airports, reliable power supply, and telecommunications facilities to support export zones. Labour legislation should be revised to allow managerial flexibility in the hire and dismissal of workers in export-oriented sectors.

The reservation of labour intensive sectors to small-scale enterprises should simply be scrapped. The government should actively encourage inward investment in export-oriented sectors, allowing 100 per cent foreign ownership without administrative interference, and with the provision of generous tax holidays as necessary to attract internationally mobile capital from other locations.

As a general matter, Gujarat has an advantage over other states. Fortunately, there is a vast amount of economic reform that can be carried out to improve conditions in rural Gujarat. There is no reason for expensive and counter-productive charity for these parts of the state, and still less any case for holding back the fast-growing coastal regions. Perhaps the key step is to improve the most basic infrastructure so that the vast rural populations can take part in more rapid state economic growth. They will do so through increased exports to coastal regions, and greatly improved productivity for local production.

Rural Gujarat needs a new social contract, in which there will be a reliable infrastructure supplied at commercial prices rather than given for free. The Government's commitment, at the state level should be that every village will be assured at least minimal telephone service, clean water, a road to the regional market, and reliable power; but that every village will be responsible for covering the commercial costs of those services on a normal user-fee basis. Technological changes in each of these areas (telephony, water, road building and maintenance, and power) allow these key sectors to be organized, at least in part, on the basis of competitive, private-sector producers, who will provide the initial financing of the investments in return for a reliable stream of user charges over time. The availability of infrastructure services, such as power, telecom, and roads in rural Gujarat can significantly help develop rural industry in Gujarat.

The Township and Village Enterprises operate outside of the state plan, and largely without funds from state banks. Therefore, they are subject to quite rigorous market competition and hard budget constraints. TVEs should be linked with the urban areas for development. This will facilitate the transportation of goods between rural and urban areas, and rising income and productivity in rural areas. As for urban enterprises, this link would open up a bigger market and help in diversification or restructuring which is currently under constraint due to area limitations.

Rural enterprises can also compete in the cities with their products having the advantage of relatively low labour costs. In this way, they will help absorb surplus labour locally, thereby resulting in less rural-to-urban migration (population in urban areas have reached levels far above what the urban cities can efficiently accommodate given their capacity to provide urban infrastructure services). Urban enterprises will also provide more employment opportunities since they would have a larger market. In addition, the linkage will benefit the rural industries via flow of technology and information.

SEZ - LESSONS FOR GUJARAT

- To attain and sustain high rates of economic growth, follow a two-pronged growth strategy, wherein the first prong is export-led growth, and the second prong is rural improvement. For the first prong, lessons from the Chinese coastal provinces are particularly instructive, since the Chinese provinces achieved in the past twenty years the kind of export-led growth that Indian states could have achieved, but have so far failed to achieve because of poor public policies. With regard to the second prong, Gujarat needs a specific strategy to bring modern economic growth to rural Gujarat, through a concerted campaign of infrastructure upgrading and appropriate re-design of state policy.

- Establish SEZs all along the Gujarat coast on an expedited time table. This is critical in view of the fact that several Indian states are in the process of setting-up such SEZs and the sooner Gujarat's SEZs are up and running, the better it will be for attracting both potential domestic and foreign investors. These SEZ companies of Gujarat should not be bound by minimum export performance requirements. Companies need to balance or have positive net foreign exchange earnings. Put briefly, when benchmarked against Chinese SEZs, broadly, the Indian SEZs are by and large at par with them.
- Identify key sectors where Gujarat offers comparative advantage for investors relative to other Indian states;
- Working with the federal government move expeditiously to reform labour laws, especially with respect to the SEZs. Labour laws in Chinese SEZs are more favourable, allowing labour contracts to be modified or rescinded through consultations between both parties.
- An exit policy needs to be formulated such that firms can exit from the market freely. While it would be incorrect to ignore the need for, and potential merit of, certain safeguards while designing an exit policy, it is also important to recognize that safeguards, if wrongly designed and/or poorly enforced would turn into barriers which may adversely affect the health of the firms. Exit policy needs to be designed in a way that it removes exit barriers and at the same time protects the necessary internal order in the firms.
- Make investments on a much higher level to upgrade

existing major port facilities and to use minor ports more efficiently.

- Make the necessary changes to align Gujarat's incentives structures in line with other competitor Indian states.
- The State Government should develop networks with Gujarati Non-resident Indians for them to invest in Gujarat. As a follow-up of the Global Investors Summit, quick and timely follow-up action is critical
- The State Government should explore if Township and Village enterprises (TVEs) can be set-up in rural Gujarat. The TVEs have huge potential to fuel growth in rural Gujarat.

(B) *Good governance results in better performance*: The governments' role can be outlined as follows. They provide the necessary legal framework and potentially, the initial bureaucratic effort such as launching a feasibility study, encouraging domestic private sector involvement and marketing the zone abroad.

In drawing up the legal and administrative framework for a zone, the government should be fully appraised of the nature of incentives offered and the type of industries they might attract (light or heavy industry, long or short-term investments, etc) to ensure that they match the government's general policy framework and expectations.

In a majority of cases the governments invest in the creation or upgrading of the infrastructure necessary for the zone. These include improvement of roads, ports, and airports near the designated zone location. Generally, governments have to secure a steady supply of electricity and water (building of new power plant/dam), and expanding the country's international communication capacity.

Once the initial legal, bureaucratic and physical framework has taken shape, the government provides (and shoulder the cost of) the ongoing services such as customs, regulatory and supervisory duties, leaving the running of the business to a private corporation or managerial group.

SEZs in Gujarat should be streamlined, prompt and efficient bureaucracy and customs control in all stages of the creation and running of an EPZ is crucial to its success. It greatly influences the attractiveness of the zone to foreign and domestic investors and the eventual performance and success of the firms established in it.

All points to the fact that, regardless of whether the zones are private or public, governance is key to the success of EPZs. The provision of efficient bureaucratic and economic services, a clear and transparent legal and regulatory structure, an unfettered and stable policy framework, and non-preferential treatment of economic actors allow an arena prone to success.

(C) *Government holds the key*: *Industrial Policy*: While the policies announced by the State govt. is quite dynamic and pragmatic and is basically growth driven yet the implementation of policy is halting and hesitant. It leaves much to be desired in respect of promotion of Industries large, medium and small, infrastructure development, employment intensive parks, Hi-tech parks, investment parks, trade centres as well as backward area development, environmental protection, and export promotion. Tardy progress made in these directions so far indicates poor and weak follow up and lack of publicity of the incentives and facilities available to industries. Corrective measures are therefore required to be taken to sustain and accelerate industrial growth in Gujarat so that with maximisation of larger manufacturing capacities and productivity, enhanced employment opportunities could be generated and enlargement of exports could be achieved.

Leads and Lags in Industrial Growth

It has to be realised that Gujarat's inherent advantages of low labour cost, intelligent man power, highly qualified and trained man power in the form of pool of scientists, prolonged period of industrial peace, entrepreneurial edge of the people, good grasp of technology and proactive govt. attitude and approach and supportive bureaucracy etc. should have taken it right to the top of the league on the industrial firmament of the country. This potential has not been realised reflects that there are still problem areas on which govt. needs to pay special attention to enhance competitiveness of our products both in the domestic and international market. This is the crux of the matter which should not be ignored while evolving and implementing

Power Availability and Rates

Periodical inadequate and irregular supply of power and high cost thereof obstructs industrial growth and hampers competitiveness. The power cost to total expenditure in major industrial units in Gujarat works out to 4.3% to 11.77% whereas in chemical industry units it comes to 13.15% to 37.3%. Power cost works out to about 7.5% to 8% of the sales which is very high. Besides high cost of power, the quality and reliability of power supply leaves much to be desired due to periodical interruptions, failure, voltage fluctuation and power cut and staggering. What is worse, because of restriction on sale of captive power and private sector investment in IPP's is not coming despite the fact that power is cheaper.

While on the one hand there is heavy shortage of power, the industries and agriculture are facing many problems due to shortage of power in the peak of the summer. The net result is that excess capacity in captive power units is not fully utilised. Even power is not available to exporting units at international price of Rs.2 per unit/kw as is being done in China. Concrete actions are needed for augmenting power supply and for reducing cost there of including duties and it is apprehended that large number of chemical and other units will face closure.

Infrastructural Constraints

Infrastructure bottlenecks and costs thereof are prohibitive and hamper competitiveness of our industries and exports. Inadequate facilities and congestion at ports, condition of roads being far from satisfactory, ineffective working of railways and antiquated facilities at airport etc. operate as impediments and add to the cost of the transaction and ultimately make goods uncompetitive both in the domestic and international market. Since this makes it difficult to ensure timely delivery and honour commitments, the exporters have to permanently lose the buyer. Rapid improvement of infrastructure with the help and assistance of funds both domestic and FDI and effective and efficient maintenance thereof is essential for promotion in capturing market share for our industries and trade in India and abroad. When Hyderabad is already promoting itself as the hub of chemical and pharma industry in the country and is willing to take all possible steps, it is high time that this issue be given priority it deserves so that existing or new units do not migrate over there from Gujarat.

Tax Structure

The old economy industries viz. Textiles, chemicals and petro-chemicals, mineral based industries and others have already started losing their competitive edge. Despite the predominance of chemical and petro-chemical industries in the industrial structure of Gujarat, it is facing serious problems of multiple taxation.

Technology

It is now universally acknowledged that success and survival of industries in the new millennium largely depends on the advances made on the technology innovation front and upgradation of technology in the existing industries both large and small so that they can achieve productivity and competitiveness at the earliest. Meagre measures like strengthening of R&D institutions or linkage with industry or setting up of incubation centre at IIM or encouragement to product development are not enough.

The emerging challenges in the context of globalisation, liberalisation and privatisation all over the world in post WTO era warrant that Gujarat which has all the wherewithal to make rapid advances in the IT and bio-technology is languishing in this vital field. If we do not leapfrog in this direction then it is apprehended that as suggested, be left out and will be relegated in the background vis-â-vis some of the southern states viz. Andhra:Pradesh, Karnataka and Tamilnadu Surprisingly, there issues have not been addressed in the approach paper which is the crying need of the day.

Finance

It is distressing to note that out of 2.65 lakh SSI units registered in Gujarat at present, about 76% are working and about 20% are closed.

The percentage of disbursement to SSI via-a-vis total disbursement for priority sector had dropped from 49.19% to 32.24%. The same situation of deceleration had continued in 2000 and 2001 and still continuing. The major constraint is non availability of working capital. Despite the fact that banks are flush with funds and credit policy advocates liberalisation of finance for SSI, the picture in reality is otherwise and SSI units are starving for want of funds.

While interest rates have shown signs of softening and prime lending rate has been revised down ward to 11%, the actual lending rates which SSI units have to pay varies from 12% to 16% which are still way above international bench mark. It is therefore reasonable and necessary that interest costs for SSI be reduced by making available finance between 8 to 10%. Even the bank charges and guarantee cost for sanctioned limit works out to about 2% which are required to be reduced. Pressure to be brought on nationalised banks, not only to augment credit deposit ratio from 45% to 65% but also finance for SSI be augmented at highly concessional rate.

If SSI units are encouraged, then lot of backward integration can be carried out for the SEZ units rather than importing it directly. Moreover, NRI investment is minimal and they need to be attracted to invest in the SEZs, for which Government should think of various attractive plans.

Cluster Development

Although Gujarat has developed 73 product clusters which include clusters like brass parts industry in Jamnagar, oil engine in Rajkot, ceramic tiles industry in Morbi, Ship breaking industry at Alang, rerolling mills in Sihor, cotton powerloom industry in Ahmedabad artsilk powerloom industry in Surat and, diamond cutting and polishing industry in Surat and Ahmedabad, yet none of them have been declared as centres of economic and export excellence in the New Exim policy such as Tirupur, for hosiery, woollen blanket in Panipat, woollen knitwear in Ludhiana. These latter centres have been provided various advantages by GOI viz. facility of EPCG plan for common service, market access funds, central assistance for infrastructural gap and entitlement of export house status at Rs.5 crores instead of Rs.15 crores for others which should be sought for main Gujarat clusters also in the Tenth plan. Despite better performance, Gujarat clusters woefully lack the aforesaid facilities for organic growth and export development.

Exports

Even though Gujarat accounts for about 17% of the total exports of the country, a lot more needs to be done to diversify and consolidate manufacturing capacity, enhance productivity and competitiveness and increase market access to newer markets which are opening up due to globalisation and liberalisation.

What is more distressing is the fact although govt. of India had approved 20 agri -export zones for various local commodities of export in various states in the country out of which 4 are in Maharashtra, 3 in U.P. and 2 in West Bengal whereas Gujarat has been granted approval for Agro export zone only recently. This is the position despite the fact that Gujarat has enough to offer in terms of processed fruits and vegetables. Out of above, work on 15 agro export zones has already started while Gujarat has lagged far behind in this regard. Govt. of Gujarat will have to reinvent and reinforce export strategy for Gujarat so that industries and trade of Gujarat achieve enhanced productivity and competitiveness in the export market. Govt. will have to move fast locally by taking prompt remedial measures particularly keeping in view international vision. This implies for a comprehensive policy for promotion of exports, to attract investments both domestic and foreign and to enhance employment on an urgent basis.

Labour Reforms

Despite the talk of India/Gujarat having lower wages, the labour productivity in India/Gujarat compares very unfavourably with many other countries like Pakistan, China, Fiji, Japan, Malaysia etc. as also compared to many leading states in the country. It is understood that out of 12 countries for which comparison of productivity indices are available, India is at the 8th position. Even compared to China we are lagging behind in labour productivity in all most all industrial sectors to the extent of 7% to 180%.

It is high time to introduce hire and fire policy and link wages with productivity and efficiency so as to enhance competitiveness of our products both in domestic market and international markets. Even pragmatic exit policy also needs to be implemented with social concern in view.

Priority Areas for Action

- Since the Indian economy and Gujarat are rapidly moving from shortages to surpluses, it is in the fitness of things that SEZ and Agro export zones approved in the state should not only be established expeditiously but also requisite incentives and facilities be provided to export industries so as to enable them to be competitive in the international market. Urgent steps are required to be taken in this direction so as to speed up recovery of Gujarat's economy and achieve target for enhancement of exports and employment in Gujarat. In short level playing field is ensured to the industries of Gujarat.
- Water intensive industries are not developing in Gujarat and are not given proper encouragement due to shortage and high cost of water. When 31% of the chemical industries of India are located in Gujarat, it is in the fitness of things to make water rates cost competitive. Paper making units located in Southern

Gujarat are facing closure due to scarcity of water. For water intensive industries urgent steps be taken to augment water supply through establishment of desalination plants.

Looking ahead and beyond warrant that both state and central govt. together should resolve to buck the global slowdown and bring about rapid resurgence of Gujarat in this turbulent times and show to the world that Gujarat State and India as a nation can overcome all odds. Adversity can not be cause for despair as tough times do not last long. Rather, it is a summon and a stimulus for action - indeed for bold but constructive and aggressive action to forge ahead on the path of progress and prosperity trouble free and struggle free. Such positive and pragmatic actions will produce visible recovery for Gujarat in the times ahead. The business community of Gujarat is totally dedicated, devoted and determined to be partner with govt. in a joint and complementary action to revive the Gujarat's economy and to take it on high growth path.

SEZ promoters underline that thanks to such zones foreign investors have been encouraged to invest and create employment in countries that would not be the natural choice for direct foreign investment if it were not for the incentives offered. But will these investors remain in such countries if the financial incentives are with- drawn, if the cost of labour increases or the quota-based trading system for garments comes to an end?

The host governments devote considerable funds to the infrastructure and operations of these zones without collecting any taxes for a given period. In return, they manage to attract investment, sometimes receive employers. Contributions to pensions, generate foreign currency earnings, and create jobs.

Yet the benefits are limited in the following ways:

- The investors usually limit their activities in the EPZs to simple processing operations, thus limiting the transfer of technologies and skills
- Most jobs are poorly paid, low quality and involve few skills

- A very small share of the foreign currency earnings generated remain in the country; the foreign investments are not secure and can be withdrawn from the country with relative ease, as seen with the numerous companies that have left the EPZs of various countries to relocate in China, where there is particularly little respect for workers rights
- The investors often import all they need and source very little from the local market.

With the SEZ ACT coming into existence and permission given to establish as many as 45 new zones in the private and joint sector, it is quite apparent that the future industrialization of the country will be closely interlinked to and concentrated in the Special Economic Zones. At present foreign exchange earned by all the 811 units in the 8 Zones put together came to Rs 18,309 crores, (4.08 billion dollars) a mere 5% of India's exports during the fiscal 2004-05.But a lot of costs are associated with this revenue: As much as two-thirds of this is used by them for imports of raw materials and components. Add to that the profits transferred from the country by wholly owned foreign companies, the revenue loss from tax concessions, and the hidden costs of the natural resources used up by the Zones - and the SEZs actually appear to be a net drain on the economy.

On the face of it SEZs do not seem to be driving export growth and coupled with the fact that a lot of worker related issues are bogging it in a mire, the future of SEZs in India seems uncertain. All in all, SEZs have the potential to script the China success story and for this reason alone they are worth the bet. By the incorporation of Redressal mechanisms, improving investment climate, improving infrastructural facilities and ensuring better working conditions, the future of SEZs in India doesn't seem anywhere bleak as it is perhaps made out to be.

10

SEBI Guidelines Relating to Capital Issues

In the case of new companies with foreign equity participation, the public offer should not be less than 20% of the issued capital, and the Indian promoter's share should not be more than 40% of the issued capital. For new companies without any foreign equity participation, the public offer is required to be at least 60% of the issued capital. Finance companies would be eligible to make an issue only if they have a minimum track record of 2 years operations or they have been granted registration as a non-banking financial company by RBI or as an intermediary by SEBI.

Stock exchanges are required to ensure that the companies concerned, have a valid acknowledgment card issued by SEBI. SEBI vets the offer document, to ensure that all disclosures have been made by the company, in the offer document, at the time the company applies for listing of its securities to the stock exchange.

Following the abolition of the office of Controller of Capital Issues and the consequent removal of administrative control over the pricing of new issues, the capital markets now enjoy a considerable degree of freedom. New companies, being set up by existing companies; with a five year track record of profitability, are free to price issues, provided the participation of the promoters is not less than 25% of the equity of the new company and the pricing is made applicable to all new investors symmetrically. Where a new company is set up by existing private sector companies along with a state level agency, or a government company, or a foreign collaborator, it will be sufficient if the private sector companies alone satisfy the requirements of five year track record of profitability. Existing profitable companies issuing capital for augmenting their own capital base are free to price their issue. At the same time, the practice of making preferential allotment of shares, unrelated to the prevailing market prices was stopped by SEBI.

In any capital issue to the public, there is a specified minimum capital contribution to be made by the promoters. To reduce the cost of the issue, underwriting by issues has been made optional, subject to the condition that if an issue is not underwritten, and is not able to collect 90% of the amount offered to the public, the entire amount collected would be refunded to the investors.

Where fully convertible debentures (FCDs) are to be issued, the interest rate can be freely determined by the issuer. Companies are required to create a Debenture Redemption Reserve (DRR) equivalent to 50% of the amount of debenture issue before debenture redemption commences. The cost of issuing capital, as of December 1992, was estimated at approximately 9-19% of the issue. This included fees for issue management, underwriting fees, stationary costs, advertisement and publicity costs, mailing costs, brokerage, etc. Companies have a variety of options which entail lower issue costs, such as GDR issues, private placement, and bought-out deals.

SEBI's intention of passing on some part of its responsibility to the lead managers is reflected in the new guidelines announced in May 1995.

The major decisions were:

- SEBI has decided to stop vetting of rights issues all together. The onus of this responsibility will now rest with Th. lead managers. The procedure for clearance would be that the merchant banker would have to file the offer document with SEBI six weeks prior to the proposed date of offer of rights issue. If SEBI does not ask for clarifications within 21 days from the date of filing, the company and the lead manager can proceed with the issue.

- SEBI revised the guidelines for reservation in public issues. As per the new guidelines which took effect from 1 June 1995, half of the net public offer should be reserved for small applicants, i.e. those applying for less than 1,000 shares/securities. The other half would be reserved for the corporate applicants.
- A committee comprising chiefs of senior executive directors of the five divisions of SEBI has been formed which will clear all public issues which are more than Rs. 1 billion. Formerly, all the issues were cleared by the primary markets division. Issues less than Rs. 200 million would be cleared by the division chiefs, those between Rs. 200 million and Rs. 500 million by the executive directors and those between Rs. 500 million and Rs. 1 billion by the senior executive director.

11

Public Sector in India

Public sector has played an important role in the industrial development of India. Before independence there were a few public sector enterprises in India such as Railways, the Posts and Telegraphs, the Port Trusts, the Ordinance Factories, and All India Radio etc. In the early years of independence, capital was scarce and the entrepreneurial resource was not strong enough.

Therefore, the 1956 Industrial Policy Resolution gave primacy to the role of the State which was directly responsible for industrial development. The public sector provided the required thrust to the economy and developed and nurtured the human resources. During this era public sector enterprises came to be known as the commanding heights of the Indian economy.

In 1991, when the government decided to shift to a liberalized economy with greater reliance upon market forces, a larger role for the private sector was envisaged. Since then the policy thrust has been on reforms such as reduction in the scope of industrial licensing, reforms in the Monopolies and Restrictive Trade Practices (MRTP) Act, reduction of areas reserved exclusively for public sector, disinvestment of equity of selected public sector enterprises (PSEs).

Central Public Sector Enterprises (CPSEs) were classified into two categories - strategic and non-strategic.

Strategic CPSEs were identified in the areas of:

- Arms & Ammunition and the allied items of defence equipments, defence air-crafts and warships
- Atomic Energy (except in the areas related to the

operation of nuclear power and applications of radiation and radio-isotopes to agriculture, medicine and non-strategic industries).

- *Railway transport*: All other public sector enterprises were considered as non-strategic. Industrial licensing by the Central Government has been almost abolished except for a few hazardous and environmentally sensitive industries.

List of industries reserved for the public sector and where private companies cannot enter

- Atomic energy.
- The substances specified in the scheduled to the notification of the Government of India in the Department of Atomic Energy number S.O.212(E), dated the 15th March, 1995.
- Railway transport.

There are certainly many factors that could drive foreign funding into hospitals in India. The most important driving factor is the demand-supply mismatch and the huge amount of private sector investment that is required in this sector to raise its infrastructure even marginally to meet international metrics.

With the growing economy, rising incomes, increased willingness among Indian consumers to pay for quality healthcare and to go to institutional providers, the comparably lower costs of establishment in India, and the healthcare packages offered by companies which are increasing affordability of healthcare for consumers, this is a potentially attractive sector for both foreign and domestic investors.

Also, with the prospects for setting up hospitals in Special Economic Zones and large-scale Medicities, there are opportunities for foreign investors to finance such projects. The growing presence of private healthcare in some developed countries also creates opportunities for foreign investment in the healthcare sector of developing countries such as India. However, there are external and domestic factors, which constrain foreign investment, especially foreign direct investment in India's hospital segment.

EXTERNAL FACTORS

One of the external factors, which was noted is that notwithstanding trends towards privatization in healthcare in major developed countries, this is a sector that is undergoing reform and internal problems in those economies. In many countries, the number of private players who can establish hospitals overseas is limited. Hence, the potential number of overseas institutions that can invest in emerging markets may be rather limited. A second factor that was commonly noted was that the hospital business requires localized and in-depth knowledge of the host country's market and thus entry as an independent overseas institution is very difficult. Joint ventures may be a better way of entering a foreign market when setting up hospitals. But there are problems in maintaining partnerships, as there are issues of financial control and differences in expectations and management styles.

A third fact is that foreign investors would consider many competing destinations and would tend to go to markets which they are more familiar with and where there is clarity about policies not only regarding FDI but also regarding the healthcare sector overall. As several respondents pointed out, the Indian government does not have a clear roadmap for the healthcare sector, has not considered it as a core sector, and is perceived to be non transparent in terms of its regulatory environment and corrupt and inefficient in its procedures for establishing business, all of which do deter foreign investors.

A quote from one foreign health sector expert sums up the perception of India as an investment destination. "Investors can have two roles. There are those who want to invest in physical infrastructure and others who see this as a profitable development opportunity and thus want certainty of returns. Thus minimization of risk and a regulatory environment that permits that is important. The regulatory environment must permit certainty of revenue flows to repay debt.

The obvious and immediate attractiveness of India is its population, its GDP growth, its expanding market ... The main factors that make India unattractive is the uncertainty of its regulatory environment, issues of income flow, license and red tape, difficulties in developing business, and corruption. Investing in service industries is different from that in production industries...There are two reasons why investors are waiting and watching. One is the lack of infrastructure and the second is the bureaucracy for setting up." The discussions suggested, however, that it is primarily domestic factors that are specific to the hospital business that have limited the extent of FDI in India's hospitals.

These include initial establishment related factors as well as post-establishment related operational issues, which affect the returns to investment. The single most important constraint is the high cost involved in setting up hospitals, the long gestation period of such investment, and the relatively low returns on investment. Several senior persons at leading corporate hospitals stated that hospitals are a very expensive business involving huge upfront very capital-intensive investments and very high running costs.

It takes some 4 to 5 years to break even and some 7 – 8 years to make reasonable profits, although depending on the model adopted and efficiencies, it may be possible to break even and make profits in a shorter period. One senior doctor noted that an estimated Rs. 50 lakhs is required per bed, which works out to Rs. 100 crores for a 200-bed hospital. If this cost could be reduced to even Rs. 40 lakhs per bed, then the break-even period could be quicker. In addition, rising operating costs (due to shortages and high procurement costs of certain inputs as discussed later) further squeeze margins.

Thus, investment in hospitals is characterized by low returns, high capital intensity, and long-term commitment. This is not the most attractive combination for foreign investors when also coupled with the various external factors discussed earlier. Several hospitals noted that profit rates are around 13 per cent, lower than that in other high growth sectors such as IT, finance, or retail. The financials for six selected hospitals, some of which have foreign funding, mainly through FII and equity sources. The key features of investment and returns in the hospital business and highlight some of the main factors, albeit interrelated, which affect this segment.

12

Privatization

PREAMBLE

The millennium offers a vantage point from which to reexamine the priorities of the Government of India (GOI). The new government and the opposition parties are united in their determination to increase the spending on human development and welfare in primary and secondary education and basic health care for all. The target is to increase the current spending which is at 1% of GDP to 6% of GDP over a period of five years. Simultaneously, GOI is interested in privatization of public sector to improve the efficiency and productivity of the Indian economy.

Subsidies for the public sector units is expected to rise significantly in the coming years. We believe that more than $100 billion can be raised (in potential market capitalization) over the next three years by a workable privatization initiative. We see the two goals — enabling investment in human capital and unlocking the value of past public sector investments — as two sides of the same coin. We suggest that GOI see the task as one of shifting priorities from owning, managing and subsidizing commercial ventures which mostly benefit the few to investments in human infrastructure that benefits all, especially the poor and the needy.

PRINCIPLES

We believe that a task of this magnitude cannot be managed without a clear framework of principles. Ad hoc, partial or expediency-driven actions will not do. The broad principles that should govern the privatization initiative. We believe that these principles address not only the economic but political and social issues arising out of privatization of the public sector in India.

- The goal of privatization should be improve the competitiveness of India's industrial infrastructure and enable it to become world class. Privatization should not be motivated only by our current account deficits.
- All commercial public sector units should be privatized over a five-year period. Speed is the essence. The longer we wait, the lower will be the market value of public sector assets in today's terms. Also quicker privatization will allow for faster investment in healthcare and education of the current generation.
- The social implications of privatization, namely, unemployment and the need for a social safety net must be dealt with openly and fairly. We should strive for a process of privatization that represents a "win-win" for all. To this end, current employees of public sector units should be allowed to share in the benefits of privatization. Further, part of the proceeds of privatization should be earmarked to provide for unemployment compensation, retraining, and reemployment of employees displaced by privatization. In particular, privatization can provide more prosperity and stability for employees whose human capital is currently locked up in over-manned and under-performing units with an uncertain future.
- There should be a nodal point for the privatization effort. Accountability must be fixed in one senior minister reporting to the Prime Minister. This minister should have the authority to expedite and approve all privatization efforts. Responsibility for the effort will be focused. The multiplicity of ministries and authorities currently involved should be disassociated with the initiative.

- In sectors that are natural monopolies or involve public safety, privatization will require some regulatory infrastructure. Independent regulatory authority is critical to regain the trust of the public, create transparency, and for the market to function effectively.
- Implementation should be decentralized. The Board of individual units should be responsible for implementation of privatization within the broad framework of principles laid down by the Privatization Ministry. If necessary, Boards of public sector units should be strengthened so that they are well equipped to perform this function.
- Government should choose the first set of public sector units for privatization using the following criteria:
  - Degree of demand for these assets (e.g. petroleum, hotels)
  - Influence that the efficient operation of this sector will have on the rest of the Indian economy (e.g. telecom, infrastructure)
  - Degree of capital intensity and size of investment required in this sector to be globally competitive (e.g. mines, shipping, steel)

The goal should be to attain early successes, rapidly improve the competitiveness of Indian industry (not jus the public sector) and accelerate resource realization.

- To make sure that employees will benefit from privatization, and also have the incentive to improve value so as to fetch the best price to the nation, all public sector units should be allowed to allocate up to 20% of the stock, free of charge, to the entire workforce as of a target date; say march 31st., 2000. All employees of record on that day should become co-owners of the company along with GOI.
- Once a unit is chosen for privatization, its Board should be expected to submit, to the Privatization Minister, within a period of 6 months, its plan to

restructure and revitalize the unit. Each unit should examine its portfolio to identify its core and non-core businesses, as well as the general approach to revitalizing the unit will be as follows:

- Identify the portfolio of businesses, products and services, which the Board and management feel can propel the company into an efficient operation that can sustain itself without any help from the GOI. Each unit must retain only the minimum complement of employees needed to make that unit very efficient. For this unit all subsidies in all forms will be cut off from the date of completion of its privatization.
- The Board should identify and group all surplus employees. Preferably, they will be housed in a different location. These employees should be provided a safety net of up to two years. Their current salaries and benefits should be protected for that period. During that time, they should be retrained and encouraged to seek other opportunities. They may choose to receive their benefits as a lump sum. Each unit should be encouraged to offer outplacement services. The private sector should be given tax incentives to retrain and employ displaced public sector workers.
- Non-core businesses may be offered as a Management Buyout option to its current managers and associates, or divested.
- The Board may seek any external assistance in determining their actions and timetable.

- A portion of the shares of the privatized firm, say 25%, will be available to the Indian investing public. Public participation, at the time of privatization, may be a way of allowing the upside to be widely shared.
- The Board should be free to form alliances, JVs or seek domestic and foreign investment subject to the current laws of the country. If a substantial stake is

to be sold to a strategic investor, earn out arrangements should be used to alleviate potential concerns regarding the sale price. Also, wherever possible, attempts should be made to establish a market price for shares before a strategic sale.

The Boards should be required to abide by governance procedures that protect the interests of minority shareholders.

- The Privatization Ministry should review all plans before they are put in motion. The Ministry will be supported, in its judgments, by a group of 12 eminent individuals who prescribe to the basic principles of privatization and fervently believe in making India a preeminent industrial power. The Ministry can take up to a maximum of two months to respond. If the Ministry does not raise any objections to proposals from the Board of the public sector unit, within this time period, the unit should have the authority to proceed with the proposal.
- These proposals must be seen as an integrated package. If the policy makers "pick and choose", the benefits of the privatization initiative will not be fully realised.
- We believe that our proposal addresses several important issues that stymied past privatization efforts in India.
- It clearly addresses the potential benefits of privatization to the Indian public - redirecting public investments to education and healthcare, and creating an economy that is concerned about creating efficiency and jobs. Such articulation is likely to increase public support for privatization.
- It addresses the concern of public sector employees. It makes them stakeholders in the privatization process, and it provides for a safety net for displaced workers.
- We recommend separating people from assets in the privatization process. This allows us to create a very efficient public sector enterprise, before it is

privatized, increasing its market capitalization significantly. All benefit from this process - GOI, current employees, and the Indian public. Secondly, we protect the interests of the employees - by protecting their wages for two years and retraining and out placing them.

- It deals with the potential concern that he sale prices may be too low in two ways. First, we require 25% of the shares to be sold to the Indian public, so that they benefit from subsequent price appreciation if the share price at sale is too low. Second, we recommend earn-out provisions that will help GOI receive a portion of the post sale profits.
- Our proposal recommends centralized supervision and decentralized implementation. As a result, we think that the privatization process is likely to be quick and transparent. It is also, likely to encourage experimentation and learning.
- Because our proposal is geared towards increasing the efficiency of the current public sector units, rather than as a mere fiscal exercise in bridging the budget gap, it will reduce the overall cost of doing business in India and increase the competitiveness of the Indian industry as a whole. Therefore, our proposal is likely to get the support of the private sector as well.
- Since the proposal focuses on the creation of an efficient and profitable industrial sector, rather than merely balancing the budget, it creates a favourable climate for foreign investment. The long- term effects of this process go beyond the benefits of privatization.

13

Joint Sector and Cooperative Sector in India

Adoption of planning in India led to a variety of initiatives by the state to promote and regulate industrialisation. For this, the overall framework was provided by the Five Year Plans. The essence of planning, while comprising of enlarged investments, is in achieving new pattern of investments. The pattern of resource allocation under a planned process, in contrast to market oriented economies, is governed by long term and a variety of socio-economic concerns and not by the market demand.

The process of planning implies determination of a set of relative priorities and ensuring effective and timely implementation of plan targets. To translate the plan objectives the policies and programmes can broadly be categorised under three heads, namely, (i) Regulatory; (ii) Promotional; and (iii) Direct participation.

The regulatory systems are by their very nature restrictive, but the nature and degree of restrictions vary from one regulatory policy to another. Regulatory mechanisms provide a positive support to the desired activities by warding off the undesired. Reservation policies, similarly, seek to place a premium on some; in effect placing the non-qualifying at a relative disadvantage. The regulatory mechanisms, however, cannot generate investments on the desirable lines.

It may be possible to restrict one type of economic activity but this does not follow that the activities of the desired types would start taking place on their own. There would, therefore, be a justification, along with regulations, for evolving of promotional and support mechanisms in the processes of planned socio-economic development. The wide network of financial, technical and developmental institutions whose primary task is to finance easy and cheap credit can rightly be categorised as promotional. The same holds true of fiscal and monetary concessions and agencies which provide risk capital to new ventures or render technical guidance and assistance to new entrepreneurs.

The third category of state action for promotion of overall industrialisation in a plan framework would be in the activities undertaken by way of direct participation in economic activity by the state. This may be in the form of creating new economic infrastructure (transport, power, banking) or in the form of state enterprises. This is irrespective of the fact whether the enterprises are established as commercial establishments or not. Of the three types of state interventions in the economy a good deal of work has been done to examine the functioning and efficacy of different regulatory mechanisms. The state regulatory mechanisms in India have come under frequent reviews for various reasons. The ones who are deprived can only be expected to react and plead for abolition of these systems. By their very character criticism of regulatory mechanisms should be a predictable phenomenon. The shortcomings of the system would be highlighted by those who fail to enjoy the preferences they expected from the regulatory policies and mechanisms.

The Hazari Report, Industrial Licensing Policy Inquiry Committee (ILPIC) Report, Memoranda submitted to Government by the Federation of Indian Chambers of Commerce and Industry (FICCI) and a number of other individual studies on the functioning of industrial licensing system in India are an indicator of the scrutiny that the industrial regulatory mechanisms have received over the past three decades Similarly, the third type of state activity, that is, direct state intervention in economic activities, attracts considerable public attention and scrutiny that goes with public accountability. There are a multiple of institutions which continue to monitor and evaluate the functioning of activities undertaken directly by the state. The Bureau of Public Enterprises (BPE), Parliamentary Committee on Public Undertakings (COPU), and the Comptroller and Auditor General of India (C&AG), are engaged in annual reviews on the working of Public Enterprises. There is, however, one category of policies and programmes which gets very little attention; the category is that of 'promotional' activities.

While we have drawn a distinction between regulatory, promotional and direct intervention it is true that the distinctions are not always easily discernable in many concrete situations. For instance, the difference between direct participation and promotional policies can be a thin one. To emphasise, one would find it difficult to say if the fact of having a substantial share in the risk capital in a private sector company should be equated with direct participation with regulatory motive or undertaken as a promotional measure. It is well known that public sector financial institutions hold a substantial share in the risk capital of the Indian corporate sector in general and the large private corporations, in particular.

The present situation has emerged out of three types of independent developments. *One,* due to nationalisation of insurance and large private commercial banks the public sector institutions have emerged as important share holders. *Two,* the public sector financial institutions had to take up the 'left overs' due to the underwriting activity of the public issues floated by the private sector companies. Also, the financial institutions had to acquire shares in the open market not only for earning higher returns but also to bail out some of the private enterprises and to ensure the stability of the stock market.

Three, in a few cases loans provided to private sector companies were converted into equity as per the initial understanding. And *four,* public sector institutions acquired significant shares to provide security to new investments. The last category is a follow-up of the policies to promote joint enterprises where in public sector and a private entrepreneur set up a new enterprise and the risk capital is so shared as to have almost equal stake of both. One does not need to dwell on the fact that geographic spread of industries in India is not a balanced or a logical one. There are States with rich resource endowment to support high level of manufacturing and other commercial activities; but due to historical and other reasons these States have not witnessed the emergence of new entrepreneurial class.

The consequence is the absence of the process of industrialisation. In some cases public interest demands new investments but there are no private takers. There are also situations when it appears more logical to have public ownership but leave the actual operation of activities to some private managements. Such situations provide a rationale for 'joint sector', in addition to the cooperative, private and public sectors.

JOINT SECTOR: THE CONCEPT

The concept of joint sector wherein Government and private entrepreneurs join hands to establish new enterprises is indeed an old one. It was quite normal for many of the erstwhile princely States (the state of Baroda, Travancore & Cochin and Hyderabad to name only a few) to share risk capital in large industrial projects. At the international level, however, positive contribution by the Japanese Government in promoting new commercial enterprises is only too well known.

Even prior to India's political independence it was a widely shared view that the state in the independent India would have to play an active role in providing financial and other support to new and small entrepreneurs. The need for the establishment of Industrial Finance Corporation to promote and assist new enterprises was underlined by the National Planning Committee as also by the Economic Programmes Committee, both under the Chairmanship of Jawahar Lal Nehru — the first Prime Minister of India. The World Bank Team which visited India in 1954 recommended that India needed financial institutions which can promote as also provide initial risk capital to those who have no support of the already well established business families. While the Industrial Finance Corporation of India (IFCI) was established by the Government in 1948, the recommendations of the World Bank team led to establishment of the Industrial Credit and Investment Corporation of India (ICICI) in 1955.

LATER IN 1964 INDUSTRIAL DEVELOPMENT

Bank of India (IDBI) was established. In addition to these, India has three major public sector investment bodies, namely, (a) the Life Insurance Corporation of India (LIC); (b) the General Insurance Corporation of India (GIC); and (c) the Unit Trust of India (UTI). Besides these, there is Industrial Reconstruction Corporation of India (IRCI) which provides term finance to rehabilitate sick industrial units. In the early 'fifties it was also realised that in view of the large size of the country the task of promoting new and small entrepreneurs could not be left to a few national level institutions. Thus, State Financial Corporations Act was enacted in 1952 to "assist smaller industries in different provinces".

As a consequence of this legislation there are by now (i.e. the year 1986) 18 State Financial Corporations (SFCs) and 25 State Industrial Development Corporations (SIDCs). The functions of these institutions are wide ranging in nature, covering different aspects of promotional and developmental activities in addition to advancing of term loans and financing of industrial projects. The State Financial Corporations (SFCs), were basically visualised to extend assistance to small and medium level industries. The SIDCs were expected to provide assistance by conducting techno-economic surveys, identification of projects, selection and training of entrepreneurs, development of backward areas, constructing industrial sheds, providing infrastructural facilities and directly participating in the share capital of new enterprises.

The State Industrial Development Corporations (SIDCs) and State Industrial Investment Corporations (SIICs) have come to occupy an important place in most of the States of India. There are, however, variations in the nature and size of their operations. The SIDCs, generally speaking, obtain Letters of Intent/Industrial Licenses for setting up industries in the fields where there is scope for development and in particular where private risk capital is not easily forthcoming for establishment of new industries. After obtaining the necessary permission/licence from the Government of India, the SIDCs identify private parties which could implement the industrial projects in the form of 'joint sector' enterprises (JSEs).

THE JOINT SECTOR ENTERPRISES IN INDIA

The main thrust to the joint sector came during the post-1970 period. Prior to India's independence a number of Joint Enterprises were established by a few erstwhile Princely States. Air India International provides another notable example. The company was established by the Tatas in 1948. The Government of India provided 49 per cent share in its equity. The Government subsequently acquired an additional 2 per cent equity from the Tata Sons Ltd to convert it into a government company. In spite of the government holding 51 per cent of the equity the Air India continued to be under the management of the Tatas until it was fully taken over by the Government of India in 1953.

There were twelve other undertakings in 1966-67, in which the Central Government had a substantial stake in equity capital without having direct managerial control. In a few cases equity participation by foreign enterprises in the public sector enterprises was also allowed. Madras Fertilizers Ltd. for example, was established as a joint enterprise in participation with Amoco Inc. (USA) and National Iranian Oil Co.(Iran). The same foreign companies were partners in Madras Refineries Ltd too.

Cochin Refineries Ltd. was established with the participation of the Phillips Petroleum Co. (USA) and Duncan Brothers Ltd.; Lubrizol India Ltd.; with the Lubrizol Corporation (USA); and Triveni Structurals Ltd., with Voest Alpine (Austria). Maruti Udyog Ltd., is one of the latest cases where a foreign private corporation has been invited to join hands with the Government. A feature of all the above cases appears to be that public sector holdings are of majority nature and these are managed by Government nominated boards. The Industrial Policy Resolution (IPR) of 1956 had classified industries into three main categories, depending on the role that the state was to play in each industry;

- The industries, the future development of which will be the exclusive responsibility of the state are referred to as Schedule-A industries.
- The industries which will be progressively state-owned and in which the state will generally take the initiative in establishing new undertakings and wherein private enterprise will be expected to supplement the efforts of the state in developing these industries are specified in Schedule - B.
- The non-scheduled Industries are left to the initiative and enterprise of the private sector. The IPR, 1956 envisaged that the state would help the private sector in fulfilling the role assigned to it within the planning framework and the industrial policy in force from time to time. In doing so, the state will continue to foster institutions to provide financial aid to these industries, and special assistance will be given to enterprises organised on co-operative lines for industrial and agricultural purposes.

In suitable cases, the State may also grant assistance to the private sector. Such assistance, especially when the amount involved is substantial, will preferably be in the form of participation in equity capital, though it may also be in part in the form of debenture capital.

14

Social Environment

THE CONSUMER PROTECTION ACT, 1986

An Act to provide for better protection of the interests of consumers and for that purpose to make provision for the establishment of consumer councils and other authorities for the settlement of consum-ers' disputes and for matters connected therewith.

BE it enacted by Parliament in the Thirty-seventh Year of the Republic of India as follows:

- Short title, extent, commencement and application.
  - This Act may be called the Consumer Protection Act, 1986.
  - It extends to the whole of India except the State of J ammu and Kashmir.
  - It shall come into force on such date as the Central Government may, by notification, appoint and different dates may be appointed for different States and for different provisions of this Act.
  - Save as otherwise expressly provided by the Central Government by notification, this Act shall apply to all goods and services.
- *Definitions*: (1) In this Act, unless the context otherwise requires:
  - "Appropriate laboratory" means a laboratory or organisation.
    - (a) Recognised by the Central Government;
    - (b) Recognised by a State Government, subject to

such guide-lines as may be prescribed by the Central Government in this behalf; or

(c) Any such laboratory or organisation established by or under any law for the time being in force, which is maintained, financed or aided by the Central Government or a State Government for carrying out analysis or test of any goods with a view to determining whether such goods suffer from any defect;

– "Branch office" means

(a) Any establishment described as a branch by the opposite party; or

(b) Any establishment carrying on either the same or substan-tially the same activity as that carried on by the head office of the establishment;

– "Complainant" means:

(a) A consumer; or

(b) Any voluntary consumer association registered under the Companies Act, 1956 (1of 1956)or under any other law for the time being in force; or

(c) The Central Government or any State Government,

(d) One or more consumers, where there are numerous consum-ers having the same interest;

(e) In case of death of a consumer, his legal heir or representative; who or which makes a complaint;

– "Coalaint" means any allegation in writing made by a complain-ant that

(a) An unfair trade practice or a restrictive trade practice has been adopted by any trader or service provider;

(b) The goods bought by him or agreed to be bought by him; suffer from one or more defects;

(c) The services hired or availed of or agreed to be hired or availed of by him suffer from deficiency in any respect;

(d) A trader or service provider, as the case may be, has charged for the goods or for the service mentioned in the com-plaint a price in excess of the price:

(i) Fdreed between the parties;

(ii) Displayed on the goods or any package containing such goods ;

(iii) Displayed on the price list exhibited by him by or under any law for the time being in force;

(iv) Agreed between the parties;

– Goods which will be hazardous to life and safety when used or being offered for sale to the public:

(a) In contravention of any standards relating to safety of such goods as required to be complied with, by or under any law for the time being in force;

(b) If the trader could have known with due diligence that the goods so offered are unsafe to the public;

– Services which are hazardous or likely to be hazardous to life and safety of the public when used, are being offered by the service provider which such person could have known with due diligence to be injurious to life and safety;";

(c) "Consumer" means any person who:

– Buys any goods for a consideration which has been paid or promised or partly paid and partly promised, or under any system of deferred payment and includes any user of such goods other than the person who buys such goods for consideration paid or promised or partly paid or partly promised, or under any system of deferred payment when such use is made with the approval of such person, but does not include a person who obtains such goods for resale or for any commercial purpose; or

- Hires or avails of any services for a consideration which has been paid or promised or partly paid and partly prom-ised, or under any system of deferred payment and includes any beneficiary of such services other than the person who 'hires or avails of the services for consideration paid or promised, or partly paid and partly promised, or under any system of deferred payment, when such services are availed of with the approval of the first mentioned person *but does not include a person who avails of such services for any commercial purposes;*

Explanation: For the purposes of this clause, "commercial purpose" does not include use by a person of goods bought and used by him and services availed by him exclusively for the purposes of earning his livelihood by means of self-employment;

- "Consumer dispute" means a dispute where the person against whom a complaint has been made, denies or disputes the allega-tions contained in the complaint.
- "Defect" means any fault, imperfection or shortcoming in the quality, quantity, potency, purity or standard which is required to be maintained by or under any law for the time being in force under any contract, express or implied or as is claimed by the trader in any manner whatsoever in relation to any goods;
- "Deficiency" means any fault, imperfection, shortcoming or inade-quacy in the quality, nature and manner of performance which is required to be maintained by or under any law for the time being in force or has been undertaken to be performed by a person in pursuance of a contract or otherwise in relation to any service;
- "District Forum" means a Consumer Disputes

Redressal Forum established under clause (a) of section 9;

- "Goods" means goods as defined in the Sale of Goods Act, 1930 (3 of 1930);
- "Manufacturer" means a person who
  - (a) Makes or manufactures any goods or part thereof;
  - (b) Does not make or manufacture any goods but assembles parts thereof made or manufactured by others; or
  - (c) Puts or causes to be put his own mark on any goods made or manufactured by any other manufacturer;

Explanation: Where a manufacturer dispatches any goods or part thereof to any branch office maintained by him, such branch office shall not be deemed to be the manufacturer even though the parts so dispatched to it are assembled at such branch office and are sold or distributed from such branch office;

- "Member" includes the President and a member of the National Commission or a State Commission or a District Forum, as the case may be;
- "National Commission" means the National Consumer Disputes Redressal Commission established under clause (c) of section 9;
- "Notification" means a notification published in the Official Gazette;
- "Person" includes,—
  - (a) A firm whether registered or not;
  - (b) A Hindu undivided family;
  - (c) A co-operative society;
  - (d) Every other association of persons whether registered under the Societies Registration Act, 1860 (21 of 1860) or not;
- "Prescribed" means prescribed by rules made by the State Gov-ernment, or as the case may be, by the Central Government under this Act;

- "Regulation" means the regulations made by the National Commission under this Act;
- "Restrictive trade practice" means a trade practice which tends to bring about manipulation of price or conditions of delivery or to affect flow of supplies in the market relating to goods or services in such a manner as to impose on the consumers unjustified costs or restrictions and shall include
  - (a) The period agreed to by a trader in supply of such goods or in providing the services which has led or is likely to lead to rise in the price;
  - (b) Any trade practice which requires a consumer to buy, hire or avail of any goods or, as the case may be, services as condition precedent to buying, hiring or availing of other goods or services;
- "Service" means service of any description which is made avail-able to potential users and includes, but not limited to, the provision of facilities in connection with banking, financing insurance, transport, processing, supply of electrical or other energy, board or lodging or both, housing construction, entertainment, amusement or the purveying of news or other information, but does not include the rendering of any service free of charge or under a contract of personal service;
- "Spurious goods and services" mean such goods and services which are claimed to be genuine but they are actually not so;
- "State Commission" means a Consumer Disputes Redressal Commission established in
  - (a) State under clause
  - (b) Of section 9;
- "Trader" in relation to any goods means a person who sells or distributes any goods for sale and includes the manufacturer thereof, and where

such goods are sold or distributed in package form, includes the packer thereof;

- "Unfair trade practice" means a trade practice which, for the purpose of promoting the sale, use or supply of any goods or for the provision of any service, adopts any unfair method or unfair or deceptive practice including any of the following practices, namely:

- The practice of making any statement, whether orally or in writing or by visible repre-sentation which:
  - Falsely represents that the goods are of a particular standard, quality, quantity, grade, composition, style or model.
  - Falsely represents that the services are of a particular standard, quality or grade.
  - Falsely represents any re-built, second-hand, reno-vated, reconditioned or old goods as new goods.
  - Represents that the goods or services have sponsor-ship, approval, performance, characteri-stics, accesso-ries, uses or benefits which such goods or services do not have.
  - Represents that the seller or the supplier has a spon-sorship or approval or affiliation which such seller or supplier does not have.
  - Makes a false or misleading representation concern-ing the need for, or the usefulness of, any goods or services.
  - Gives to the public any warranty or guarantee of the performance, efficacy or length of life of a product or of any goods that is not based on an adequate or proper test thereof.

    Provided that where a defence is raised to the effect that such warranty or guarantee is based on adequate or proper test, the burden of proof of such defence shall lie on the person raising such defence.
  - *Makes to the public a representation in a form that purports to be:*

(a) A warranty or guarantee of a product or of any goods or services.

(b) A promise to replace, maintain or repair an article or any part thereof or to repeat or continue a service until it has achieved a specified result, if such purported warranty or guarantee or prom-ise is materially misleading or if there is no reasonable prospect that such warranty, guaran-tee or promise will be carried out.

– Materially misleads the public concerning the price at which a product or like products or goods or services, have been or are, ordinarily sold or provided, and, for this purpose, a representation as to price shall be deemed to refer to the price at which the product or goods or services has or have been sold by sellers or provided by suppliers generally in the relevant market unless it is clearly specified to be the price at which the product has been sold or services have been provided by the person by whom or on whose behalf the representation is made.

– Gives false or misleading facts disparaging the goods, services or trade of another person.

Explanation: For the purposes of clause.

1. *A statement that is:*

- Expressed on an article offered or displayed for sale, or on its wrapper or container.
- Expressed on anything attached to, inserted in, or accompanying, an article offered or displayed for sale, or on anything on which the article is mounted for display or sale.
- Contained in or on anything that is sold, sent, delivered, transmit-ted or in any other manner whatsoever made available to a member of the public, shall be deemed to be a statement made to the public by, and only by, the person who

had caused the statement to be so expressed, made or contained.

2. Permits the publication of any advertisement whether in any news-paper or otherwise, for the sale or supply at a bargain price, of goods or services that are not intended to be offered for sale or supply at the bargain price, or for a period that is, and in quantities that are, reasonable, having regard to the nature of the market in which the business is carried on, the nature and size of business, and the nature of the advertisement.

Explanation: For the purpose of clause.

2. *"Bargaining price" means*:
   - A price that is stated in any advertisement to be a bargain price, by reference to an ordinary price or otherwise.
   - A price that a person who reads, hears or sees the advertisement, would reasonably understand to be a bargain price having regard to the prices at which the product advertised or like products are ordinarily sold.
3. *Permits*:
   - The offering of gifts, prizes or other items with the intention of not providing them as offered or creating impression that something is being given or offered free of charge when it is fully or partly covered by the amount charged in the transaction as a whole.
   - The conduct of any contest, lottery, game of chance or skill, for the purpose of promoting, directly or indirectly, the sale, use or supply of any product or any business interest.
     (a) Withholding from the participants of any plan offering gifts, prizes or other items free of charge, on its closure the information about final results of the plan.

Explanation: For the purposes of this sub-clause, the participants of a plan shall be deemed to have been informed of the final results of the plan where such results are within a reasonable time, published, prominently in the same newspapers in which the plan was originally advertised.

- Permits the sale or supply of goods intended to be used, or are of a kind likely to be used, by consumers, knowing or having reason to believe that the goods do not comply with the standards prescribed by competent authority relating to performance, composition, contents, design, constructions, finishing or packaging as are necessary to prevent or reduce the risk of injury to the person using the goods.
- Permits the hoarding or destruction of goods, or refuses to sell the goods or to make them available for sale or to provide any service, if such hoarding or destruction or refusal raises or tends to raise or is intended to raise, the cost of those or other similar goods or services.
- Manufacture of spurious goods or offering such goods for sale or adopts deceptive practices in the provision of services.
- Any reference in this Act to any other Act or provision thereof which is not in force in any area to which this Act applies shall be construed to have a reference to the corresponding Act or provision thereof in force in such area.
- Act not in derogation of any other law.—The provisions of this Act shall be in addition to and not in derogation of the provisions of any other law for the time being in force.

CONSUMER PROTECTION COUNCILS

4. The Central Consumer Protection Council.—(1) The Central Government *shall*, by notification, establish with effect from such date as it may specify in such notification, a Council to be known as the Central Consumer Protection Council (hereinafter referred to

as the Central Council). (2) The Central Council shall consist of the following members, namely: (a) the Minister in charge of the consumer affairs in the Central Government, who shall be its Chairman, and (b) such number of other official or non-official members represent-ing such interests as may be prescribed.

5. Procedure for meetings of the Central Council.—(1) The Central Council shall meet as and when necessary, but at least one meeting of the Council shall be held every year. (2)The Central Council shall meet at such time and place as the Chairman may think fit and shall observe such procedure in regard to the transaction of its business as may be prescribed.
6. *Objects of the Central Council*: The objects of the Central Council shall be to promote and protect the rights of the consumers such as:
   - The right to be protected against the marketing of goods and services which are hazardous to life and property;
   - The right to be informed about the quality, quantity, potency, purity, standard and price of goods or services, as the case may be so as to protect the consumer against unfair trade practices;
   - The right to be assured, wherever possible, access to a variety of goods and services at competitive prices;
   - The right to be heard and to be assured that consumer's interests will receive due consideration at appropriate forums;
   - The right to seek redressal against unfair trade practices or restrictive trade practices or unscrupulous exploitation of con-sumers; and
   - The right to consumer education.
7. The State Consumer Protection Councils: (1) The State Government shall, by notification, establish with

effect from such date as it may specify in such notification, a Council to be known as the Consumer Protection Council for..................... (hereinafter referred to as the State Council). (2) The State Council shall consist of the following members, namely:

- The Minister incharge of consumer affairs in the State Government who shall be its Chairman;
- Such number of other official or non-official members representing such interests as may be prescribed by the State Government.
- Such number of other official or non-official members, not exceeding ten, as may be nominated by the Central Government. (3) The State Council shall meet as and when necessary but not less than two meetings shall be held every year. (4) The State Council shall meet at such time and place as the Chairman may think fit and shall observe such procedure in regard to the transaction of its business as may be prescribed by the State Government.

8. Objects of the State Council. — The objects of every State Council shall be to promote and protect within the State the rights of the consumers laid down in clauses (a) to (f) of section 6.

8a. (1) The State Government shall establish for every district, by notification, a council to be known as the District Consumer Protection Council with effect from such date as it may specify in such notification. (2) The District Consumer Protection Council (hereinafter referred to as the District Council) shall consist of the following members, namely: (a) the Collector of the district (by whatever name called), who shall be its Chairman; and (b) such number of other official and non-official members representing such interests as may be prescribed by the State Government. (3) The District Council shall meet as and when necessary but not less than two meetings shall be held every year. (4) The District Council shall meet at such time and place within the district as the Chairman may think fit and shall observe such procedure in regard to the transaction of its business as may be prescribed by the State Government.

8b. The objects of every District Council shall be to promote and protect within the district the rights of the consumers laid down in clauses (a) to (f) of section 6.

CONSUMER DISPUTES REDRESSAL AGENCIES

9. Establishment of Consumer Disputes Redressal Agencies. There shall be established for the purposes of this Act, the following agencies, namely:
   (a) A Consumer Disputes Redressal Forum to be known as the "District Forum" established by the State Government in each district of the State by notification:
   Provided that the State Government may, if it deems fit, establish more than one District Forum in a district.
   (b) A Consumer Disputes Redressal Commission to be known as the "State Commission" established by the State Government in the State by notification; and
   (c) A National Consumer Disputes Redressal Commission established by the Central Government by notification.
10. Composition of the District Forum. (1) Each District Forum shall consist of,
   (a) A person who is, or has been, or is qualified to be a District Judge, who shall be its President;
   (b) Two other members, one of whom shall be a woman, who shall have the following qualifications, namely:
   (i) Be not less than thirty-five years of age,

(ii) Possess a bachelor's degree from a recognised university,

(iii) Be persons of ability, integrity and standing, and have adequate knowledge and experience of at least ten years in dealing with problems relating to economics, law, commerce, accountancy, industry, public affairs or administration:

Provided that a person shall be disqualified for appointment as a member if he:

- Has been convicted and sentenced to imprisonment for an offence which, in the opinion of the state Government involves moral turpitude; or
- Is an undischarged insolvent; or
- Is of unsound mind and stands so declared by a competent court; or
- Has been removed or dismissed from the service of the Government or a body corporate owned or controlled by the Government; or
- Has, in the opinion of the state Government, such financial or other interest as is likely to affect prejudicially the discharge by him of his functions as a member; or
- Has such other disqualifications as may be prescribed by the State Government; (1A) Every appointment under sub-section (I) shall be made by the State Government on the recommendation of a selection committee consisting of the following, namely:
  (a) The President of the State Commission – Chairman.
  (b) Secretary, Law Department of the State – Member.
  (c) Secretary incharge of the Department dealing with consumer affairs in the State – Member.

Provided that where the President of the State Commission is, by reason of absence or otherwise, unable to act as Chairman of the Selection Committee, the State Government may refer the matter to the Chief Justice of the

High Court for nominating a sitting Judge of that High Court to act as Chairman. (2) Every member of the District Forum shall hold office for a term of five years or up to the age of sixty-five years, whichever is earlier: Provided that a member shall be eligible for re-appointment for another term of five years or up to the age of sixty-five years, whichever is earlier, subject to the condition that he fulfills the qualifications and other conditions for appointment mentioned in clause (b) of sub-section (1) and such re-appointment is also made on the basis of the recommendation of the Selection Committee:

Provided further that a member may resign his office in writing under his hand addressed to the State Government and on such resignation being accepted, his office shall become vacant and may be filled by appointment of a person possessing any of the qualifications mentioned in sub-section (1) in relation to the category of the member who is required to be appointed under the provisions of sub-section (1A) in place of the person who has resigned:

Provided also that a person appointed as the President or as a member, before the commencement of the Consumer Protection (Amendment) Act, 2002, shall continue to hold such office as President or member, as the case may be, till the completion of his term. (3) The salary or honourarium and other allowances payable to, and the other terms and conditions of service of the members of the District Forum shall be such as may be prescribed by the State Government.

Provided that the appointment of a member on whole-time basis shall be made by the State Government on the recommendation of the President of the State Commission taking into consideration such factors as may be prescribed including the work load of the District Forum.

11. Jurisdiction of the District Forum.—(1) Subject to the other provisions of this Act, the District Forum shall have jurisdiction to entertain complaints where the value of the goods or services and the compensation, if any, claimed "does not exceed rupees twenty lakhs. (2) A complaint shall be instituted in a District Forum within the local limits of whose jurisdiction,—

(a) The opposite party or each of the opposite parties, where there are more than one, at the time of the institution of the complaint, actually and voluntarily resides or carries on business or has a branch office or personally works for gain, or

(b) Any of the opposite parties, where there are more than one, at the time of the institution of the complaint, actually and voluntarily resides, or carries on business or has a branch office, or personally works for gain, provided that in such case either the permission of the District Forum is given, or the opposite parties who do not reside, or carry on business or have a branch office, or personally work for gain, as the case may be, acquiesce in such institution; or

(c) The cause of action, wholly or in part, arises.

12. Manner in which complaint shall be made.—(1) A complaint in relation to any goods sold or delivered or agreed to be sold or delivered or any service provided or agreed to be provided may be filed with a District Forum by:

(*a*) The consumer to whom such goods are sold or delivered or agreed to be sold or delivered or such service provided or agreed to be provided;

(b) Any recognised consumer association whether the consumer to whom the goods sold or delivered or agreed to be sold or delivered or service provided or agreed to be provided is a member of such association or not;

(c) One or more consumers, where there are numerous consumers having the same interest, with the permission of the District Forum, on behalf of, or for the benefit of, all consumers so interested; or

(d) The Central Government or the State Government, as the case may be, either in its individual capacity or as a representative of interests of the consumers in general.

(2) Every complaint filed under sub-section (1) shall be accompanied with such amount of fee and payable in such manner as may be prescribed. (3) On receipt of a complaint made under sub-section (1), the District Forum may, by order, allow the complaint to be proceeded with or rejected: Provided that a complaint shall not be rejected under this section unless an opportunity of being heard has been given to the complainant: Provided further that the admissibility of the complaint shall ordinarily be decided within twenty-one days from the date on which the complaint was received. (4) Where a complaint is allowed to be proceeded with under sub-section (3), the District Forum may proceed with the complaint in the manner provided under this Act: Provided that where a complaint has been admitted by the District Forum, it shall not be transferred to any other court or tribunal or any authority set up by or under any other law for the time being in force. Explanation. - For the purpose of this section "recognised consumer association" means any voluntary consumer association registered under the Companies Act, 1956 or any other law for the time being in force".

13. Procedure on admission of complaint. — (1) The District Forum shall, on admission of a complaint, if it relates to any goods:

(a) Refer a copy of the admitted complaint, within twenty-one days from the date of its admission to the opposite party mentioned in the complaint directing him to give his version of the case within a period of thirty days or such extended period not exceeding fifteen days as may be granted by the District Forum;

(b) Where the opposite party on receipt of a complaint referred to him under clause *(a)* denies or disputes the allegations contained in the complaint, or omits or fails to take any action to represent his case within the time given by the District Forum, the District Forum shall proceed to settle the consumer dispute in the manner specified in clauses (c) to (g);

(c) Where the complaint alleges a defect in the goods

which cannot be determined without proper analysis or test of the goods, the District Forum shall obtain a sample of the goods from the complainant, seal it and authenticate it in the manner prescribed and refer the sample so sealed to the appropriate laboratory along with a direction that such laboratory make an analysis or test, whichever may be necessary, with a view to finding out whether such goods suffer from any defect alleged in the complaint or from any other defect and to report its findings thereon to the District Forum within a period of forty-five days of the receipt of the reference or within such extended period as may be granted by the District Forum;

(d) Before any sample of the goods is referred to any appropriate laboratory under clause (c), the District Forum may require the complainant to deposit to the credit of the Forum such fees as may be specified, for payment to the appropriate laboratory for carrying out the necessary analysis or test in relation to the goods in question;

(e) The District Forum shall remit the amount deposited to its credit under clause (d) to the appropriate laboratory to enable it to carry out the analysis or test mentioned in clause (c) and on receipt of the report from the appropriate laboratory, the District Forum shall forward a copy of the report along with such remarks as the District Forum may feel appropriate to the opposite party;

(f) If any of the parties disputes the correctness of the findings of the appropriate laboratory, or disputes the correctness of the meth-ods of analysis or test adopted by the appropriate laboratory, the District Forum shall require the opposite party or the complain-ant to submit in writing his objections in regard to the report made by the appropriate laboratory;

(g) The District Forum shall thereafter give a reasonable

opportunity to the complainant as well as the opposite party of being heard as to the correctness or otherwise of the report made by the appro-priate laboratory and also as to the objection made in relation thereto under clause (*l*) and issue an appropriate order under section 14. (2) The District Forum shall, if the complaint admitted by it under section 12 relates to goods in respect of which the procedure specified in sub-section (1) cannot be followed, or if the complaint relates to any services,

(a) Refer a copy of such complaint to the opposite party directing him to give his version of the case within a period of thirty days or such extended period not exceeding fifteen days as may be granted by the District Forum;

(b) Where the opposite party, on receipt of a copy of the complaint, referred to him under clause *(a)* denies or disputes the allegations contained in the complaint, or omits or fails to take any action to represent his case within the time given by the District Forum, the District Forum shall proceed to settle the consumer dispute,—

(i) On the basis of evidence brought to its notice by the complainant and the opposite party, where the opposite party denies or disputes the allegations contained in the complaint, or

(ii) Ex parle on the basis of evidence brought to its notice by the complainant where the opposite party omits or fails to take any action to represent his case within the time given by the Forum.

(c) where the complainant fails to appear on the date of hearing before the District Forum, the District Forum may either dismiss the complaint for default or decide it on merits.

(3) No proceedings complying with the procedure laid down in sub-sections [1] and [2] shall be called in question in any court on the ground that the

principles of natural justice have not been complied with. (3A)Every complaint shall be heard as expeditiously as possible and endeavour shall be made to decide the complaint within a period of three months from the date of receipt of notice by opposite party where the complaint does not require analysis or testing of commodities and within five months if it requires analysis or testing of commodities:

Provided that no adjournment shall be ordinarily granted by the District Forum unless sufficient cause is shown and the reasons for grant of adjournment have been recorded in writing by the Forum: Provided further that the District Forum shall make such orders as to the costs occasioned by the adjournment as may be provided in the regulations made under this Act.

Provided also that in the event of a complaint being disposed of after the period so specified, the District Forum shall record in writing, the reasons for the same at the time of disposing of the said complaint. (3B) Where during the pendency of any proceeding before the District Forum, it appears to it necessary, it may pass such interim order as is just and proper in the facts and circumstances of the case. (4) For the purposes of this section, the District Forum shall have the same powers as are vested in a civil court under Code of Civil Procedure, 1908 while trying a suit in respect of the following matters, namely:

(i) The summoning and enforcing the attendance of any defendant or witness and examining the witness on oath;
(ii) The discovery and production of any document or other material object producible as evidence;
(iii) The reception of evidence on affidavits;
(iv) The requisitioning of the report of the concerned analysis or test from the appropriate laboratory or from any other relevant source;
(v) Issuing of any commission for the examination of any witness.
(vi) Any other matter which may be prescribed.

(5) Every proceeding before the District Forum shall be deemed to be a judicial proceeding within the meaning of sections 193 and 228 of the Indian Code (45 of 1860), and the District Forum shall be deemed to be a civil court for the purposes of section 195, and Chapter XXVI of the Code of Criminal Procedure, 1973 (2 of 1974). (6) Where the complainant is a consumer referred to in sub-clause (iv) of clause (b) of sub-section (1) of section 2, the provisions of rule 8 of Order I of the First Schedule to the Code of Civil Procedure, 1908 (5 of 1908) shall apply subject to the modification that every reference therein to a suit or decree shall be construed as a reference to a complaint or the order of the District Forum thereon. (7) In the event of death of a complainant who is a consumer or of the opposite party against whom the complaint has been filed, the provisions of Order XXII of the First Schedule to the Code of Civil Procedure, 1908 (5 of 1908) shall apply subject to the modification that every reference therein to the plaintiff and the defendant shall be construed as reference to a complainant or the opposite party, as the case may be.

14. *Finding of the District Forum*: (1) If, after the proceeding conducted under section 13, the District Forum is satisfied that the goods complained against suffer from any of the defects specified in the complaint or that any of the allegations contained in the complaint about the services are proved, it shall issue an order to the opposite party directing him to do one or more of the following things, namely:

(a) To remove the defect pointed out by the appropriate laboratory from the goods in question;

(b) To replace the goods with new goods of similar description which shall be free from any defect;

(c) To return to the complainant the price, or, as the case may be, the charges paid by the complainant;

(d) To pay such amount as may be awarded by it as compensation to the consumer for any loss or injury suffered by the consumer due to the negligence of the opposite party. Provided that the District Forum shall have the power to grant punitive damages in such circumstances as it deems fit;

(e) To remove the defects in goods or deficiencies in the services in question;

(f) To discontinue the unfair trade practice or the restrictive trade practice or not to repeat it;

(g) Not to offer the hazardous goods for sale;

(h) To withdraw the hazardous goods from being offered for sale; (ha)to cease manufacture of hazardous goods and to desist from offering services which are hazardous in nature; (hb)to pay such sum as may be determined by it if it is of the opinion that loss or injury has been suffered by a large number of consumers who are not identifiable conveniently: Provided that the minimum amount of sum so payable shall not be less than five per cent. of the value of such defective goods sold or service provided, as the case may be, to such consumers: Provided further that the amount so obtained shall be credited in favour of such person and utilized in such manner as may be prescribed; (hc)to issue corrective advertisement to neutralize the effect of misleading advertisement at the cost of the opposite party responsible for issuing such misleading advertisement; (i) To provide for adequate costs to parties.

(2) Every proceeding referred to in sub-section (1) shall be conducted by the President of the District Forum and at least one member thereof sitting together: Provided that where a member, for any reason, is unable to conduct a proceeding till it is completed, the President and the other member shall continue the proceeding from the stage at which it was last heard by the previous member.

(2A) Every order made by the District Forum under sub-section (1) shall be signed by its President and the member or members who conducted the proceeding:

Provided that where the proceeding is conducted by the President and one member and they differ on any point or points, they shall state the point or points on which they differ and refer the same to the other member for hearing on such point or points and the opinion of the majority shall be the order of the District Forum.

(3) Subject to the foregoing provisions, the procedure relating to the conduct of the meetings of the District Forum, its sittings and other matters shall be such as may be prescribed by the State Government.

15. *Appeal*: Any person aggrieved by an order made by the District Forum may prefer an appeal against such order to the State Commission within a period of thirty days from the date of the order, in such form and manner as may be prescribed:

Provided that the State Commission may entertain an appeal after the expiry of the said period of thirty days if it is satisfied that there was sufficient cause for not finding it within that period.

Provided further that no appeal by a person, who is required to pay any amount in terms of an order of the District Forum, shall be entertained by the State Commission unless the appellant has deposited in the prescribed manner fifty per cent. of that amount or twenty-five thousand rupees, whichever is less:

16. *Composition of the State Commission*: (1) Each State Com-mission shall consist of—

(a) A person who is or has been a Judge of a High Court, appointed by the State Government, who shall be its President: Provided that no appointment under this clause shall be made except after consultation with the Chief Justice of the High Court;

(b) Not less than two, and not more than such number of members, as may be prescribed, and one of whom shall be a woman, who shall have the following qualifications, namely:

(i) Be not less than thirty-five years of age;

(ii) Possess a bachelor's degree from a recognised university; and

(iii) Be persons of ability, integrity and standing, and have adequate knowledge and experience of at least ten years in dealing with problems relating to economics, law, commerce, accountancy, industry, public affairs or administration: Provided that not more than fifty per cent. of the members shall be from amongst persons having a judicial background.

Explanation: For the purposes of this clause, the expression "persons having judicial background" shall mean persons having knowledge and experience for at least a period of ten years as a presiding officer at the district level court or any tribunal at equivalent level:

Provided further that a person shall be disqualified for appointment as a member if he:

(a) Has been convicted and sentenced to imprisonment for an offence which, in the opinion of the State Government, involves moral turpitude; or

(b) Is an undischarged insolvent; or

(c) Is of unsound mind and stands so declared by a competent court; or

(d) Has been removed or dismissed from the service of the Government or a body corporate owned or controlled by the Government; or

(e) Has, in the opinion of the State Government, such financial or other interest, as is likely to affect prejudicially the discharge by him of his functions as a member; or

(f) Has such other disqualifications as may be prescribed by the State Government.

(1A)Every appointment under sub-section (1) shall be made by the State Government on the recommendation of a Selection Committee consisting of the following members, namely:

(i) President of the State Commission — Chairman;

(ii) Secretary of the Law Department of the State — Member;

(iii) Secretary incharge of the Department dealing with Consumer Affairs in the State — Member:

Provided that where the President of the State Commission is, by reason of absence or otherwise, unable to act as Chairman of the Selection Committee, the State Government may refer the matter to the Chief Justice of the High Court for nominating a sitting Judge of that High Court to act as Chairman. (1B) (i) The jurisdiction, powers and authority of the State Commission may be exercised by Benches thereof. (ii) A Bench may be constituted by the President with one or more members as the President may deem fit. (iii) If the members of a Bench differ in opinion on any point, the points shall be decided according to the opinion of the majority, if there is a majority, but if the Members are equally divided, they shall state the point or points on which they differ, and make a reference to the President who shall either hear the point or points himself or refer the case for hearing on such point or points by one or more or the other members and such point or points shall be decided according to the opinion of the majority of the members who have heard the case, including those who first heard it.

(2) The salary or honourarium and other allowances payable to, and the other terms and conditions of service of, the members of the State Commission shall be such as may be prescribed by the State Government. Provided that the appointment of a member on whole-time basis shall be made by the State Government on the recommendation of the President of the State Commission taking into consideration such factors as may be prescribed including the work load of the State Commission.

(3) Every member of the State Commission shall hold office for a term of five years or up to the age of sixty-seven years, whichever is earlier:

Provided that a member shall be eligible for re-appointment for another term of five years or up to the age of sixty-seven years, whichever is earlier, subject to the condition that he fulfills the qualifications and other conditions for appointment mentioned in clause (b) of sub-section (1) and such re-appointment is made on the basis of the recommendation of the Selection Committee: Provided further that a person appointed as a President of the State Commission shall also be eligible for re-appointment in the manner provided in clause (a) of sub-section (1) of this section:

Provided also that a member may resign his office in writing under his hand addressed to the State Government and on such resignation being accepted, his office shall become vacant and may be filled by appointment of a person possessing any of the qualifications mentioned in sub-section (1) in relation to the category of the member who is required to be appointed under the provisions of sub-section (1A) in place of the person who has resigned.

(4) Notwithstanding anything contained in sub-section (3), a person appointed as the President or as a member, before the commencement of the Consumer Protection (Amendment) Act, 2002, shall continue to hold such office as President or member, as the case may be, till the completion of his term.

17. Jurisdiction of the State Commission. – *(1)* Subject to the other provisions of this Act, the State Commission shall have jurisdiction

(a) *To entertain:*

(i) Complaints where the value of the goods or services and compensation, if any, claimed exceeds rupees twenty lakhs but does not exceed rupees one crore; and

(ii) Appeals against the orders of any District Forum within the State; and

(b) To call for the records and pass appropriate orders in any con-sumer dispute which is pending before or has been decided by any District Forum within the State, where it appears to the State Commission that such District Forum has exercised a jurisdiction not vested in it by law, or has failed to exercise a jurisdiction so vested or has acted in exercise of its jurisdiction illegally or with material irregularity.

(2) A complaint shall be instituted in a State Commission within the limits of whose jurisdiction:

(a) The opposite party or each of the opposite parties, where there are more than one, at the time of the institution of the complaint, actually and voluntarily resides or carries on business or has a branch office or personally works for gain; or

(b) Any of the opposite parties, where there are more than one, at the time of the institution of the complaint, actually and voluntarily resides, or carries on business or has a branch office or personally works for gain, provided that in such case either the permission of the State Commission is given or the opposite parties who do not reside or carry on business or have a branch office or personally work for gain, as the case may be, acquiesce in such institution; or

(c) The cause of action, wholly or in part, arises.

17A. Transfer of cases. - On the application of the complainant or of its own motion, the State Commission may, at any stage of the proceeding, transfer any complaint pending before the District Forum to another District Forum within the State if the interest of justice so requires.

17B. Circuit Benches.-The State Commission shall ordinarily function in the State Capital but may perform its functions at such other place as the State Government may, in consultation with the State Commission, notify in the Official Gazette, from time to time.

18. Procedure applicable to State Commissions.—The provisions of Sections 12, 13 and 14 and the rules made thereunder for the disposal of complaints by the District Forum shall, with such modifications as

may be necessary, be applicable to the disposal of disputes by the State Commission. (1A. Omitted)

19. Appeals.—Any person aggrieved by an order made by the State Commission in exercise of its powers conferred by sub-clause (i) of clause (a) of section 17 may prefer an appeal against such order to the National Commission within a period of thirty days from the date of the order in such form and manner as may be prescribed:

Provided that the National Commission may entertain an appeal after the expiry of the said period of thirty days if it is satisfied that there was sufficient cause for not filing it within that period. Provided further that no appeal by a person, who is required to pay any amount in terms of an order of the State Commission, shall be entertained by the National Commission unless the appellant has deposited in the prescribed manner fifty per cent. of the amount or rupees thirty-five thousand, whichever is less:

19A. Hearing of Appeal - An appeal filed before the State Commission or the National Commission shall be heard as expeditiously as possible and an endeavour shall be made to finally dispose of the appeal within a period of ninety days from the date of its admission: Provided that no adjournment shall be ordinarily granted by the State Commission or the National Commission, as the case may be, unless sufficient cause is shown and the reasons for grant of adjournment have been recorded in writing by such Commission:

Provided further that the State Commission or the National Commission, as the case may be, shall make such orders as to the costs occasioned by the adjournment as may be provided in the regulations made under this Act.

Provided also that in the event of an appeal being disposed of after the period so specified, the State Commission or, the National Commission, as the case may be, shall record in writing the reasons *for the same at the time of disposing of the said appeal.*

20. Composition of the National Commission.—(1) The National Commission shall consist of—

(a) a person who is or has been a Judge of the Supreme Court, to be appointed by the Central Government, who shall be its President; Provided that no appointment under this clause shall be made except after consultation with the Chief Justice of India;

(b) not less than four, and not more than such number of members, as may be prescribed, and one of whom shall be a woman, who shall have the following qualifications, namely:

(i) Be not less than thirty-five years of age;

(ii) Possess a bachelor's degree from a recognised university; and

(iii) Be persons of ability, integrity and standing and have adequate knowledge and experience of at least ten years in dealing with problems relating to economics, law, commerce, accountancy, industry, public affairs or administration:

Provided that not more than fifty per cent. of the members shall be from amongst the persons having a judicial background.

Explanation: For the purposes of this clause, the expression "persons having judicial background" shall mean persons having knowledge and experience for at least a period of ten years as a presiding officer at the district level court or any tribunal at equivalent level:

Provided further that a person shall be disqualified for appointment if he:

(a) Has been convicted and sentenced to imprisonment for an offence which, in the opinion of the Central Government, involves moral turpitude; or

(b) Is an undischarged insolvent; or

(c) Is of unsound mind and stands so declared by a competent court; or

(d) Has been removed or dismissed from the service of the Government or a body corporate owned or controlled by the Government; or

(e) Has in the opinion of the Central Government such financial or other interest as is likely to affect prejudicially the discharge by him of his functions as a member; or

(f) Has such other disqualifications as may be prescribed by the Central Government:

Provided also that every appointment under this clause shall be made by the Central Government on the recommendation of a selection committee consisting of the following, namely:—

(a) *A person who is a Judge of the Supreme Court*: Chairman; To be nominated by the Chief Justice of India

(b) *The Secretary in the Department of Legal Affairs*: Member; In the Government of India

(c) *Secretary of the Department dealing with consumer:* Member; Affairs in the Government of India

(1A)(i) The jurisdiction, powers and authority of the National Commission may be exercised by Benches thereof.

(ii) A Bench may be constituted by the President with one or more members as the President may deem fit.

(iii) if the Members of a Bench differ in opinion on any point, the points shall be decided according to the opinion of the majority, if there is a majority, but if the members are equally divided, they shall state the point or points on which they differ, and make a reference to the President who shall either hear the point or points himself or refer the case for hearing on such point or points by one or more or the other Members and such point or points shall be decided according to the opinion of the majority of the Members who have heard the case, including those who first heard it.

(2) The salary or honourarium and other allowances payable to and the other terms and conditions of service of the members of the National Commission shall be such as may be prescribed by the Central Government.

(3) Every member of the National Commission shall hold office for a term of five years or up to the age of seventy years, whichever is earlier:

Provided that a member shall be eligible for re-appointment for another term of five years or up to the age of seventy years, whichever is earlier, subject to the condition that he fulfills the qualifications and other conditions for appointment mentioned in clause (b) of sub-section (1) and such re-appointment is made on the basis of the recommendation of the Selection Committee:

Provided further that a person appointed as a President of the National Commission shall also be eligible for re-appointment in the manner provided in clause (a) of sub-section (1):

Provided also that a member may resign his office in writing under his hand addressed to the Central Government and on such resignation being accepted, his office shall become vacant and may be filled by appointment of a person possessing any of the qualifications mentioned in sub-section (1) in relation to the category of the member who is required to be appointed under the provisions of sub-section (1A) in place of the person who has resigned.

(4) Notwithstanding anything contained in sub-section (3), a person appointed as a President or as a member before the commencement of the Consumer Protection (Amendment) Act, 2002 shall continue to hold such office as President or member, as the case may be, till the completion of his term.

21. Jurisdiction of the National Commission. — Subject to the other provisions of this Act, the National Commission shall have jurisdiction:

(a) *To entertain:*

(i) complaints where the value of the goods or services and compensation, if any, claimed exceeds rupees one crore; and

(ii) appeals against the orders of any State Commission; and

(b) To call for the records and pass appropriate orders in any con-sumer dispute which is pending before or has been decided by any State Commission where it appears to the National Commission that such State Commission has exercised a jurisdiction not vested in it by law, or has failed to exercise a jurisdiction so vested, or has acted in the exercise of its jurisdiction illegally or with material irregularity.

22. Power of and procedure applicable to the National Commission.

(1) The provisions of sections 12, 13 and 14 and the rules made thereunder for the disposal of complaints by the District Forum shall, with such modifications as may be considered necessary by the Commission, be applicable to the disposal of disputes by the National Commission.

(2) Without prejudice to the provisions contained in sub-section (1), the National Commission shall have the power to review any order made by it, when there is an error apparent on the face of record.

22A. *Power to set aside ex parte orders*: Where an order is passed by the National Commission ex parte against the opposite party or a complainant, as the case may be, the aggrieved party may apply to the Commission to set aside the said order in the interest of justice.

22B. Transfer of cases - On the application of the complainant or of its own motion, the National Commission may, at any stage of the proceeding, in the interest of justice, transfer any complaint pending before the District Forum of one State to a District Forum of another State or before one State Commission to another State Commission.

22C. Circuit Benches - The National Commission shall ordinarily function at New Delhi and perform its functions at such other place as the Central Government may, in consultation with the National Commission, notify in the Official Gazette, from time to time.

22D. Vacancy in the Office of the President - When the office of President of a District Forum, State Commission, or of the National Commission, as the case may be, is vacant or a person occupying such office is, by reason of absence or otherwise, unable to perform the duties of his office, these shall be performed by the senior-most member of the District Forum, the State Commission or of the National Commission, as the case may be:

Provided that where a retired Judge of a High Court is a member of the National Commission, such member or where the number of such members is more than one, the senior-most person among such members, shall preside over the National Commission in the absence of President of that Commission.

23. *Appeal*: Any person, aggrieved by an order made by the National Commission in exercise of its powers conferred by sub-clause (i) of clause *(a)* of section 21, may prefer an appeal against such order of the Supreme Court within a period of thirty days from the date of the order:

Provided that the Supreme Court may entertain an appeal after the expiry of the said period of thirty days if it is satisfied that there was sufficient cause for not filing it within that period. Provided further that no appeal by a person who is required to pay any amount in terms of an order of the National Commission shall be entertained by the Supreme Court unless that person has deposited in the prescribed manner fifty per cent. of that amount or rupees fifty thousand, whichever is less.

24. *Finality of orders*: Every order of a District Forum, the State Commission or the National Commission shall, if no appeal has been preferred against such order under the provisions of this Act, be final.

24A. Limitation period. - (l) The District Forum, the State Commis-sion or the National Commission shall not admit a complaint unless it is filed within two years from the date on which the cause of action has arisen.

(2) Notwithstanding anything contained in sub-section (1), a complaint may be entertained after the period specified in sub-section (l), if the complainant satisfies the District Forum, the State Commission or the National Commission, as the case may be, that he had sufficient cause for not filing the complaint within such period: Provided that no such complaint shall be entertained unless the National Commission, the State Commission or the District Forum, as the case may be, records its reasons for condoning such delay.

24B. Administrative Control.—(1) The National

Commission shall have administrative control over all the State Commissions in the following matters, namely:

(i) Calling for periodical return regarding the institution, disposal pendency of cases;

(ii) Issuance of instructions regarding adoption of uniform pro-cedure in the hearing of matters, prior service of copies of documents produced by one party to the opposite parties, furnishing of English translation of judgments written in any language, speedy grant of copies of documents;

(iii) Generally overseeing the functioning of the State Commis-sions or the District Fora to ensure that the objects and purposes of the Act are best served without in any way interfering with their *quasi-judicial* freedom.

(2) The State Commission shall have administrative control over all the District Fora within its jurisdiction in all matters referred to in sub-section (1).

25. Enforcement of orders of the District Forum, the State Commission or the National Commission. — (1) Where an interim order made under this Act, is not complied with the District Forum or the State Commission or the National Commission, as the case may be, may order the property of the person, not complying with such order to be attached.

(2) No attachment made under sub-section (1) shall remain in force for more than three months at the end of which, if the non-compliance continues, the property attached may be sold and out of the proceeds thereof, the District Forum or the State Commission or the National Commission may award such damages as it thinks fit to the complainant and shall pay the balance, if any, to the party entitled thereto.

(3) Where any amount is due from any person under an order made by a District Forum, State Commission or the National Commission, as the case may be, the

person entitled to the amount may make an application to the District Forum, the State Commission or the National Commission, as the case may be, and such District Forum or the State Commission or the National Commission may issue a certificate for the said amount to the Collector of the district (by whatever name called) and the Collector shall proceed to recover the amount in the same manner as arrears of land revenue.

26. Dismissal of frivolous or vexatious complaints. — Where a complaint instituted before the District Forum, the State Commission or as the case may be, the National Commission, is found to be frivolous or vexatious, it shall, for reasons to be recorded in writing, dismiss the complaint and make an order that the complainant shall pay to the opposite party such cost, not exceeding ten thousand rupees, as may be specified in the order

27. Penalties. — *(1)* Where a trader or a person against whom a complaint is made or the complainant fails or omits to comply with any order made by the District Forum, the State Commission or the National Commission, as the case may be, such trader or person or complainant shall be punishable with imprisonment for a term which shall not be less than one month but which may extend to three years, or with fine which shall not be less than two thousands rupees but which may extend to ten thousand rupees, or with both:

(2) Notwithstanding anything contained in the Code of Criminal Procedure, 1973, (2 of 1974), the District Forum or the State Commission or the National Commission, as the case may be, shall have the power of a Judicial Magistrate of the first class for the trial of offences under this Act, and on such conferment of powers, the District Forum or the State Commission or the National Commission, as the case may be, on whom the powers are so conferred, shall be deemed to be a Judicial Magistrate of the first class for the purpose of the

Code of Criminal Procedure, 1973 (2 of 1974). (3) All offences under this Act may be tried summarily by the District Forum or the State Commission or the National Commission, as the case may be.

27A. Appeal against order passed under section 27 - (1) Notwithstanding anything contained in the Code of Criminal Procedure, 1973 (2 of 1974), an appeal under section 27, both on facts and on law, shall lie from -

(a) *The order made by the District Forum to the State Commission;*

(b) *The order made by the State Commission to the National Commission;*

(c) *The order made by the National Commission to the Supreme Court.*

(2) Except as aforesaid, no appeal shall lie to any court from any order of a District Forum or a State Commission or the National Commission.

(3) Every appeal under this section shall be preferred within a period of thirty days from the date of an order of a District Forum or a State Commission or, as the case may be, the National Commission:

Provided that the State Commission or the National Commission or the Supreme Court, as the case may be, may entertain an appeal after the expiry of the said period of thirty days, if, it is satisfied that the appellant had sufficient cause for not preferring the appeal within the period of thirty days.

OTHER LAWS

28. Protection of action taken in good faith. — No suit, prosecution or other legal proceedings shall lie against the members of the District Forum, the State Commission or the National Commission or any officer or person acting under the direction of the District Forum, the State Commission or the National Commission for executing any order made by it or in respect of anything which is in good faith done or intended to be done by such member, officer or person under this Act or under any rule or order made thereunder.

28A. Service of notice, etc. - (1) All notices required by this Act to be served shall be served in the manner hereinafter mentioned in sub-section (2).

(2) The service of notices may be made by delivering or transmitting a copy thereof by registered post acknowledgment due addressed to opposite party against whom complaint is made or to the complainant by speed post or by such courier service as are approved by the District Forum, the State Commission or the National Commission, as the case may be, or by any other means of transmission of documents (including FAX message).

(3) When an acknowledgment or any other receipt purporting to be signed by the opposite party or his agent or by the complainant is received by the District Forum, the State Commission or the National Commission, as the case may be, or postal article containing the notice is received back by such District Forum, State Commission or the National Commission, with an endorsement purporting to have been made by a postal employee or by any person authorized by the courier service to the effect that the opposite party or his agent or complainant had refused to take delivery of the postal article containing the notice or had refused to accept the notice by any other means specified in sub- section (2) when tendered or transmitted to him, the District Forum or the State Commission or the National Commission, as the case may be, shall declare that the notice had been duly served on the opposite party or to the complainant: Provided that where the notice was properly addressed, pre-paid and duly sent by registered post acknowledgment due, a declaration referred to in this sub-section shall be made notwithstanding the fact that the acknowledgment has been lost or mislaid, or for any other reason, has not been received by the District Forum, the State Commission or the National Commission, as the case

may be, within thirty days from the date of issue of notice.

(4) All notices required to be served on an opposite party or to complainant shall be deemed to be sufficiently served, if addressed in the case of the opposite party to the place where business or profession is carried and in case of complainant, the place where such person actually and voluntarily resides.

29. *Power to remove difficulties*:

(l) If any difficulty arises in giving effect to the provisions of this Act, the (Central Government may, by order in the official Gazette, make such provisions not inconsistent with the provisions of this Act as appear to it to be necessary or expedient for removing the difficulty: Provided that no such order shall be made after the expiry of a period of two years from the commencement of this Act

(2) Every order made under this part shall, as soon as may be after it is made be laid before each House of Parliament

(3) If any difficulty arises in giving effect to the provisions of the Consumer Protection (Amendment) Act, 2002, the Central Government may, by order, do anything not inconsistent with such provisions for the purpose of removing the difficulty: Provided that no such order shall be made after the expiry of a period of two years from the commencement of the Consumer Protection (Amendment) Act, 2002.

(4) Every order made under sub-section (3) shall be laid before each House of Parliament.

29A. Vacancies or defects in appointment not to invalidate orders.—No act or proceeding of the District Forum, the State Commission or the National Commission shall be invalid by reason only of the existence of any vacancy amongst its member or any defect in the constitution thereof.

30. Power to make rules. - (1) The Central Government may, by notification, make rules for carrying out the provisions contained in clause (a) of sub-section (1) of section 2, clause (b) of sub-section (2) of section 4, sub-section (2) of section 5, sub-section (2) of section 12, clause (vi) of sub-section (4) of section 13, clause (hb) of sub-section (1) of section 14, section 19, clause (b) of sub-section (1) and sub-section (2) of section 20, section 22 and section 23 of this Act.

(2) The State Government may, by notification, make rules for carrying out the provisions contained in clause (b) of sub-section (2) and sub-section (4) of section 7, clause (b) of sub-section (2) and sub-section (4) of section 8A, clause (b) of sub-section (1) and sub-section (3) of section 10, clause (c) of sub-section (1) of section 13 clause (hb) of sub-section (1) and sub-section (3) of section 14, section 15 and clause (b) of sub-section (1) and sub-section (2) of section 16 of this Act.

30A. Power of the National Commission to make regulations - (1) The National Commission may, with the previous approval of the Central Government, by notification, make regulations not inconsistent with this Act to provide for all matters for which provision is necessary or expedient for the purpose of giving effect to the provisions of this Act.

(2) In particular and without prejudice to the generality of the foregoing power, such regulations may make provisions for the cost of adjournment of any proceeding before the District Forum, the State Commission or the National Commission, as the case may be, which a party may be ordered to pay.

31. Rules and regulations to be laid before each House of Parliament - (1) Every rule and every regulation made under this Act shall be laid, as soon as may be after it is made, before each House of Parliament, while it is in session, for a total period of thirty days which may be comprised in one session or in two or more successive sessions, and if, before the expiry of the session immediately following the session or the successive sessions aforesaid, both Houses agree in making any modification in the rule or regulation or both Houses agree that the rule or regulation should

not be made, the rule or regulation shall thereafter have effect only in such modified form or be of no effect, as the case may be; so, however, that any such modification or annulment shall be without prejudice to the validity of anything previously done under that rule or regulation.

(2) Every rule made by a State Government under this Act shall be laid as soon as may be after it is made, before the State Legislature.

THE ENVIRONMENT PROTECTION ACT 1986

An Act to provide for the protection and improvement of environment and for matters connected there with:

WHEREAS the decisions were taken at the United NationsConference on the Human Environment held at Stockholm in June, 1972, in which India participated, to take appropriate steps for the protection and improvement of human environment;

AND WHEREAS it is considered necessary further to implement the decisions aforesaid in so far as they relate to the protection and improvement of environment and the prevention of hazards to human beings, other living creatures, plants and property;

BE it enacted by Parliament in the Thirty-seventh Year of the Republic of India as follows:

PRELIMINARY:

- Short Title, Extend And Commencement
  - This Act may be called the Environment (Protection) Act, 1986.
  - It extends to the whole of India.
  - It shall come into force on such date as the Central Government may, by notification in the Official Gazette, appoint and different dates may be appointed for different provisions of this Act and for different areas.
- *Definitions*: *In this Act, unless the context otherwise requires*:

- "Environment" includes water, air and land and the inter- relationship which exists among and between water, air and land, and human beings, other living creatures, plants, micro-organism and property;
- "Environmental pollutant" means any solid, liquid or gaseous substance present in such concentration as may be, or tend to be, injurious to environment;
- "Environmental pollution" means the presence in the environment of any environmental pollutant;
- "Handling", in relation to any substance, means the manufacture, processing, treatment, package, storage, transportation, use, collection, destruction, conversion, offering for sale, transfer or the like of such substance;
- "Hazardous substance" means any substance or preparation which, by reason of its chemical or physico-chemical properties or handling, is liable to cause harm to human beings, other living creatures, plant, micro-organism, property or the environment;
- "Occupier", in relation to any factory or premises, means a person who has, control over the affairs of the factory or the premises and includes in relation to any substance, the person in possession of the substance;
- "Prescribed" means prescribed by rules made under this Act.

GENERAL POWERS OF THE CENTRAL GOVERNMENT

- Power Of Central Government To Take Measures To Protect And Improve Environment
  - Subject to the provisions of this Act, the Central Government, shall have the power to take all such measures as it deems necessary or expedient for the purpose of protecting and

improving the quality of the environment and preventing controlling and abating environmental pollution.

- In particular, and without prejudice to the generality of the provisions of sub-section (1), such measures may include measures with respect to all or any of the following matters, namely:—

(a) Co-ordination of actions by the State Governments, officers and other authorities—

i. Under this Act, or the rules made thereunder, or

ii. Under any other law for the time being in force which is relatable to the objects of this Act;

(b) Planning and execution of a nation-wide programme for the prevention, control and abatement of environmental pollution;

(c) Laying down standards for the quality of environment in its various aspects;

(d) Laying down standards for emission or discharge of environmental pollutants from various sources whatsoever:

Provided that different standards for emission or discharge may be laid down under this clause from different sources having regard to the quality or composition of the emission or discharge of environmental pollutants from such sources;

(e) Restriction of areas in which any industries, operations or processes or class of industries, operations or processes shall not be carried out or shall be carried out subject to certain safeguards;

(f) Laying down procedures and safeguards for the prevention of accidents which may cause environmental pollution and remedial measures for such accidents;

(g) Laying down procedures and safeguards for the handling of hazardous substances;

(h) Examination of such manufacturing processes, materials and substances as are likely to cause environmental pollution;

(i) Carrying out and sponsoring investigations and research relating to problems of environmental pollution;

(j) Inspection of any premises, plant, equipment, machinery, manufacturing or other processes, materials or substances and giving, by order, of such directions to such authorities, officers or persons as it may consider necessary to take steps for the prevention, control and abatement of environmental pollution;

(k) Establishment or recognition of environmental laboratories and institutes to carry out the functions entrusted to such environmental laboratories and institutes under this Act;

(l) Collection and dissemination of information in respect of matters relating to environmental pollution;

(m) Preparation of manuals, codes or guides relating to the prevention, control and abatement of environmental pollution;

(n) Such other matters as the Central Government deems necessary or expedient for the purpose of securing the effective implementation of the provisions of this Act.

– The Central Government may, if it considers it necessary or expedient so to do for the purpose of this Act, by order, published in the Official Gazette, constitute an authority or authorities by such name or names as may be specified in the order for the purpose of exercising and performing such of the powers and functions (including the power to issue directions under section 5) of the Central Government under this

Act and for taking measures with respect to such of the matters referred to in sub-section (2) as may be mentioned in the order and subject to the supervision and control of the Central Government and the provisions of such order, such authority or authorities may exercise and powers or perform the functions or take the measures so mentioned in the order as if such authority or authorities had been empowered by this Act to exercise those powers or perform those functions or take such measures.

- Appointment Of Officers And Their Powers And Functions
  - Without prejudice to the provisions of sub-section (3) of section 3, the Central Government may appoint officers with such designation as it thinks fit for the purposes of this Act and may entrust to them such of the powers and functions under this Act as it may deem fit.
  - The officers appointed under sub-section (1) shall be subject to the general control and direction of the Central Government or, if so directed by that Government, also of the authority or authorities, if any, constituted under sub- section (3) of section 3 or of any other authority or officer.
- *Power To Give Directions*: Not with standing anything contained in any other law but subject to the provisions of this Act, the Central Government may, in the exercise of its powers and performance of its functions under this Act, issue directions in writing to any person, officer or any authority and such person, officer or authority shall be bound to comply with such directions.

  Explanation: For the avoidance of doubts, it is hereby declared that the power to issue directions under this section includes the power to direct—
  - The closure, prohibition or regulation of any industry, operation or process; or

- Stoppage or regulation of the supply of electricity or water or any other service.

- Rules To Regulate Environmental Pollution
  - The Central Government may, by notification in the Official Gazette, make rules in respect of all or any of the matters referred to in section 3.
  - In particular, and without prejudice to the generality of the foregoing power, such rules may provide for all or any of the following matters, namely:—
    - (a) The standards of quality of air, water or soil for various areas and purposes;
    - (b) The maximum allowable limits of concentration of various environmental pollutants (including noise) for different areas;
    - (c) The procedures and safeguards for the handling of hazardous substances;
    - (d) The prohibition and restrictions on the handling of hazardous substances in different areas;
    - (e) The prohibition and restriction on the location of industries and the carrying on process and operations in different areas;
    - (f) The procedures and safeguards for the prevention of accidents which may cause environmental pollution and for providing for remedial measures for such accidents.

PREVENTION, CONTROL, AND ABATEMENT OF ENVIRONMENTAL POLLUTION

- Persons Carrying On Industry Operation, Etc., Not To Allow Emission Or Discharge Of Environmental Pollutants In Excess Of The Standards No person carrying on any industry, operation or process shall discharge or emit or permit to be discharged or emitted any environmental pollutants in excess of such standards as may be prescribed.

- Persons Handling Hazardous Substances To Comply With Procedural Safeguards
  No person shall handle or cause to be handled any hazardous substance except in accordance with such procedure and after complying with such safeguards as may be prescribed.
- Furnishing Of Information To Authorities And Agencies In Certain Cases
  - Where the discharge of any environmental pollutant in excess of the prescribed standards occurs or is apprehended to occur due to any accident or other unforeseen act or event, the person responsible for such discharge and the person in charge of the place at which such discharge occurs or is apprehended to occur shall be bound to prevent or mitigate the environmental pollution caused as a result of such discharge and shall also forthwith—
    (a) Intimate the fact of such occurrence or apprehension of such occurrence; and
    (b) Be bound, if called upon, to render all assistance, to such authorities or agencies as may be prescribed.
  - On receipt of information with respect to the fact or apprehension on any occurrence of the nature referred to in sub-section (1), whether through intimation under that sub-section or otherwise, the authorities or agencies referred to in sub-section (1) shall, as early as practicable, cause such remedial measures to be taken as necessary to prevent or mitigate the environmental pollution.
  - The expenses, if any, incurred by any authority or agency with respect to the remedial measures referred to in sub-section (2), together with interest (at such reasonable rate as the Government may, by order, fix) from the date when a demand for the expenses is made until it is paid, may be recovered by such authority

or agency from the person concerned as arrears of land revenue or of public demand.

- Powers Of Entry And Inspection
  - Subject to the provisions of this section, any person empowered by the Central Government in this behalf shall have a right to enter, at all reasonable times with such assistance as he considers necessary, any place—
    (a) For the purpose of performing any of the functions of the Central Government entrusted to him;
    (b) For the purpose of determining whether and if so in what manner, any such functions are to be performed or whether any provisions of this Act or the rules made thereunder orany notice, order, direction or authorisation served, made, given or granted under this Act is being or has been complied with;
    (c) for the purpose of examining and testing any equipment, industrial plant, record, register, document or any other material object or for conducting a search of any building in which he has reason to believe that an offence under this Act or the rules made thereunder has been or is being or is about to be committed and for seizing any such equipment, industrial plant, record, register, document or other material object if he has reason to believe that it may furnish evidence of the commission of an offence punishable under this Act or the rules made thereunder or that such seizure is necessary to prevent or mitigate environmental pollution.

(2) Every person carrying on any industry, operation or process of handling any hazardous substance shall be bound to render all assistance to the person empowered by the Central Government under sub-section (1) for carrying out the functions under that sub-section and

if he fails to do so without any reasonable cause or excuse, he shall be guilty of an offence under this Act.

(3) If any person wilfully delays or obstructs any persons empowered by the Central Government under sub-section (1) in the performance of his functions, he shall be guilty of an offence under this Act.

(4) The provisions of the Code of Criminal Procedure, 1973, or, in relation to the State of Jammu and Kashmir, or an area in which that Code is not in force, the provisions of any corresponding law in force in that State or area shall, so far as may be, apply to any search or seizures under this section as they apply to any search or seizure made under the authority of a warrant issued under section 94 of the said Code or as the case may be, under the corresponding provision of the said law.

- Power To Take Sample And Procedure To Be Followed In Connection Therewith
  - The Central Government or any officer empowered by it in this behalf, shall have power to take, for the purpose of analysis, samples of air, water, soil or other substance from any factory, premises or other place in such manner as may be prescribed.
  - The result of any analysis of a sample taken under sub-section (1) shall not be admissible in evidence in any legal proceeding unless the provisions of sub-sections (3) and (4) are complied with.
  - Subject to the provisions of sub-section (4), the person taking the sample under sub-section (1) shall

    (a) Serve on the occupier or his agent or person in charge of the place, a notice, then and there, in such form as may be prescribed, of his intention to have it so analysed;

    (b) In the presence of the occupier of his agent or person, collect a sample for analysis;

    (c) Cause the sample to be placed in a container or containers which shall be marked and sealed and shall also be signed both by the person taking the sample and the occupier or his agent or person;

(d) Send without delay, the container or the containers to the laboratory established or recognised by the Central Government under section 12.

– When a sample is taken for analysis under sub-section (1) and the person taking the sample serves on the occupier or his agent or person, a notice under clause (a) of sub-section (3), then,—

(a) In a case where the occupier, his agent or person wilfully absents himself, the person taking the sample shall collect the sample for analysis to be placed in a container or containers which shall be marked and sealed and shall also be signed by the person taking the sample, and

(b) In a case where the occupier or his agent or person present at the time of taking the sample refuses to sign the marked and sealed container or containers of the sample as required under clause

(c) Of sub-section (3), the marked and sealed container or containers shall be signed by the person taking the samples, and the container or containers shall be sent without delay by the person taking the sample for analysis to the laboratory established or recognised under section 12 and such person shall inform the Government Analyst appointed or recognised under section 12 in writing, about the wilfull absence of the occupier or his agent or person, or, as the case may be, his refusal to sign the container or containers.

ENVIRONMENTAL LABORATORIES

(1) The Central Government may, by notification in the Official Gazette,

(a) Establish one or more environmental laboratories;

(b) Recognise one or more laboratories or institutes as environmental laboratories to carry out the functions entrusted to an environmental laboratory under this Act.

(2) The Central Government may, by notification in the Official Gazette, make rules specifying—

(a) The functions of the environmental laboratory;

(b) The procedure for the submission to the said laboratory of samples of air, water, soil or other substance for analysis or tests, the form of the laboratory report thereon and the fees payable for such report;

(c) Such other matters as may be necessary or expedient to enable that laboratory to carry out its functions.

13. Government Analysts: The Central Government may by notification in the Official Gazette, appoint or recognise such persons as it thinks fit and having the prescribed qualifications to be Government Analysts for the purpose of analysis of samples of air, water, soil or other substance sent for analysis to any environmental laboratory established or recognised under sub-section (1) of section 12.

14. *Reports Of Government Analysts*: Any document purporting to be a report signed by a Government analyst may be used as evidence of the facts stated therein in any proceeding under this Act.

15. Penalty For Contravention Of The Provisions Of The Act And The Rules, Orders And Directions

(1) Whoever fails to comply with or contravenes any of the provisions of this Act, or the rules made or orders or directions issued thereunder, shall, in respect of each such failure or contravention, be punishable with imprisonment for a term which may extend to five years with fine which may extend to one lakh rupees, or with both, and in case the failure or contravention continues, with additional fine which

may extend to five thousand rupees for every day during which such failure or contravention continues after the conviction for the first such failure or contravention.

(2) If the failure or contravention referred to in sub-section (1) continues beyond a period of one year after the date of conviction, the offender shall be punishable with imprisonment for a term which may extend to seven years.

16. Offences By Companies:

(1) Where any offence under this Act has been committed by a company, every person who, at the time the offence was committed, was directly in charge of, and was responsible to, the company for the conduct of the business of the company, as well as the company, shall be deemed to be guilty of the offence and shall be liable to be proceeded against and punished accordingly:

Provided that nothing contained in this sub-section shall render any such person liable to any punishment provided in this Act, if he proves that the offence was committed without his knowledge or that he exercised all due diligence to prevent the commission of such offence.

(2) Notwithstanding anything contained in sub-section (1), where an offence under this Act has been committed by a company and it is proved that the offence has been committed with the consent or connivance of, or is attributable to any neglect on the part of, any director, manager, secretary or other officer of the company, such director, manager, secretary or other officer shall also deemed to be guilty of that offence and shall be liable to be proceeded against and punished accordingly.

Explanation: For the purpose of this section:

(a) "company" means any body corporate and includes a firm or other association of individuals;

(b) "Director", in relation to a firm, means a partner in the firm.

17. Offences by government departments

(1) Where an offence under this Act has been committed by any Department of Government, the Head of the Department shall be deemed to be guilty of the offence and shall be liable to be proceeded against and punished accordingly.

Provided that nothing contained in this part shall render such Head of the Department liable to any punishment if he proves that the offence was committed without his knowledge or that he exercise all due diligence to prevent the commission of such offence.

(2) Notwithstanding anything contained in sub-section (1), where an offence under this Act has been committed by a Department of Government and it is proved that the offence has been committed with the consent or connivance of, or is attributable to any neglect on the part of, any officer, other than the Head of the Department, such officer shall also be deemed to be guilty of that offence and shall be liable to be proceeded against and punished accordingly.

Miscellaneous

18. *Protection Of Action Taken In Good Faith*: No suit, prosecution or other legal proceeding shall lie against the Government or any officer or other employee of the Government or any authority constituted under this Act or any member, officer or other employee of such authority in respect of anything which is done or intended to be done in good faith in pursuance of this Act or the rules made or orders or directions issued thereunder.
19. *Cognizance Of Offences*: No court shall take cognizance of any offence under this Act except on a complaint made by:
    (a) The Central Government or any authority or officer authorised in this behalf by that Government, or
    (b) Any person who has given notice of not less than sixty days, in the manner prescribed, of the alleged offence and of his intention to make a

complaint, to the Central Government or the authority or officer authorised as aforesaid.

20. *Information, reports or returns*: The Central Government may, in relation to its function under this Act, from time to time, require any person, officer, State Government or other authority to furnish to it or any prescribed authority or officer any reports, returns, statistics, accounts and other information and such person, officer, State Government or other authority shall be bound to do so.
21. *Members, officers and employees of the authority constituted under section 3 to be public servants*: All the members of the authority, constituted, if any, under section 3 and all officers and other employees of such authority when acting or purporting to act in pursuance of any provisions of this Act or the rules made or orders or directions issued thereunder shall be deemed to be public servants within the meaning of section 21 of the Indian Penal Code (45 of 1860).
22. Bar of Jurisdiction: No civil court shall have jurisdiction to entertain any suit or proceeding in respect of anything done, action taken or order or direction issued by the Central Government or any other authority or officer in pursuance of any power conferred by or in relation to its or his functions under this Act.
23. *Powers to delegate*: Without prejudice to the provisions of sub-section (3) of section 3, the Central Government may, by notification in the Official Gazette, delegate, subject to such conditions and limitations as may be specified in the notifications, such of its powers and functions under this Act [except the powers to constitute an authority under sub-section (3) of section 3 and to make rules under section 25] as it may deem necessary or expedient, to any officer, State Government or other authority.
24. Effect Of Other Laws:

(1) Subject to the provisions of sub-section (2), the provisions of this Act and the rules or orders made therein shall have effect notwithstanding anything inconsistent therewith contained in any enactment other than this Act.

(2) Where any act or omission constitutes an offence punishable under this Act and also under any other Act then the offender found guilty of such offence shall be liable to be punished under the other Act and not under this Act.

25. Power To Make Rules

(1) The Central Government may, by notification in the Official Gazette, make rules for carrying out the purposes of this Act.

(2) In particular, and without prejudice to the generality of the foregoing power, such rules may provide for all or any of the following matters, namely—

(a) The standards in excess of which environmental pollutants shall not be discharged or emitted under section 7;

(b) The procedure in accordance with and the safeguards in compliance with which hazardous substances shall be handled or caused to be handled under section 8;

(c) The authorities or agencies to which intimation of the fact of occurrence or apprehension of occurrence of the discharge of any environmental pollutant in excess of the prescribed standards shall be given and to whom all assistance shall be bound to be rendered under sub-section (1) of section 9;

(d) The manner in which samples of air, water, soil or other substance for the purpose of analysis shall be taken under sub-section (1) of section 11;

(e) The form in which notice of intention to have a sample analysed shall be served under clause (a) of sub section (3) of section 11;

(f) The functions of the environmental laboratories, the procedure for the submission to such laboratories of samples of air, water, soil and other substances for analysis or test; the form of laboratory report; the fees payable for such report and other matters to enable such laboratories to carry out their functions under sub-section (2) of section 12;

(g) The qualifications of Government Analyst appointed or recognised for the purpose of analysis of samples of air, water, soil or other substances under section 13;

(h) The manner in which notice of the offence and of the intention to make a complaint to the Central Government shall be given under clause (b) of section 19;

(i) The authority of officer to whom any reports, returns, statistics, accounts and other information shall be furnished under section 20;

(j) Any other matter which is required to be, or may be, prescribed.

26. *Rules made under this act to be laid before parliament*: Every rule made under this Act shall be laid, as soon as may be after it is made, before each Hose of Parliament, while it is in session, for a total period of thirty days which may be comprised in one session or in two or more successive sessions, and if, before the expiry of the session immediately following the session or the successive sessions aforesaid, both Houses agree in making any modification in the rule or both Houses agree that the rule should not be made, the rule shall thereafter have effect only in such modified form or be of no effect, as the case may be; so, however, that any such modification or annulment shall be without prejudice to the validity of anything previously done under that rule.

15

Technological Environment

The US and the UK have well-defined and comprehensive laws on data security and privacy. The US has sector-specific laws and laws at the federal and the state level.

The UK has a comprehensive Data Protection Act covering all sectors. While India lacks specific laws on privacy and data protection, there are proxy laws and other indirect safeguards, which provide adequate protection to companies offshoring work.

Further, the Indian Government is proactively strengthening the existing legal system to cover data protection issues. A few of the proxy laws are Section 65, 66 and 72 of the Indian IT Act, the Indian Contract Act, Section 406 and 420 of the Indian Penal Code, and the Indian Copyright Act.

Key Laws Governing in Formation Security in India

Information Technology Act, 2000 In May 2000 the Indian Parliament passed the Information Technology Bill now known as the Information Technology Act, 2000. The Act covers cyber and related information technology laws in India.

Some of the issues addressed by the Information Technology Act, 2000 include:

- Any subscriber can authenticate an electronic record with his digital signature, and subsequently any person can verify that document by using the subscriber's public key.
- That all electronic records and digital signatures have legal acceptance. The substance also confers rights

to the Central Government to make rules with respect to digital signatures.

- Deals with the attribution, acknowledgement and dispatch of electronic records and digital signatures.
- Deals with the regulation of the certifying authorities. The substance also lists the powers of the controller to investigate any contraventions to the provisions of the Act.
- State the conditions under which a digital signature may be suspended or revoked.
- States that any person who accesses, downloads, copies, extracts data without authorized means or permission is punishable. The part also states that any person tampering with, damaging, denying unwarranted access to or manipulating any computer/computer system shall be liable to pay damages by way of compensation not exceeding INR 10 million to the affected persons. Introducing viruses or causing disruptions in a computer are also punishable under the Act.
- Describes the role of the Cyber Regulations Appellate Tribunal.
- Deals with offences such as wrongful loss or damage or destruction of information, deletion or alteration of any information in a computer network, 'hacking' etc and prescribes their punishment. It also includes offences such as tampering with computer source documents; publishing obscene information, misrepresentation, and breach of confidentiality and privacy.
- States that if a network provider/ intermediary can prove that he has taken diligent steps to prevent the offence he has been charged with, or that it was unintentional, he is not punishable under the Act.

Digital Signatures

Digital signatures were accorded legal acceptance by the IT Act. The Controller of Certifying Authorities, set up to implement the IT Act, has issued licenses to four players who can issue digital signatures. These are Safescrypt Limited, National Informatics Centre (NIC), Institute for Development and Research in Banking Technology (IDRBT), and Tata Consultancy Services (TCS).

In July 2001 a set of laws known as the Information Technology (Certifying Authority) Regulations, 2001 were issued by the Government of India. These regulations detail the functioning of the certifying authorities in issuing digital signatures.Intellectual Property Right Laws for Computer Software Under Indian law, computer programmes have copyright protection, but no patent protection. A software programme is an algorithm and patent law does not protect algorithms per se. The term 'software' includes computer programmes, databases, computer files, preparatory design material and associated printed documentation, such as users' manuals. Under the Indian Copyright Act, copying from an engraving is an infringement of the copyright, but an engraving produced independently from the same picture is not. Copyright laws generally do not protect the owner from independent creation or reverse engineering. Therefore, many software and hardware companies have been able to take advantage of the copyright law's lack of protection against reverse engineering.

INDIAN COPYRIGHT ACT

India has one of the most modern copyright protection laws in the world. A major development in the area of copyright was the amendment to the Copyright Act of 1957 in 1999, to make it fully compatible with the provisions of the TRIPS Agreement. Known as the Copyright (Amendment) Act, 1999, this Act came into force on January 15, 2000.

The 1994 amendment of the Copyright Act of 1957 brought sectors such as satellite broadcasting, computer software and digital technology under Indian copyright protection. The present Copyright Act conforms fully to the TRIPS obligations. The other important development during 1999 was the issuance of the International Copyright Order, 1999, which extended the provisions of the Copyright Act to nationals of all World Trade Organization (WTO) member countries. As per the provision in the Indian Copyright Act, 1957 and as amended in 1994-1995, any person who knowingly makes use on a computer of an infringing copy of computer programme shall be punishable. Section 63 B, copyright infringement attracts a minimum jail term of seven days. The Act further provides for fines, which shall not be less than INR 50,000, but may extend up to INR 200,000, and a jail term up to three years or both.The Ministry of Information Technology has taken also several initiatives to upgrade security standards in India. These include setting up organizations such as the Standardization, Testing and Quality Certification (STQC) Directorate, the Computer Emergency Response Team (CERT), the Information Security Technology Development Council (ISTDC), etc.

TECHNOLOGICAL POLICY

Preamble

Political freedom must lead to economic independence and the alleviation of the burden of poverty. We have regarded science and technology as the basis of economic progress. As a result of three decades of planning, and the Scientific Policy Resolution of 1958, we now have a strong agricultural and industrial base and a scientific manpower impressive in quality, numbers and range of skills. Given clear-cut objectives and the necessary support, our science has shown its capacity to solve problems. The frontiers of knowledge are being extended at incredible speed, opening up wholly new areas and introducing new concepts. Technological advances are influencing life-styles as well as societal expectations. The use and development of technology must relate to the people's aspirations. Our own immediate needs in India are the attainment of technological self-reliance, a swift and tangible improvement in the conditions of the weakest sections of the population and the speedy development of backward regions. India is known for its diversity. Technology must suit local needs and to make an impact on the lives of ordinary citizens, must give constant thought to even small improvements which could make better and more cost-effective use of existing materials and methods of work. Our development must be based on our own culture and personality. Our future depends on our ability to resist the imposition of technology which is obsolete or unrelated to our specific requirements and of policies which tie us to systems which serve the purposes of others rather than our own, and on our success in dealing with vested interests in our organizations: governmental, economic, social and even intellectual, which bind us to outmoded systems and institutions.

Technology must be viewed in the broadest sense, covering the agricultural and the services sectors along with the obvious manufacturing sector. The latter stretches over a wide spectrum ranging from village, small-scale and cottage industries (often based on traditional skills) to medium, heavy and sophisticated industries. Our philosophy of a mixed economy involves the operation of the private, public and joint sectors, including those with foreign equity participation. Our directives must clearly define systems for the choice of technology, taking into account economic, social and cultural factors along with technical considerations; indigenous development and support to technology, and utilization of such technology; acquisition of technology through import and its subsequent absorption, adaptation and upgradation; ensuring competitiveness at international levels in all necessary areas; and establishing links between the various elements concerned with generation of technology, its transformation into economically utilizable form, the sector responsible for production (which is the user of such technology), financial institutions concerned with the resources needed for these activities, and the promotional and regulating arms of the Government.

This Technology Policy Statement is in response to the need for guidelines to cover this wide-ranging and complex set of inter-related areas. Keeping in mind the capital-scarce character of a developing economy it aims at ensuring that our available natural endowments, especially human resources, are optimally utilized for a continuing increase in the well-being of all sections of our people. We seek technological advancement not for prestige or aggrandisement but to solve our multifarious problems and to be able to safeguard our independence and our unity. Our modernization, far from diminishing the enormous diversity of our regional traditions should help to enrich them and to make the ancient wisdom of our nation more meaningful to our people. Our task is gigantic and calls for close co-ordination between the different departments of the Central and State Governments and also of those concerned, at all levels, with any sector of economic, scientific or technological activity, and, not least, the understanding and involvement of the entire Indian people. We look particularly to young people to bring a scientific attitude of mind to bear on all our problems.

Aims and Objectives

Aims: The basic objectives of the Technology Policy will be the development of indigenous technology and efficient absorption and adaptation of imported technology appropriate to national priorities and resources. Its aims are to:

- Attain technological competence and self-reliance, to reduce vulnerability, particularly in strategic and critical areas, making the maximum use of indigenous resources;
- Provide the maximum gainful and satisfying employment to all strata of society, with emphasis on the employment of women and weaker parts of society;
- Use traditional skills and capabilities, making them commercially competitive;
- Ensure the correct mix between mass production technologies and production by the masses;
- Ensure maximum development with minimum capital outlay;
- Identify obsolescence of technology in use and

arrange for modernization of both equipment and technology;

- Develop technologies which are internationally competitive, particularly those with export potential;
- Improve production speedily through greater efficiency and fuller utilization of existing capabilities, and enhance the quality and reliability of performance and output;
- Reduce demands on energy, particularly energy from non-renewable sources;
- Ensure harmony with the environment, preserve the ecological balance and improve the quality of the habitat;
- Recycle waste material and make full utilization of by-products.

Self-reliance

In a country of India's size and endowments, self-reliance is inescapable and must be at the very heart of technological development. We must aim at major technological break-throughs in the shortest possible time for the development of indigenous technology appropriate to national priorities and resources. For this, the role of different agencies will be identified, responsibilities assigned and the necessary linkages established.

Strengthening the Technology Base

Research and Development, together with science and technology education and training of a high order, will be accorded pride of place. The base of science and technology consists of trained and skilled manpower at various levels, covering a wide range of disciplines, and an appropriate institutional, legal and fiscal infrastructure. Consolidation of the existing scientific base and selective strengthening of thrust areas in it are essential. Special attention will be given to the promotion and strengthening of the technology base in newly emerging and frontier areas such as information and materials sciences, electronics and bio-technology. Education and

Some Specific Areas

In technology development special emphasis will be focused on food, health, housing, energy and industry.

In particular, stress will be laid on:

- Agriculture including dry-land farming;
- Optimum use of water resources, increased production of pulses and oilseeds;
- Provision of drinking water in rural areas, improvement of nutrition, rapid reduction in the incidence of blindness, eradication of the major communicable diseases (such as leprosy and tuberculosis), and population stabilization;
- Low-cost housing;
- Development and use of renewable non-conventional sources of energy; and
- Industrial development

Indigenous Technology

Importance of Technology Development

Fullest support will be given to the development of indigenous technology to achieve technological self-reliance and reduce the dependence on foreign inputs, particularly in critical and vulnerable areas and in high value-added items in which the domestic base is strong. Strengthening and diversifying the domestic technology base are necessary to reduce imports and to expand exports for which international competitiveness must be ensured.

Inventions

The spirit of innovation and invention is the driving force behind all technological change. We must awaken our science and technology to the exciting challenges of our times, provide incentives to encourage inventors, and direct their efforts to areas of special importance. The system of rewards and incentives will be strengthened for inventions, innovations and technological breakthroughs and their utilization. The fullest opportunity will be provided to make use of inventions.

Enhancing Traditional Skills and Capabilities

Traditional skills and capabilities will need to be upgraded and enhanced, using knowledge and techniques generated by advances in science and technology. Technologies which will result in low-cost production and in products marketable close to the point of manufacture, particularly in the rural sector, will be promoted. Support will be given to technologies which reduce pressure on items in short supply and utilize improved local materials and methods. Government will give preference to products of such technologies in its own purchases. The adoption of technologies that can promote decentralized production will be helped through the support to design, marketing, quality control and other services.

Ensuring Timely Availability

The time cycle from scientific research to utilization is a long one. Hence the need to initiate action well in advance to identify and ensure timely availability and delivery of new technologies. Encouragement and support (fiscal, commercial and administrative) will be given to the production and user organizations to be associated with and participate in technology development efforts at appropriate stages.

Upgradation to Prevent Obsolescence

Technology is constantly on the move. The base of indigenous technology should be capable of utilizing world-wide advances and adapting them to local needs. The creation and strengthening of institutional structures for keeping track of international developments will receive urgent attention. A strong central group will be constituted to undertake technology forecast and technology assessment studies and will inter alia draw up programmes of purposeful research. Arrangements will be made to provide high-level scientific advice in major sectors of the economy.

Where big investments are involved or a large volume of production is envisaged, it will be incumbent on the Ministry or agency concerned to provide a technology forecast covering its requirements over a ten-year or longer period and evolve a strategy for development based on priorities.

Increasing the Demand for Indigenous Technology

Our country has already invested significant amounts in setting up research and development facilities as well as design consultancy and engineering capabilities. The technological potential inherent in this system of interlinked capabilities must be fully utilized, and in turn provide a fillip for further development from within the system. Incentives will, therefore, be provided to users of indigenously developed technology, and for products and processes resulting for such use.

Preferential Treatment

In view of the cost of technology development and the time necessary for successful marketing of a new or improved product, indigenously developed items are invariably at a disadvantage compared with imported products or those based on imported technologies and brand names.

Support must therefore be provided through fiscal and other measures, for a limited period, in favour of products made through indigenously developed technologies, care being taken to ensure quality.

Fiscal Incentives

Suitable financial mechanisms will be established to facilitate investment on pilot plants, process demonstration units and prototype development in order to enable rapid commercial exploitation of technologies developed in laboratories.

Linkages between scientific and technological institutions and development banks will be strengthened. Gaps in technology will be identified and suitable corrective measures taken with adequate allocation of resources. Fiscal incentives will be provided in particular to: promote inventions; increase the use of indigenously developed technology; enhance in-house Research and Development in industry; and efforts directed to absorb and adapt imported technology.

Design Engineering

Capabilities in design engineering are essential for the translation of know-how to commercial production. This is particularly important in areas relating to: agricultural production; agro-industries; metallurgical, chemical and petrochemical processes; machine tools; industrial machinery and capital goods; as well as for the construction and erection of entire plants. Building up and enhancing these capabilities will have a catalytic beneficial impact on the utilization of indigenous efforts that have resulted in product and process know-how. Existing design engineering capabilities will be strengthened and upgraded, and interaction encouraged between design engineering organizations, academic and research institutions and industry. Wherever gaps exist, design engineering capabilities will be developed and nurtured.

Engineering Consultancy

Engineering consultancy is a vital area for ensuring speedy technological and industrial development. It ensures the appropriate utilization of indigenous materials, plant and machinery. Engineering consultancy provides an essential link between R&D institutions and industry, and thus promotes effective transfer of technology. Capability for total systems engineering, process development and project management should be developed with collaboration if required. Wherever capability exists, utilization of Indian consultancy engineering organizations will be promoted. Even where foreign technical collaboration or consultancy is considered unavoidable, association of designated Indian consulting engineering organizations would be preferred. Indigenous engineering consultancy, in both private and public sectors, will be promoted on a sound professional basis in the context of the overall national perspective of technological self-reliance.

In-house R&D

In-house R&D units in industry provide a desirable and essential interface between efforts within the national laboratories and the educational sector as well as production in industry. Appropriate incentives will be given to the setting up of R&D units in industry and for industry including those on a cooperative basis. Enterprises will be encouraged to set up R&D units of a size to permit the accomplishment of major technological tasks.

Technology Acquisition

Mix of Indigenous and Imported Technology

A policy directed towards technological self-reliance does not imply technological self-sufficiency. The criterion must be national interest. Government policy will be directed towards reducing technological dependence in key areas. Advantage should be taken of technological developments elsewhere. This can also be achieved through well-defined collaborative arrangements in research and development.

At any given point of time, there will be a mix of indigenous and imported technology. However, technology acquisition from outside shall not be at the expense of national interest. Indigenous initiative must receive due recognition and support. In the acquisition of technology, consideration will be given to the choice and sources of technology, alternative means of acquiring it, its role in meeting a major felt need, selection and relevance of the products, costs, and related conditions. A National Register on Foreign Collaboration will be developed to provide analytical inputs at various stages of technological acquisition.

Principles of Acquisition and Technology Assessment

Where the need to import technology is established, every effort should be made to ensure that it is of the highest level, consistent with requirements and resources. The technology import will be so planned as to have effective transfer of basic knowledge (know-why) and to facilitate further advancement. Where the import of technology is contemplated, the level to which technology has been developed, or is in current use, within the country, shall be first evaluated.

Lists of technologies that have been adequately developed to the extent that import is unnecessary will be prepared and periodically updated; in such areas no import of technology would normally be permitted; and the onus will be on the seeker of foreign technology, be it industry or a user Ministry, to demonstrate to the satisfaction of the approval authority that import is necessary.

Technology assessment systems will be reviewed. A technology assessment mechanism consisting of competent groups will render advice in all cases of technology import relating to highly sophisticated technology, large investments and national security. Aspects of employment, energy, efficiency and environment will be kept in view.

The basic principles governing the acquisition of technology will be:

- Import of technology, and foreign investment in this regard, will continue to be permitted only on a selective basis where: need has been established; technology does not exist within the country; the time taken to generate the technology indigenously would delay the achievement of development targets.
- Government may, from time to time, identify and notify such areas of high national priority, in respect of which procedures would be simplified further to ensure timely acquisition of the required technology.
- There shall be a firm commitment for absorption, adaptation and subsequent development of imported know-how through adequate investment in Research and Development to which importers of technology will be expected to contribute.

  Unpackaging: Technology to fulfil a particular need consists of many components. It is necessary to develop capability to break down the total package of technology required for a purpose into components, some of which may be readily available or could be indigenously developed, and other that will need to be imported. Norms and guidelines for such unpackaging will be evolved.

Absorption of Technology

There shall be a commitment to ensure an adequate scale of investment in R&D for the absorption, adaptation and, wherever possible, improvement on and generation of new technology, making fullest use of overall national capabilities. Only thus can self-reliance be ensured and a technology generation process established firmly. Appropriate mechanisms will be evolved at the stage of technology assessment to ensure the absorption of imported technology.

Technological Information

The availability of an efficient system of collection and analysis of relevant technological information, including cost and other economic aspects, is a prerequisite for the appropriate choice of technologies. This will considerably enhance the possibility of obtaining favourable terms and conditions in acquisition of technology. Such a technology information base will be established.

Technology Transfer

Diffusion

Special efforts need to be made for the diffusion of technology in use to all beneficiaries who can employ them optimally. Appropriate measures shall be evolved to facilitate technology diffusion, including: horizontal transfer; technological support for ancillaries from large units; technology inputs to small units; and upgradation of traditional skills and capabilities.International Competitiveness and Technology Exports It is necessary to maintain international competitiveness in products, services and technologies that have export potential. Conditions for the marketing of indigenous technology and of products based on it will be improved. It is important in all such cases to conform to the highest international standards.

Technical Cooperation Among Developing Countries

A concerted effort will be made to participate fully in

technical cooperation among developing countries. Encouragement will be provided for participation in technology development programmes with other developing countries which can contribute to mutual national development.

Protection: Legislative Framework

Development of technology calls for large investments and often involves considerable risk. Encouragement will be given to obtaining necessary protection in all cases of indigenous technology development. A mechanism will be set up to ensure that national interests arising from the generating of technology are fully protected internationally in terms of industrial property rights.

Implementation

The success of the Technology Policy and the speed with which the various facets of the policy are implemented will depend to a considerable extent on a system for efficient monitoring, review and guidance and a plan of incentives and disincentives. Government will evolve instruments for the implementation of this Technology Policy and spell out in detail guidelines for Ministries and agencies of Government as well as for industries and entrepreneurs. Success in implementation demands a conscious integrated approach covering technology assessment, development, acquisition, absorption, utilization and diffusion, and connected aspects of financing, based on overall national interests, priorities and the attainment of the most challenging technological goals.

The entire population must be imbued with self-confidence and pride in national capacity. Indian Science and Technology must unlock the creative potential of our people and help in building the India of our dreams.

INTERNATIONAL ENVIRONMENT

International business is a term used to collectively describe all commercial transactions (private and governmental, sales, investments, logistics,and transportation) that take place between two or more nations. Usually, private companies undertake such transactions for profit; governments undertake them for profit and for political reasons. It refers to all those business activities which involves cross border transactions of goods, services, resources between two or more nations. Transaction of economic resources include capital, skills, people etc. for international production of physical goods and services such as finance, banking, insurance, construction etc. A multinational enterprise (MNE) is a company that has a worldwide approach to markets and production or one with operations in more than a country. An MNE is often called multinational corporation (MNC) or transnational company (TNC). Well known MNCs include fast food companies such as McDonald's and Yum Brands, vehicle manufacturers such as General Motors, Ford Motor Company and Toyota, consumer electronics companies like Samsung, LG and Sony, and energy companies such as ExxonMobil, Shell and BP. Most of the largest corporations operate in multiple national markets. Areas of study within this topic include differences in legal systems, political systems, economic policy, language, accounting standards, labour standards, living standards, environmental standards, local culture, corporate culture, foreign exchange market, tariffs, import and export regulations, trade agreements, climate, education and many more topics. Each of these factors requires significant changes in how individual business units operate from one country to the next.

The conduct of international operations depends on companies' objectives and the means with which they carry them out. The operations affect and are affected by the physical and societal factors and the competitive environment.

Operations:

- Objectives: sales expansion, resource acquisition, risk minimization

Means:

- *Modes*: importing and exporting, tourism and transportation, licensing and franchising, turnkey operations, management contracts, direct investment and portfolio investments.

- *Functions*: marketing, global manufacturing and supply chain management, accounting, finance, human resources
- Overlaying alternatives: choice of countries, organization and control mechanisms

Physical and societal factors:

- Political policies and legal practices
- Cultural factors
- Economic forces
- Geographical influences

Competitive factors:

- Major advantage in price, marketing, innovation, or other factors.
- Number and comparative capabilities of competitors
- Competitive differences by country

There has been growth in globalization in recent decades due to the following eight factors:

- Technology is expanding, especially in transportation and communications.
- Governments are removing international business restrictions.
- Institutions provide services to ease the conduct of international business.
- Consumers know about and want foreign goods and services.
- Competition has become more global.
- Political relationships have improved among some major economic powers.
- Countries cooperate more on transnational issues.
- Cross-national cooperation and agreements.

Studying international business is important because:

- Most companies are either international or compete with international companies.
- Modes of operation may differ from those used domestically.
- The best way of conducting business may differ by country.

- An understanding helps you make better career decisions.
- An understanding helps you decide what governmental policies to support.

Managers in international business must understand social science disciplines and how they affect all functional business fields.

Tom Travis, the managing partner of Sandler, Travis & Rosenberg, PA. and international trade and customs consultant, uses the Six Tenets when giving advice on how to globalize one's business.

The Six Tenets are as follows:

1. Take advantage of trade agreements: think outside the border
    - Familiarize yourself with preference programmes and trade agreements.
    - Read the fine print.
    - Participate in the process.
    - Seize opportunities when they arise.
2. Protect your brand at all costs
    - You and your brand are inseparable.
    - You must be vigilant in protecting your intellectual property both at home and abroad.
    - You must be vigilant in enforcing your IP rights.
    - Protect your worldwide reputation by strict adherence to labour and human rights standards.
3. Maintain high ethical standards
    - Strong ethics translate into good business.
    - Forge ethical strategic partnerships.
    - Understand corporate accountability laws.
    - Become involved with the international business self-regulation movement.
    - Develop compliance protocols for import and export operations.
    - Memorialize your company's code of ethics and compliance practices in writing.
    - Appoint a leader.
4. Stay secure in an insecure world

- Security requires transparency throughout the supply chain.
- Participate in trade-government partnerships.
- Make the most of new security measures.
- Secure your data.
- Keep your personnel secure.

5. Expect the Unexpected
   - The unexpected will happen.
   - Do your research now.
   - Address your particular circumstances.
6. All global business is personal
   - Go to the source.
   - Keep communications open.
   - Keep the home office operational.
   - Fly the flag at your overseas locations.
   - Relate to offshore associates on a personal level.
   - Be available to overseas clients and customers 24/7.

Index